LETS GO!

PUBLISH

America 4 Dummmies

*Your first book to read to refresh your knowledge of America &
how our government works*

***Read America 4 Dummmies so you don't sign up for anything
stupid!!***

Learn about America by reading America 4 Dummmies! It is the best
thing you can do to understand our great form of government.

This book is the best starter book for anybody wanting to refresh their
knowledge or learn about the government of America and to be better
prepared to react to the overreach of corrupt politicians. Without the
knowledge that you can gain easily in this book, for example, you might
unknowingly sign up for a socialist progressive government that takes
away your rights, and makes you dependent on government employees
all your life. I kid you not.

Today more than ever with US chief executives ignoring the
Constitution and executing the office in a lawless fashion, Americans
need to know their rights and the protections built into the basic
framework of our government.

Just because one powerful person chooses to ignore our rights and
freedoms does not mean we must endure the tyranny. The first step of
course is to understand the most basic written precepts. Reading this
book is a must for every US citizen.

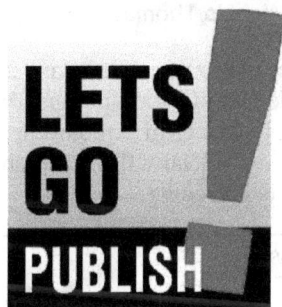

**LETS
GO !
PUBLISH**

BRIAN W. KELLY

Copyright © 2014,2016   Brian W. Kelly
Editor: Brian P. Kelly
America 4 Dummmies!   Author Brian W. Kelly

Disclaimer: Though judicious care was taken throughout the writing and
the publication of this work that the information contained herein is
accurate, there is no expressed or implied warranty that all information in
this book is 100% correct. Therefore, neither LETS GO PUBLISH, nor
the author accepts liability for any use of this work.

Trademarks: A number of products and names referenced in this book
are trade names and trademarks of their respective companies.

Referenced Material :   Standard Disclaimer: The information in
this book has been obtained through personal and third party observations, interviews, and
copious research. Where unique information has been provided or extracted from other sources,
those sources are acknowledged within the text of the book itself or at the end of the chapter in
the Sources Section. Thus, there are no formal footnotes nor is there a bibliography section.
Any picture that does not have a source was taken from various sites on the Internet with no
credit attached. If resource owners would like credit in the next printing, please email publisher.

Published by: LETS GO PUBLISH!
Editor   Brian P. Kelly
Email: info@letsgopublish.com
Web site   www.letsgopublish.com

Library of Congress Copyright Information Pending
Book Cover Design by Michele Thomas

ISBN Information: The International Standard Book Number (ISBN) is a
unique machine-readable identification number, which marks any book
unmistakably. The ISBN is the clear standard in the book industry. 159
countries and territories are officially ISBN members. The Official ISBN
For this book is on the outside cover:

The price for this work is: **$13.88 USD**
10   9   8   7   6   5   4   3   2   1

Release Date: June 2016

Dedication

To my two best friends,

Dennis Grimes and Gerry Rodski.

Thank you for all of your support in my writing and publishing efforts.

You guys are the best.

Acknowledgments

In every book that I write or edit, I publicly acknowledged all of the help that I have received from many sources. Some of these wonderful people are still on earth and others have made their way to heaven.

I would like to thank many people for helping me in this effort. I appreciate all the help that I received in putting this book together, along with the 66 other books from the past.

My printed acknowledgments were once so large that book readers needed to navigate too many pages to get to page one of the text. To permit me more flexibility, I put my acknowledgment list online at www.letsgopublish.com. The list of acknowledgments continues to grow. Believe it or not, it once cost about a dollar more to print each book.

Thank you all on the big list in the sky and God bless you all for your help.

Please check out www.letsgopublish.com to read the latest version of my heartfelt acknowledgments updated for this book. Thank you all!

In this book, I received some extra special help from many avid Notre Dame supporters including Bruce Ikeda, Dennis Grimes, Gerry Rodski, Wily Ky Eyely, Angel Irene McKeown Kelly, Angel Edward Joseph Kelly Sr., Angel Edward Joseph Kelly Jr., Ann Flannery, Angel James Flannery Sr., Mary Daniels, Bill Daniels, Robert Gary Daniels, Angel Sarah Janice Daniels, Angel Punkie Daniels, Joe Kelly, Diane Kelly, Brian P. Kelly, Mike P. Kelly, Katie P. Kelly, Ben Kelly, and Budmund (Buddy) Arthur Kelly.

Preface

Here we are citizens in a truly exceptional country. Yet, even here in America all is not perfect. But, if we don't smarten up, things will get a lot worse and they may never get better again.

Taxes are too high, elected officials are out of touch, government is too big, spending is out of control; the new healthcare program is a train wreck, the federal government is incompetent, the people have no voice in government, too many people are too lazy to hold government accountable, too many are on the take… There's lots more!

Learn about America by reading this book. It is the best thing you can do to understand our great country and our great form of government, before the bad guys take it away from us.

This book is the best starter book for anybody wanting to refresh their knowledge or learn about the government of the United States of America and to be better prepared to react to the overreach of today's corrupt politicians. Without the knowledge that you can gain so easily in this book, for example, you might unknowingly sign up for a socialist progressive government that takes away your rights, and makes you dependent on government employees for the rest of your natural life. I kid you not.

Today more than ever with our chief executive ignoring the Constitution and administering the office in lawless fashion, Americans need to know their rights and protections built into the basic framework of our government.

Just because one powerful person chooses to ignore our rights and freedoms does not mean we must endure the tyranny. The first step of course is to understand America's revolution, its founding, and its most basic written precepts. Reading this book is a must for every US citizen.

If you have been paying attention to what is going on in America today, you know that we are in trouble. We have a busted economy, high unemployment, no jobs, and our basic rights to freedoms such as speech, religion, the press, and our right-to-bear-arms are being impinged upon. The founders saw it as a civic duty for Americans to *pay attention* to our government so that we can avoid being chumps and being snookered by crooked politicians.

You and I know that there are more issues than just those noted above, and we better fix them quickly while we still have an America. Isn't this a shame on US? I think that is why you bought this book. Thank you very much.

We are on the same side, and together we can all help. We first must understand what is going on and we then must understand our rights. Even before you and I and everybody else are on board, you must start the first wave of solutions by opening your windows all the way and shouting as loud as you can: "I am mad as hell, and I am not going to take it anymore." Now, didn't that feel better?

Then, after you read this book, you must make sure that you talk to all of the other dummmies out there that you know— people like you and I and others, and let's help them know that it is time. It is time to get off the couch and act. Unless we all fully engage in America, when we wake up from our deep fog, there may be no America left for our progeny. We will have blown it for sure if that is permitted to happen.

In this book, we unabashedly recommend to stop trusting government, run by Republicans or Democrats, since it is clearly not working for our best interests. The sooner we can understand the active threat from the left and the passive threat from the right, the sooner we can move on to solving the problem for our values, our country, and our freedom.

It will be tough to wage this war against the corrupt politicians and the corrupt media if we are not even permitted to help on the battlefield when America is hanging by just a thread. The smarter we are, the more chances we have for success.

Brian W. Kelly monitors what is happening to our government and he has written extensively on the major problems our country faces. Kelly is one of America's most outspoken and eloquent conservative spokesmen. He is the author of No Amnesty! No Way!, Saving America, Taxation Without Representation, , Kill the EPA!, Jobs! Jobs! Jobs!, The Federalist Papers—a total of 67 books. All books are available at www.bookhawkers.com. Many are available at Amazon and Kindle.

Like many Americans, Brian is fed up with a stifling socialist progressive Marxists sitting in the top seat in Washington, DC. The progressives place the needs of everybody else in front of the needs of Americans. Like many Americans, Kelly is shocked at how brazen our President has become in ignoring our Constitution.

Brian Kelly has read the founding documents, the underlying intelligence reports, and he has researched and written about such topics for years. Brian has written sixty-seven books and hundreds of articles. He is deeply concerned about how intolerable the results of poor government policy can be within our neighborhoods and our lives. His comprehensible and sane recommendations in this book are explained in detail within the covers of this soon-to-be classic edition.

More and more Americans are clamoring for jobs but all that has been given by the government to the people is lip service. Both parties permit it. Americans want to keep their health insurance and pick their own doctors, and they want to be able to afford the insurance. If Obama put his name to a plan like that, he might have had our support. Instead, he lied to the people and everything in healthcare is worse than in 2009.

Unfortunately there is reason to believe that our president, who is a fine politician, would like nothing more than to be the dictator of America so that he does not have to abide by our Constitution and our American values. Unbelievable as it may seem, too often than not, even Republicans give him what he wants. Americans who know their rights vote out scoundrels from office to protect America and Americans.

In his eight years, this president has tried to take away our guns; ram a health scam on Americans that includes death panels for the elderly and infirm; grant illegals citizenship while handing them benefits paid by hard working Americans, including free education; and finally he encourages foreigners to take more American jobs and there is no punishment.

America for Dummmies! is a title to get your attention. I hope my dad got it. In addition to reviewing the founding history, Brian W. Kelly has included a major civics lesson in this book to bring you up to date on the national scene. Additionally, he has included copies of the founding documents so that you can read them in this book, rather than on the Internet.

You are going to love this book since it is designed by an American for Americans. Few books are a must-read but America for Dummies will quickly appear at the top of America's most read list.

Sincerely,

Brian P. Kelly, Editor

Table of Contents

About the Author

Brian W. Kelly retired as an Assistant Professor in the Business Information Technology (BIT) program at Marywood University, where he also served as the IBM i and midrange systems technical advisor to the IT faculty. Kelly has designed, developed, and taught many college and professional courses. He is also a contributing technical editor to a number of IT industry magazines, including "The Four Hundred" and "Four Hundred Guru" published by IT Jungle.

Kelly is a former IBM Senior Systems Engineer and he has been a candidate for US Congress and the US Senate from Pennsylvania. He has an active information technology consultancy. He is the author of 67 books and numerous articles. Kelly is a frequent speaker at COMMON, IBM conferences, and other technical conferences. Ask him to speak at your next Conservative / Populist rally!

Over the past eight years, Brian Kelly has become America's most outspoken and eloquent conservative protagonist. Besides *Just Say No to Chris Christie for President*, Kelly is also the author of No Amnesty! No Way!, Taxation Without Representation, and many other patriotic books.

Endorsed by the Independence Hall Tea Party in 2010, Kelly ran for Congress against a 13-term Democrat; took zero campaign contrib-utions, spent enough to buy signs and T-shirts, and as a virtual unknown, he captured 17% of the vote—www.briankellyforcongress.com. Kelly then supported Republican challenger Lou Barletta, a conservative leader on immigration policy, and helped him win a resounding victory in the general election.

Part I Why Is This Book Necessary Today?

Chapter 1   Are You Mad as Hell About Government!

I'm Mad as Hell!

Do you remember back in November, 1976 when Howard Beale, as played by Peter Finch, the long-time anchor in the movie "Network News," gets the bad news that eventually causes him to utter one of the most famous movie lines of all time? Beale gets fired and is given two weeks. The long-time anchor has a very poor reaction to this personal news and he cannot control himself during the next broadcast. He "goes off the deep end."

He promises to commit suicide on the air. The company immediately fires him—no second chances for a repeat performance. Beale is devastated and remorseful. He begs for the opportunity to say good-by to his fans with dignity, and he is given his last opportunity ever for air time so that he can say his good-by's respectfully and also apologize. Nobody expects it to happen but Beale gets his chance, and it is billed as a *last chance.*

Despite his promises, once on the air, Beale is overwhelmed by his circumstance. He goes into another diatribe starting off with a rant claiming that "Life is bullshit." He is so passionate that his ratings spike as he persuades his viewers to shout out of their windows: "I'm as mad as hell, and I'm not going to take this anymore!" Like the shot at Lexington and Concord, this is *the line heard round the world.*

Well, my fellow Americans, I bet you saw this coming, and I am going to deliver it as passionately in words as I can: "I am mad as hell, and I am not going to take this anymore." I bet you are too. Let me remind you of why you are upset.

If you read the Preface, you may find this redundant but many do not believe that America suffers so please hear it again. Taxes are too high, elected officials are out of touch, government is too big, spending is out of control, the Obamacare program has been a train wreck from its inception, heroes are dying in the VA system,

The people see the federal government as incompetent. We have no voice in government; too many people are too lazy to hold government accountable, and too many of our finest are on the take. Only you and I can bring this back to beig OK, but not by sitting on our duffs.

Our country run by this government is a train wreck and Hillary Clinton, and Bernie Sanders promise to keep the train derailed for another eight years. They love how things are.

Corporate leaches have infiltrated our government. We have record unemployment; illegal aliens are smiling as they take American jobs; we have an unsustainable status quo with special interests having priority over the people's interests. When we look to the future we see a public education system that creates more dummies. These dummies are so dummm that they don't seem to mind being called dummmies. Scrooge would even come up with a more devastating term than "Bah Humbug." It's that bad! Can't you feel it?

We have the poorest economy since the depression, excessive welfare and income redistribution, institutionalized lying, a corrupt press carrying water for government, a debt large enough to kill America, huge student debt stopping graduate's success, tyranny v. democracy, government lawlessness, freedom and liberty in jeopardy, American stagnation, and a big loss of American world prestige.

Why we do not know about this is because we have the most corrupt press since Gutenberg invented the printing press and they work hard to propagandize all aspects of American life while being surrogates of the liberal progressive wing of the Marxist / Communist oriented new Democratic Party.

Our big government has become such a problem that it can never again be the solution. Our finest hope, our youth; go through colleges in huge numbers to become unemployed and sacked with debt. Their out of touch professors have convinced them that this is the norm but we know the American Dream is the norm. Today's millennials do not believe in the American Dream or any dreams because their elitist professors hate our America.

The student loan burden prevents borrowers from buying homes, cars, and having a family. As many as 37 million student loan borrowers are too broke to engage in life. College loans, instead of lifting people to the top, have created a new race to the bottom,

On the International stage, thanks to our elected government, America is now known a bad actor. Nobody gives us standing ovations anymore. Nobody asks us for curtain calls. Our leaders turn their backs on our friends and seem to pay homage to our enemies. Nightclubs in Orlando create major carnage while, so as not to offend the new religion of acceptability in the US, the government blames Christians and guns rather for the work of an ISIS terrorist, rather than the hate mongering perpetrators of the atrocity.

Smaller and weaker countries such as Russia, Iran, and North Korea push US around and laugh at US, and our only response is to see if somehow we may gave have offended them. For me, these are the worst days of America that I have ever witnessed, and the leadership and our government seems to be OK with being mediocre, instead of being outstanding. Our government has trained us not to fight the bad guys.

If you have been paying attention, and I sure hope you have been as it is a civic duty, you know that there are even more issues than the exhaustive list we just walked through. Isn't that a shame on US? I think that is why you bought this book. Thank you very much.

We are on the same side, and together we can all help. We first must understand what is going on and we then must understand our rights. Even before you and I and everybody else are on board, we must start the first wave of solutions by opening our windows all the way and shouting as loud as you can so all of the government perpetrators in Washington can hear us well: "I am mad as hell, and I am not going to take this anymore."

Then, make sure that you talk to all of the other dummmies out there that you know—people like you and I and others, and let's help them know that unless we all fully engage, in America, when we wake up from our deep fog, there may be no America left for our progeny. We will have blown it for sure if that is permitted to happen.

America is a Representative Democracy?

When we think of the very important notion that "America is a representative democracy," watching the clowns who occupy our central government, it is a sane question to ask if this is really true. The song, "Is that all there is?" comes to mind today. We are nothing like our parents and nothing like our founders. We should all be ashamed but then again shame is no longer permitted.

A representative democracy is the foundation of America. However, what makes America, America is that we are also a Republic, the finest form of government ever brought forth from mankind.

We also have a set of laws, beginning with our Constitution that govern all politicians in perpetuity—as long as we hold them accountable.

The big laws like the Constitution are not so that the government can hurt us or impose its will upon US. Not hardly! Our country was founded by some smart people and they knew that without constraints on government gone wild, such as a great body of law known as the Constitution, politicians and others in government would feel they had a right to deny US our liberty and freedom. They are trying real hard today to kill America so you are reading this book none too soon.

If you could figure any way to put a stranglehold on corrupt politicians, right now or in the future, would you not do it? The founders of America put such a stranglehold on all political agents of the future when it wrote and adopted the Constitution, the greatest body of law ever written in any civilization.

Of course, if we the people do not know what is written in the Constitution, it can't help us much. Can it? So, it is time to stop being dummmies and political sport for the elite. It is time to rule America as our birthright as citizens of this great country commands US. Let somebody else eat cake!

And, so, my fellow Americans, that is the number one reason that in order to form a more perfect union of the thirteen colonies / states, and with more states expected, our forefathers built the finest Constitution ever fashioned by the pen of human beings. Our President has a pen and a phone but he can't make it work the magic of the founders. Apparently, he is not interested in trying to do so anyway!

The Bible, from the hand of God, may be the greatest story ever told in the greatest book ever written, but the Constitution is as good as it gets for the goodness of man, written by the hands of our first patriots, and surely this was with the guidance of God.

In this day and age, there are everyday attempts by the government to undermine our lasting Republic, which is an almost pure constitutional representative democracy. The attacks most often come from the left side of the political spectrum.

The ideology of the progressive left favors Marxism and its simpler forms of socialism and communism. Since Americans do not vote for socialists, communists, or Marxists, these are things that nobody other than a crooked politician should want. If we are unaware of this in today's government, it is time we all paid more attention. No politician wanting to be elected will admit they are more communist than American. Yet, as much as it pains me to tell you, they are!

These overtures, which demean the Constitution, the fabric of our democracy, originate from corrupt politicians who have been caught up in the leftist movement, which would like to end capitalism, and bring on a socialist order to replace the American Dream, and all the dreams of We The People!

One midnight, I asked myself one of those haunting questions: "Isn't it about time that we real Americans actually had some real "representation" from the so-called representatives in our so-called representative government? I said to myself: "Yes it is!" It doesn't have to be a dream. If we believe, it can easily again be made a reality.

The way it now works provides far too much separation between US, the electors, and them, the elected officials who coordinate our pooled resources for the alleged benefit of "everyone." But who is everyone? And who takes credit for everything?

Do our representatives in the second decade of the twenty-first century have a genuinely compelling concern for the people and our government or is this simply a Nirvana, which in Buddhism is its final goal—a transcendent state in which there is neither suffering, desire, nor sense of self, and the subject is released from the effects of karma and the cycle of death and rebirth. If not Nirvana, perhaps it is a Disney-like Utopian myth perpetrated on US by these same "benevolent politicians?" Do any of US think they care?

I propose the latter. Our government is wholly unaccountable to We the People. Today, our government rejects the fundamental principles of our founding and has no real legitimacy the further it drifts from the precepts of the Constitution.

The US was not designed this way. It was designed by a group of artisans to not only represent their artistic touch, but to be held as the creed of the people, for the people, and by the people, forever. What thinking human being blessed to be part of America, could ask for anything more?

If you think that life, freedom, liberty, and the ability to pursue your own happiness are simple notions, and *givens* in any civilization, get out your thinking pad, and think again. Why do people from all over the world crash our gates just to get in?

Which would you first give up? Your freedom, your life, your liberty, or your ability to do what you need to be happy? Who could ask for anything more than being an American? But, if Americans do not care about it, maybe it cannot last.

If this design, which the founders labored to create for America was so great, you might ask, why is it that our current lawmakers ignore it? They have no trouble going with the flow and committing US to years of debt without even taking the time to read the debt-ridden legislation for which they vote.

Even worse, its members, our alleged civil servants, are able to get away without doing their jobs, while collecting more and more remuneration for the act of hurting the American people at large.

The true answer to that question is very unfortunate for Americans. There is tacit collaboration in undermining the principles of our Democratic Republic by our supposed representatives, their supporters, the special interests, and their corporate interests. We the people now come last. They think we are not paying attention. Maybe we have not been paying enough attention but don't you agree that is about to end. *Pay attention* is about to become the motto of the free!

Perhaps too many of US, until things got this bad, have been hoping George would do it! Well, George Washington, one of our finest patriots is long gone, and unless you know of a recent George with the time, it is up to US to do it.

And, by the way, the two George Bush's did not get it done either. But, the country drama with all Americans being the least we can be, had not yet become a cliff hanger event, either. Maybe the Bushes were not so bad after all. They could have done more but they did not cause today's morose about life in America. BHO can step up to the plate and claim that all for himself.

Can it be that too many of US and too many of our friends have been constitutional dummies for too long? Perhaps this book and your exhortations to all your friends will help many Americans awaken to what happens in a country in which government, rather than the people, has the stronger hand.

By the way, as much as they could have helped and did not do such a good job; the Bushes did not cause this problem. It rests on the shoulders of BHO. Yet, nobody wants to blame him for it, because he seems so happy screwing US all!

Chapter 2   Are Americans Simply Dummm Suckers?

Americans must not be chumps

Our representatives are in office far too long and they gain relationships with others in the ruling class. They begin to think they belong in Washington, not their home territories, where their social life exists. They begin to like the trappings of Washington more than being with their loved ones back in their home states.

Unfortunately for all Americans, the new "important" relationships trump the notion of fair representation for the people (US) from back home. When they take their oaths of office and they promise to represent US, most are sincere at the time.

Then, they come to Washington and experience the trappings and the temptations. And, because humans are only human, way too many of our finest stray from the mark and contribute to the re-creation of a country of which few thinking Americans are proud today.

Think about our forefathers, especially George Washington, who guided our troops in the revolution against England's tyranny. Think about honest Abe Lincoln, who freed the slaves and saved the union. They would weep to see what their political successors have done to our nation.

So, our fair haired representatives (figure of speech) choose to represent themselves and their special interests, rather than the territories that sent them to the Congress of the USA to represent the people. Perhaps a dose of Lincoln's "honesty," is all that is needed to save the day. Wouldn't that be nice?

Our "honorable," do not even seem to care for our well-being. They care for their leadership positions, which make them big shots, and they care for themselves for sure. Unfortunately, they just can't get it into their heads that we the people are the reason they are in their positions in the first place. We are their employers, and they serve at our pleasure. The more we all understand that the tighter the reins can be on errant politicians, the more the people will be in charge.

Then again, maybe a lot of the problem is our fault since we do not check them out well enough before we slam them into office. To make it simple to understand this notion—if there is a rotten piece of fish in the market and we select it for dinner, whose fault is it when it doesn't taste good and our guests get sick? So, when we pick a rotten person to represent US—whose fault is that? You see, we do not have to be dummmies. We simply choose to be.

It does not matter whether the government is controlled by Democrats or Republicans. The people are always short changed on the notion of representation and well, honesty! When has a representative run effectively on honesty? Is that because we do not care about honesty or we know they are kidding. Either way it is our fault.

Somebody once said that if you like your honesty, you will be able to keep it and it should save you about $2500.00 per year. But I jest, yet my jest is serious.

OK, nobody said that but some president at some time in the last four years told Americans that they could keep their doctors, their health policies, and save $2500.00.

My objective in this book is not to have you know who said that or to get you upset whether he or she did or did not. I just want you to think about what the founders promised and what American government has been delivering to the people before the liars took charge. There is a chasm.

My objective is to help smarten you up so that guys like that, whether they are the president or not, do not get to treat you like a chump.

I have the ability to imitate people's speech. In my home town, I can imitate a late Congressman, Daniel J. Flood, as if he were in the room when you heard the words. It is a gift. I can also imitate WC Fields, though not as well—but not too badly.

Can W. C. Fields help?

Some Americans know that WC Fields was the essence of Americana in his day. He found the nuances and he got a lot of laughs by pointing them out while using just a smidge of hyperbole. Fields counted on the weak and the strong alike to understand his missives, and he fired them off in his raspy voice to much acclaim.

Fields was into everybody's head, like it or not, strong willed-or not. He was not just a writer and an actor; he was also a psychologist without a degree. I would argue that only WC Fields can explain why America is falling apart today. However, I would agree to give Rod Serling his due that this may just be a bad Twilight Zone episode.

Fields did not think much of the human character of his day and age, and I suspect that he would think less of humans in our time. How about the title of one of his films? Does it not explain his perspective about how non-thinking, humans, aka, dummmies, can be exploited when they choose to not pay attention?

I would ask you all to consider his movie, *"Never Give a Sucker an Even Break."* This is a war-time 1941 Universal Pictures comedy starring the raspy voiced master of comedy himself. WC wrote the original story without taking credit in his own name. His pseudonym for this work was Otis Criblecoblis. This master played himself in the movie. His plot was that he was searching for a chance to promote a surreal screenplay he had written. Ah, Yes!

Fields based this movie on some of his earlier films, such as *Poppy* (1936) and *You Can't Cheat an Honest Man* (1939). It did not take long for the audience to know the poor regard Fields felt for his fellow man.

WC himself would refer to it as understanding the comic importance of human vulnerability. In *Poppy*, for example, he tells his sweet little daughter that "If we should ever separate, my little plum, I want to give you just one bit of fatherly advice: *Never give a sucker an even break!"*

Think about that and ask yourself if you have wondered why some of the political parties out there today may not be giving any of US an even break. Maybe they think we are too weak to demand it?

Knowing that he had hit a chord with his Americana, in the blockbuster film, *You Can't Cheat an Honest Man*, WC lays it on even thicker. He knew that people hated wussies; but he also knew that many people take on the personality of a wuss, in a moment's notice.

And, so , in this great film extravaganza, with gin breath for sure in every scene, WC tells a customer that his grandfather's last words, "just before they sprung the trap" were, "You can't cheat an honest man; never give a sucker an even break, or smarten up a chump." He could say these seven thousand times in his inimitable voice, and I know I would chuckle each time. But, maybe he was right about US?

Since this is not supposed to be a political book, though we are surely in tough political times, when trust of government is in question, I cannot tell you which of the two major political parties think that Americans have no brains. However, I will tell you that WC Fields would have had no problem identifying the culprits and delivering the goods.

Moreover, he would be pleased to cheat suckers in any way he could; while giving none a break. All chumps of course would remain dumb and gullible and capable of swallowing political propaganda, while still remaining loyal to the party that was inflicting the most harm on them. Fields in many ways behaved as the party, which I shall not mention. He lied very well. In fact, he literally made prevarication into an art form.

My job in this book is to help all Americans know that it is about time that we all pay attention and that we no longer can defer to the judgment of political "friends." Let's stop being suckers and chumps, and throw out the bums that are destroying America, from whichever party they come.

If we happen to come across an upstanding janitor in a clean building, we would be far better off enticing this fine person into representing our district than listening to the propaganda of the establishment political class. They are destroying America. Their advice is purposely directed to convince US to elect representatives of the worst character. Let's just say no!

When Fields put out this last film, he was 61 years old. Though he was probably tickled that he lasted to 62 years of age, with all the weathering he inflicted on himself over the years, he knew that alcohol and illness had taken their toll. His waist line had grown in size but not by design. He loved a nip way too much. It would do him in and soon.

He was an accomplished juggler in his teens and early days in burlesque. He had real athletic talent, and he had the determination of a poor person, hoping never again to be poor.

At one time, when in his fifties, he went through a period in which he made eight films in the space of two years. Abuse does take its toll. I bring him into this book because Americans are being played for chumps by the political class, and nobody seems to be giving US a break.

Truth and knowledge are our best hope to fight off the promises and lies of the political class. When you see a politician speaking, remember there is only one way to know if he or she is lying: "Are their lips moving?"

Then, of course in today's day and age, you have the low-information voters – the most gullible citizens, who are so good hearted, they would ask an aggressor if they could hold the nail as it was pounded through their hand on a cross. They would ask an opposing soccer striker coming towards the ball in a rush to kick it into the goal," Is this your ball sir? They would be nice rather than take what is theirs. They would not want the striker to miss out on her or his opportunity to score against him or her. Why kick it away to save the team when there is less immediate flack if you just say, "Oh, excuse me, is this your ball?"

That's just a little too nice. America was not born of niceness. It was built on fairness, goodness, and individual strength. We are not supposed to give politicians an even break, We are supposed to pay attention so our rights are not violated by grabby politicians. If you happen to be in this low information / overly nice category, thank you for visiting this book. I hope that through my writings, I can help you be more like you can be.

You gotta smarten up or we are all toast. Finish this book, please and you will understand how smart you can be and how much power you can wield against those who care nothing about you or me, or America. Always keep your eye on the ball and do not give the ball up to an opponent just because they lie and schmooze you.

Though I enjoy his work, please note that this is not a biography of WC Fields nor is it a book that attempts to hide all of his transgressions or the transgressions of the political class. Beware of false prophets.

In his day, Fields was the master in understanding his times. My goal in bringing him into this discussion as we absorb my book, *America 4 Dummmies*, is so that we can cast his knowledge forward to the people of today. With a not-so-free and very dishonest and corrupt press, the propaganda provided in the mainstream news media of today, would have US all believe in the *"Tooth Fairy."* Any of US that live by believing their rot, are un-smartened chumps.

Since I too believe in Santa Clause, and have met him once or twice in my life, I will cast aspersions only on the Tooth Fairy. I have never personally met her, though I did find a quarter under my pillow one morning and there was a missing tooth.

Ask the mainstream press about these two fine characters, which make our children very happy. Ask them if they are real or not? If you can get the press to talk to you honestly about Santa or the Tooth Ferry, ask them if they care at all about regular Americans.

Those of US living in the shadow of the post 2008 and 2012 elections are no longer suffering from a recession or a bad economy. We have been told that we are in a recovery period by a government that will say anything to protect its power. How is the recovery going for you?

We are suffering from no economy, caused by a government that wants to punish anybody or any company that is productive. Those in charge of government now tell US that this is the new normal and we are just supposed to accept it. I don't accept it and I hope you won't. This is about the worst government I have lived through. But, we still have the right to vote. Please vote.

The Affordable Health Care Act, which cynics either call the Unaffordable Health Care Act, or simply Obamacare (even the President loves the term), is one of those things that most Americans joke about in public but fear in private. Most of US get sick every now and then and we do not want a government bureaucrat deciding whether we get treatment or not.

We may joke about its conception and its most inept rollout, and the miracle of a 7.1 million count by March 31, 2014 when just the day before nobody knew how many had paid. These things are really not funny but our government sees the truth as its mortal enemy.

Some of the most attractive measures of Obamacare include the fact that it permits parents to keep their kids on the dole, since the Obama economy is so bad, until they are 26. The other great thing people like is that nobody can deny a person with pre-existing conditions.

Well, I have bad news about the little lie involved in this story. Just like you can't keep your doctor, your hospital, or your health insurance plan, and you won't save $2500, despite Obama promises, he was also kidding about the pre-existing thing. Obama said, you can get Obamacare if you have a pre-existing condition. Sorry, he was kidding again. Please forgive him as you always do because he is so good looking.

Once March 31, 2014 came, that was the end. Unless you can postpone your illness until January, 2015, and you do not die, you cannot sign up for Obamacare. With 7.1 million signed up and Obaam claiming victory, nobody can get insurance again until 2015. I am so sorry the President did not tell you that, but it is the truth.

Regardless of which party is responsible for the mess, Americans are on edge anticipating that somehow, because there are big problems, we will all get nailed by it in one way or another. Many of US think that we may lose our jobs, lose our ability to work full time, lose our health insurance policies, and not be able to afford the new government issued policies coming our way. We may get sick and we may die because of Obamacare. Thank God Obama is not under Obamacare so at least he will be available for a eulogy at any of our funerals.

Illegal immigration and amnesty is another of the jokes perpetrated on the American people. In this instance, both the Democrats and the Republicans share the same vision – *to stiff the American people,* and to give priority to illegal foreign nationals rather than American citizens. What happened to America and Americans first? What would WC say about this folks?

Some truths stand forever. Even Obama when he met with Pope Francis could not think of anything positive to say, so he quoted his buddy Harry Reid. We show the bubbled exchange with the Pope below. Pope Francis must have a great sense of humor. Don't we just love his simplicity?

HARRY REID SAID THAT I SHOULD BE MADE A SAINT BECAUSE OF OBAMACARE!

THAT'S BECAUSE IF IT EVER WORKS, IT WILL BE A MIRACLE.

HopeNChangeCartoons.com

And, so, I decided that this book about America would not be political and it shall not be. It is anti-political. But, we must tell the truth about how things really are—don't you think?

I am a Democrat, though not too proud about that fact. But it has been both Democrats and Republicans who have given us this sad state of affairs.

And, so this book will be truthful and fact-filled and it will make each political party seem like they, and they alone, along with the two party system—are responsible for the problems that America has been suffering while trying to stay America—and while trying to keep our American way of life.

Because I love America so much, I wrote this book so that I can share my sense of what America really is, and why until the millennials got shut out of the American dream, with no jobs after college, who consequently cannot start families, this was a country that not only promised an American Dream. It delivered.

I hope this book helps to wake up Americans of all ages from the fog that has affected our brains. We have not changed but we have permitted our government to change. Our representatives and our government has changed so much they have forgotten who we are and who we are supposed to be.

Government has grown so big that we the people who own the government according to a deed known as the Constitution, can no longer sort through all the lies and the empty promises. So, we must all help reduce the size of government so that the people can matter again. We get our chances each election cycle.

If all Americans understood America, and were taught to respect America in our schools, instead of blaming America—we would not have to worry about being defeated from within.

In this way, if any American political party comes-by led by Democrats or Republicans, and it wants to change America into a Communist-Russian-like, or Communist-Chinese-like, or Naxi-German-like country, we will be equipped to fire off a quick *nyet*, or a *mhai*, or simply, a hearty, guttural *nein*!

We can surely add *no-way Jose* for effect if we choose, simply because we are Americans and we are exceptional. What we cannot do is accept and believe the propaganda from the corrupt, socialist progressive Marxist owned press in the US.

America, from its inception, along with mercantilism, has used capitalism to create the strongest country in the world. Those who do not like America have already removed mercantilism from the landscape and now hope to replace capitalism with socialism. Their replacement scenario is a promise of the best of small "c" communism in our later evolution, or revolution, but they may not permit freedom lovers to live when they gain control, if we are not totally happy with them.

If you believe in any of these socialist philosophies and you also like your freedom, it might be a good time to visit the tombstone makers in your area and pick out a good one. In memoriam! You are gone!

Chapter 3   Spurn Corrupt Politicians and Be an American Patriot

Hard work pays off big time?

America has always been a capitalist country in which hard work pays off big-time, and so the same goes for our economy. If any American political party comes-by led by Democrats or Republicans, and it wants to change America into a communist, socialist, or Marxist country, once you understand America, and you are no longer part of the dummmy crowd, you will be well-equipped with the information you are absorbing to fire off a resounding "NO" in our native language of English.

As a proud American, after I wrapped up most of my IT career, I thought that I might be able to help my country with the knowledge and skills that I had picked up as an American citizen, who happened to be a well-trained and well experienced IT professional.

I was baptized at King's College with a Data Processing degree and later I was confirmed in technical and marketing skills by the IBM Corporation itself, and then later I received MBA status at Wilkes University because I wanted to know more about business.

At the time, IBM was king of all IT in the world. By the way, I was also baptized Roman Catholic and confirmed in my church, and so I mean no disrespect to Catholics or any other religions or non-religions about my comments on baptism and confirmation. I love America and I love the Catholic

Faith. I also respect other religions that honor a God of goodness.

So, here I am in an early post retirement. I stopped actively seeking IT engagements for my consulting practice, though I get some anyway, and I am actually thinking about reemerging in IT sometime in the near future. Maybe!

But, while my resources were more abundant, and I saw an America failing and becoming as poorly managed as a banana republic, I began to re-study my American heritage, with an eye to doing my part to keep our country strong.

I hoped to learn how to keep America beyond the reach and influence of treacherous politicians, who would be pleased with tyranny, simply to gain an extra nickel for their over-bulging pocket books and wallets.

That led me into making a run for the US Congress without taking a dime from relatives or friends, or anybody else. I learned many lessons from this great attempt. Unfortunately, my biggest lesson was that when a regular citizen chooses to run for national office, the bumps in the road to possible success are huge. They are not just little moguls that can be quickly overcome.

The game is rigged against regular Americans by guess-who—corrupt politicians from the last 150 years. They are not about to give up their power easily, even if we the people demand it. Our only recourse is to vote them out, while elections in the US are still free, and the workers in the crooked election stations may still be prosecuted.

Supposed representatives of the people from years past have placed obstacle after obstacle in the path of any non-political potential candidates. Their objective is for US to learn our lessons and never attempt to disrupt the harmony that all crooked politicians have among themselves.

Many of the founders engaged George III of England so America could be free without a revolution. Those from countries other than England who came to America engaged other Kings and royalty in addition to King George III. But, all came to America to be free. I hope all Americans wake up to realize that freedom is not free.

The founders never envisioned that tyranny would come from the people itself and from the press. They never expected the citizenry to stand by and permit the powerful to take away the liberties for which the revolutionaries shed blood. Our founders would not be happy with many of US today, because we sit idly and let things happen to US.

They said no to the repression of freedom and took matters into their own hands, risking life and limb, to provide US with a free America, in which all of the people are free. Go get yourself a breath of fresh air. It is free.

Unfortunately, because of neglect from our representatives, a whole new bunch of people arrived inside our country without checking in. They did not come because we are free in America, they came because they could take American jobs with the tacit acceptance of the American government. If they could not get a job, their sustenance would also be free. How nice are we while we are starving to give others our food?

Today, the well-to-do politicians, who have become very popular with the dummmest of Americans, along with sharp and cunning regular folks with political ambitions, are happy to say or do anything that would help them get elected to important offices of the city, the state or in the union.

The word "politician," is used in its most un-complimentary way to describe those who gain the people's trust and get elected to office and then turn on the people for their own self-interests.

The founders were well aware of politicians in England and other countries in Europe, and the treachery they caused. Back in the late 1700's as the Constitution was prepared for ratification, the founders were so tickled that George III was no longer in control, they somehow felt that the new America would remain pure over time and would not require another popular revolution to purify the government of scoundrels who may in later years choose to take control. Though their work was excellent, scoundrels still flourish.

The founders could not conceive of a scenario in which the recently freed people would join an oppressive and tyrannical government, such as ours is today. Where we are today, it assures that the worst of the worst get to decide which freedoms and liberties the people should be left with.

The founders had created a set of rules, known as The Constitution to assure that all the people would be left with all freedom and all liberty in all cases. They did not want any scoundrels (politicians) messing with this notion or this nation.

Unfortunately, our legislators and our president have stopped full adherence to the Constitution and consequently, our freedom is now in jeopardy. Our representatives can stop this tonight or tomorrow; but, last time I checked, they are more interested in being important in Washington than helping the folks back home.

Only Americans who hope to be in control of a socialist state advocate against the American way. Egalitarian principles of socialism simply mean that nobody gets to be the cream of the crop since the most equal spot for all is the bottom of the barrel.

Before this is fait accompli, Americans who love freedom have to do a little more than just speak up. We have to know what the founders would do to protect liberty and freedom and we simply have to do it or suffer the consequences. Reading this book is a good start.

I do not have to preach freedom to 99% of Americans out there. We all either are products of good people who came here to be free or we came here ourselves to be free.

Permitting politicians from either party to talk us out of our birthright is not only dummm; it is asinine.

Yet, we can choose to be the dummmest Americans of all time or we can choose to engage, smarten up, stop being chumps, and take on these bad guys. They do not care at all about us. Think of the leaders of the regimes that committed the atrocities that prompted our forefathers or ourselves to come here. They were evil. They were bad. They would love to have their boot on your neck right now if you would let them.

I have had the pleasure of writing a lot of patriotic books. I write tech books and patriotic / political books. This is # 52. It may be my 52-skidoo but we'll see. It is really fun to write and to help people with clear thinking.

Sometimes I do get the idea that I am talking to the wall. But, I am committed to do my part to help save America. Thank you for doing your part.

Each time I write a book, I hope that I can attract another person into a love affair with America. If you have read any of my other stuff, you know that I point out the bad guys and I pull no punches in my description of what we must do to escape from their reach. They will destroy us if we do not pay attention and escape their grasp.

In my last book, titled *The Federalist Papers, by Hamilton, Jay, and Madison*, I wrote no more than twenty pages of original introductory text to help persuade the reader that the rest of

the book for which they had paid was worth reading. I admit
I did more.

I took the patriotic essays of Alexander Hamliton, John Jay,
and James Madison, known as The Federalist Papers, and I
separated all of the two page and single page paragraphs, and
half page paragraphs, and other large paragraphs, and I
chopped them into smaller, more readable bits and pieces.
Whether you buy a book or you download these essays free
of charge, there is a lot of learning to be had in the Federalist
Papers.

I literally had to wake myself up too many times in my initial
reading because they are tough to read. Yet, they are very
insightful. I know how tough it is to get through them as
written. I did not eliminate a word of the original. I just made
it more readable. Check it out at **www.bookhawkers.com**.

By the way, just like *America 4 Dummmies*, this patriotic book
also contains the full text of the US Constitution, The
Declaration of Independence, The Articles of Confederation,
The Bill of Rights, and lots of other stuff that many of US
over the years have forgotten. Once you get back into these
writings of the founders, you will fully understand that they
are the glue that keeps Americans free and they can help
provide US all with liberty and justice forever and ever and
ever… as long as we pay attention.

Having read the Federalist Papers myself, I feel like I should
not be the one to offer this exhortation, but I shall anyway. If
you can read every one of the Federalist Papers, you have
passed a great love test for America, and if you do all the
other things you need to do to be the citizen you would be
proud to be, you then become worthy of the title, American.

Those of US who read the Federalist Papers, though it is an
arduous journey, know we have accomplished a lot. These
papers—eighty- five articles written by Alexander Hamilton,
John Jay, and James Madison, quickly show US all that the

founders were very concerned that the bad aspects of any other foreign government would not become part of the new American Democratic Republic.

The founders were well aware of politicians, but since they never put the notion of welfare, food stamps, and cell phones in the founding documents, they did not believe that the people would permit the Republic to be tainted by notions like socialism, progressivism, or Marxism.

In the early days, the people were all aware of the sacrifices the early colonials had made to secure the new America. Never in the history of man was so much patriotism shown for a notion that might not ever make it to the future. After enduring tyranny from England and other monarchies, Americans fought for and won the revolution against England et al for the cause of liberty and freedom.

Yet, here we are 200 plus years later looking for hope and change rather than looking to the spirits of our founders to rebuild our fallen country. Hope will deliver nothing when action by well spirited citizens is required but discouraged.

So, again, why did I write this book?

I have found so many people, including myself, who at one time have forgotten the sacrifices of the revolutionaries and the gifts of freedom and liberty that were bestowed on all of US at the time of the revolutionary victory. We Americans have been so blessed that we have not reminded ourselves enough over the years of our great heritage. Fourth of July celebrations are picnics, and though our parents try, the work of our founders is often lost in the celebration.

Yet, neither freedom nor liberty come cheap so the next time an engaging politician offers you something for nothing, and in your heart, you know it is wrong; stick to your guns.

Remember the words of Ben Franklin, a favorite US and Pennsylvania patriot:

"Those who desire to give up freedom in order to gain security will not have, nor do they deserve, either one."

Chapter 4 Some Things a Good American Just Feels and Just Does!

Write opinion letters and call your representatives

The purpose of this book as noted is to help US all be better Americans by understanding America and its founding. Our job of course is to learn what we can about our government and pay attention that our representatives actually spend their time representing US.

When they do not do the will of the people in between elections we need to write letters to the editors of newspapers, and write our Congressmen and Senators so they know they cannot snooker us. If they don't listen, then we do the honorable thing and we write more letters to the editor and we un-elect our leaders their next time out.

Years ago, there was a great film director, Frank Capra, who understood what America was all about. He had a great way of bringing out the proper emotions of Americans, who would see his films and get his overall uplifting message. Twice with Gary Cooper and twice with James Stewart, Capra presented simple solutions to problems about which all Americans can relate. It would be nice if it were so easy but maybe it is.

Both *Meet John Doe* (1941) and *It's A Wonderful Life* (1946) were directed by Frank Capra. This Director had a gift to make people feel as good as they possibly could feel just by watching his films. One of seven children, Frank Capra himself was an immigrant from Sicily, and his experience on the "boat," mirrors that of many early immigrants.

Though at six years old, he did not have to deal with coyotes and bribery as illegal immigrants do today, to make his trip in 1903 to America as a legal immigrant, Capra recalled quite vividly the hell of the voyage on the Big Ship Germania (1300 passengers) which sailed from Naples Italy:

> *"There's no ventilation, and it stinks like hell. They're all miserable. It's the most degrading place you could ever be. Oh, it was awful, awful. It seems to always be storming, raining like hell and very windy, with these big long rolling Atlantic waves. Everybody was sick, vomiting. God, they were sick. And the poor kids were always crying."*

There were days at Ellis Island that at least eight ships arrived at Port. Over 12,000 new immigrants needed to be processed in a single day.

Meet John Doe

Meet John Doe (1941 Cooper) is Capra's wonderful, message-laden populist melodramatic tale about the common man. We could all stand another injection of goodness by watching this film again, and again, and again. This sentimental, hard-hitting film is often grouped into a populist trilogy of Capra films about American individualism - associated with *Mr. Deeds Goes to Town* (1936 Cooper)) and *Mr. Smith Goes to Washington* (1939 Stewart), although it is generally considered the weakest of the three (not by me). The socially-aware film was derived from a 1939 film that was titled *The Life and Death of John Doe.*

Barbara Stanwyck and Gary Cooper both gave persuasive and impressive performances in *Meet John Doe.* It is a very sobering film and in many ways remains today as part of an important social commentary. Like this book, and my continual pleas for all Americans to pay attention, Capra is asking movie goers *to think critically of everything they hear on the radio or see in papers or hear from elites.* Let's all say Amen to that. Today's press is much more corrupt than it was 70 years ago.

Where are the films that show us the way today? The liberal elitist progressive Marxists in Hollywood will not produce anything in these times that touts virtue and goodness, and so they join the press in refusing to do their jobs on behalf of the people. One might conclude they their intentions are to deprive the people of the way, the truth, and the light.

Contrasted to today, a Capra film about individualism may not fit so well for the hard left residents of the government and their many minions. Individualism and goodness for the sake of being good is counter to the group-think and the notion of collectivism that has permeated our government. Yet, if we are to be saved from ourselves, it will be rugged individualism, and not group-think or statism that does it for us.

Back in Capra's day, the media, aka the press, was mostly honest and it worked with the government for the good of the country. It challenged the government on behalf of the people when necessary. It was a valid fourth estate. That's what a free press is to do. Wouldn't that be something if it could happen again today? Unless we force it, it will not happen.

You can help by the way simply by canceling any subscription which lauds the progressive socialist Marxist agenda. Then get real news from honest talk radio shows or on the Internet.

Ironically, this film was intended to combat pro-Nazi Fascist forces present in America at the time. The story was about a young female newspaper reporter (Barbara Stanwyck), who writes a completely fraudulent column after threatened with being fired. In the spoof, she invents a fictitious person as the author of a letter - a suicide-martyr who protests against an unjust political and social system. The public bought the charade and were filled with hope. Then, because of the public's interest and demand (and soaring newspaper sales), she convinces a hobo (Gary Cooper) to take on the role of John Doe as if he were real. Then the "fun" starts.

This American ex-minor-league baseball player/hobo becomes John Doe - an *Everyman* character, and he sells his services as an imposter. He does a great job of impersonating the non-existent character. Before long, John Doe becomes a national figure, and this causes the spread of "John Doe Clubs" across the country.

The public gets excited over all of the goodness represented by the notion of John Doe. But, this spirit was not seen as a good thing by the political power brokers who felt their control of the people slipping away. So, just like they would today, the powerful elite had to shut it down.

Eventually, the reformed Doe, who is now taken up fully by his own cause, and who actually has become the embodiment of the John Doe he represented, is discovered as a fraud. The corrupting, unscrupulous political forces use this against him and cut him down like a pea. A shamed Doe is forced to publicly admit to the charade.

The film hits on the dangers of a complacent nation (with hunger amidst a land of plenty) being manipulated and taken over by neo-Fascist forces and Hitler's Third Reich (a reality in the early 1940s). This notion is countered in the film by the actions of the ordinary 'little man,' the John Does of this world (people like you and I) in a very moving way.

It gives strength to the notion that every person counts, and quite frankly, that is the only way that we can ever hope to bring back the spring in our step as we free America from the shackles of socialism. Just like all the John Does in the film, we Americans must "Pay attention."

Fully humiliated upon discovery of what was intended to be an innocent perpetration, John Doe decides to prove his sincerity to the people by fulfilling the suicide promise and leaping from the top of City Hall. But the rest of the world, all the real John Does of the world, like you and I, convince him otherwise. Without killing himself, in a cliff-hanger, his sincerity is recognized on Christmas Eve and like all good films, "the star lives and all is well." Moviegoers leave the theatres with hope in their hearts and a confidence that their opinions matter.

It's a Wonderful Life

Many more have seen Capra's *It's a Wonderful Life* than *Meet John Doe*. This magically wonderful film portrays a good young man named George Bailey (James Stewart), who marries his sweetheart Mary (Donna Reed), has four wonderful children, sacrifices for his father and his brother and his family and then has a tough time one particular Christmas Eve. This puts George on the verge of suicide, thinking, with his life insurance policy, he is worth more dead than alive.

The movie starts on Christmas eve, as all of the citizens of the small town of Bedford Falls pray to the heavens to help George Bailey. It's then decided in the heavens that Clarence, an angel who hasn't earned his wings, is assigned to help George. The film is emotional and it is uplifting and it again shows the power of the little guy and the power of good over evil. Just like *Meet John Doe*, it rekindles a spirit of goodness in all of US.

Keep both films handy because in this fight against evil and corporate greed, rampant political corruption, union thuggism, and the threat of statism, plus a government takeover of healthcare and other industries, none of us want to become like Potter or the bad guys in this movie. When you win as a John Doe or a George Bailey's yourself, you want it to be for the good of the country, and not just to get even. In this spirit, the spirit of real hope and individual goodness, all Americans must take up the torch and smarten up; stop being chumps; pay attention and take back our government from our corrupt representatives.

Mr. Smith Goes to Washington

This movie reminds me a lot about what it would be like if you or I or another of our neighbors were asked to uproot our lives and go to Washington to represent our community. We would expect a lot from the important people we would meet in the hallowed chambers in Washington D.C. We would expect honesty, integrity, and goodnesss and an overriding concern for the people.

In Mr. Smith Goes to Washington, a naive man (Jefferson Smith played by James Stewart) is appointed to fill a vacancy in the US Senate. He does not experience what he expects after a short while in the nation's power seat.

The power brokers, who arranged the appointment, never thought Smith would really engage nor do anything to hurt their extracurricular earnings opportunities. Yet, Smith's plans to be a good representative promptly collide with political corruption; but he doesn't back down.

Naive and idealistic Jefferson Smith had been the leader of the Boy Rangers in his home town. He was appointed on a lark by the spineless governor of his state. When he gets to Washington, he is amazed at the history and a major overall sense of national pride overtakes him on his way to his office.

Soon he is reunited with his state's senior senator, who happens also to be a presidential hopeful, Senator Joseph

Paine (Claude Rains). Paine had been Smith's childhood hero and Smith still had the utmost respect for Paine. In fact, if all went well, he would be happy to defer to the senior senator's judgments. But, all is not well, and Paine is not all that honest.

More or less alone in Washington, Smith slowly discovers many of the shortcomings of the political process. As the former head of the Boy Rangers, he has an altruistic goal for a national boys' camp, which leads him smack into the middle of a major conflict with the state's political boss, Jim Taylor (Edward Arnold). Taylor first tries to corrupt Smith but cannot and then later attempts to destroy Smith through a trumped-up scandal. He almost succeeds.

You can get the sense of the type of American Jefferson Smith is, when he lectures the Senate in his huge overnight filibuster included in the movie: "I wouldn't give you two cents for all your fancy rules if, behind them, they didn't have a little bit of plain, ordinary, everyday kindness and a little looking out for the other fella, too..."

Smith is like you and I. And like you and I he is met with very powerful forces of corruption. We too must be more intelligent than our adversaries so we can together defeat their evil notions and we can save America. That's what it is all about you know—saving America!

Jefferson Smith prevails in a heartwarming ending to this great story, and again movie goers are able to leave the theatre upbeat about their futures.

Throw the Bums Out

Unfortunately for Americans, our representative in the Congress, the Supreme Court, and the Presidency is not Jefferson Smith. All representation has been getting progressively worse each year—not better. Over the past few years, since 2009 / 2010 especially with the healthcare debacle, it is clear that our voices are not being heard in Washington.

Just as Smith found out, the corrupt purposes of elected officials is now in the open. It is to serve themselves by serving special interests.

In the sunlight of the day, therefore, the existing Congress -- yes, both houses must go. We must bid them sayonara. And when it comes time to elect our next President, let's not forget to bring in an honest person who loves America as much as we do. If the mess we have today is not the President's intentions, and his direct fault, then whose fault, I might ask, is it?

Surprise in today's email

Every now and then, we all get encouraged when somebody speaks out exactly how we all should be speaking out. As a conservative Democrat myself, trying to make this book apolitical, I thought about redacting parts of the below email that discuss people and party in specific terms. But, it is what it is. I'll let the email speak for itself and then after you read it, we will move to Part II of this book.

Sent from my iPad

Begin forwarded message:
From: Roger
To: undisclosed-recipients:;
Subject: Fwd: FW: Two Americas

Two Americas

To add balance to the president's speech last night, read the below;

This is as well said as anything I have seen. Take the time to read it. No matter your political affiliation, Democrat, Republican, or Independent, it should be clear that this country is in a lot of trouble. Some of us will live long enough to see the consequences, but I really fear for our children and grandchildren's future. The damage that can and will be done over the next three years will likely be irreversible or take years to overcome.

In early January 2014, Bob Lonsberry, a Rochester talk radio personality on WHAM 1180 AM, said this in response to Obama's "income inequality speech":

To Americans

The Democrats are right, there are two Americas.

The America that works, and the America that doesn't. The America that contributes, and the America that doesn't. It's not the haves and the have nots, it's the dos and the don'ts. Some people do their duty as Americans, obey the law, support themselves, contribute to society, and others don't. That's the divide in America.

It's not about income inequality, it's about civic irresponsibility. It's about a political party that preaches hatred, greed and victimization in order to win elective office. It's about a political party that loves power more than it loves its country. That's not invective, that's truth, and it's about time someone said it.

The politics of envy was on proud display a couple weeks ago when President Obama pledged the rest of his term to fighting "income inequality." He noted that some people make more than other people, that some people have higher incomes than others, and he says that's not just.

That is the rationale of thievery. The other guy has it, you want it, Obama will take it for you. Vote Democrat. That is the philosophy that produced Detroit. It is the electoral philosophy that is destroying America.

It conceals a fundamental deviation from American values and common sense because it ends up not benefiting the people who support it, but a betrayal. The Democrats have not empowered their followers, they have enslaved them in a culture of dependence and entitlement, of victimhood and anger instead of ability and hope.

The president's premise - that you reduce income inequality by debasing the successful - seeks to deny the successful the consequences of their choices and spare the unsuccessful the consequences of their choices.

Because, by and large, income variations in society is a result of different choices leading to different consequences. Those who choose wisely and responsibly have a far greater likelihood of success, while those who choose foolishly and irresponsibly have a far greater likelihood of failure. Success and failure usually manifest themselves in personal and family income.

You choose to drop out of high school or to skip college - and you are apt to have a different outcome than someone who gets a diploma and pushes on with purposeful education. You have your children out of wedlock and life is apt to take one course; you have them within a marriage and life is apt to take another course. Most often in life our destination is determined by the course we take.

My doctor, for example, makes far more than I do. There is significant income inequality between us. Our lives have had an inequality of outcome, but, our lives also have had an inequality of effort. While my doctor went to college and then devoted his young adulthood to medical school and residency, I got a job in a restaurant.

He made a choice, I made a choice, and our choices led us to different outcomes. His outcome pays a lot better than mine.

Does that mean he cheated and Barack Obama needs to take away his wealth? No, it means we are both free men in a free society where free choices lead to different outcomes.

It is not inequality Barack Obama intends to take away, it is freedom. The freedom to succeed, and the freedom to fail. There is no true option for success if there is no true option for failure.

The pursuit of happiness means a whole lot less when you face the punitive hand of government if your pursuit brings you more happiness than the other guy. Even if the other guy sat on his arse and did nothing. Even if the other guy made a lifetime's worth of asinine and shortsighted decisions.

Barack Obama and the Democrats preach equality of outcome as a right, while completely ignoring inequality of effort.

The simple Law of the Harvest - as ye sow, so shall ye reap - is sometimes applied as, "The harder you work, the more you get." Obama would turn that upside down. Those who achieve are to be punished as enemies of society and those who fail are to be rewarded as wards of society.

Entitlement will replace effort as the key to upward mobility in American society if Barack Obama gets his way. He seeks a lowest common denominator society in which the government besieges the successful and productive to foster equality through mediocrity.

He and his party speak of two Americas, and their grip on power is based on using the votes of one to sap the productivity of the other. America is not divided by the differences in our outcomes, it is divided by the differences in our efforts. It is a false philosophy to say one man's success comes about unavoidably as the result of another man's victimization.

*What Obama offered was not a solution, but a separatism.
He fomented division and strife, pitted one set of
Americans against another for his own political benefit.
That's what socialists offer. Marxist class warfare wrapped
up with a bow.*

*Two Americas, coming closer each day to proving the truth
to Lincoln's maxim that a house divided against itself
cannot stand.*

Part II: Brief History of the USA

Chapter 5   Introduction to Colonial History

Americans benefit from our democracy

Our Constitutional Representative Democracy, aka, our Republic comes from the hard fought battles of the Revolutionary War plus the craft of our founders in writing our country's original laws. Everything America was and is, is because of the work of the great men who came before US.

Most Americans have a great feel for the notion of representative democracy and the sense that we elect representatives of the community to handle our affairs in the governing of the nation. We also have the privilege of a Constitution which is intended to prevent tyranny by a government gone wild. We do not have a direct democracy in that we do not conduct the activities of government ourselves in Washington.

It would be very difficult squeezing over 300 million people into a room in Washington D.C. Instead, we choose representatives among us to get the job done.

What's Next?

When you go through other sections of this book, your opinion of the purity of the act of representation may become tainted. That is OK. I hope to generate some alarm and a sense of urgency among the readers for we simply may not have much time to get it right.

Something surely went wrong with the intention of representation from the Founding Fathers to what representation means today. Something went way wrong sometime between 1492 and the present day but the evidence suggests that the problem began closer to the year 2000 than to the year 1400. That's not to say that all was hunky-dory in the 1400s and onward.

Let's now take a look how America started to set the initial stage for an explanation. Then, we will take a peek at Colonial times and then the times from our founding. Eventually we will discuss present times and the problems with corrupt representation. Along the way, we will stop several times to examine and discuss the founding documents which define our government.

In Part IV, we will take a hard look at civics, and we will all get a nice civics lesson on government choices that the founders made so we can better appreciate our republican form of democracy.

From here we will discuss some of the pitfalls that any government runs into, especially our Constitutional Republic after over 200 years in existence. We will wrap up the book by discussing our supposedly honorable elected officials and how our understanding of America can help us keep these "honorables" under control to preserve government of the people, for the people, and by the people.

Chapter 6   America Before Columbus

Was Columbus the First Man Standing?

When we learned about Columbus in grade school, we also learned a very small amount about America before 1492— before Columbus landed? We learned that our hemisphere had a very sparse population, and that the occupants were mostly nomadic tribes living off the wilderness. We also learned about some more developed cultures in Central and South America.

Author Charles C. Mann in his book, "1491" presents convincing evidence that the pre-1492 era in American was not quite so barren and in fact was a lot more sophisticated than most of US have ever imagined.

In his writings, Mann notes that from southern Maine down the East Coast even past Virginia, there was farm after farm—not just a loggers dream wilderness. Most notably, Mann says there were lots of people. Americans would later call these people Indians or Native Americans.

Unfortunately, most of these people met their deaths through pestilence and disease. Thus, when the American settlers came to inhabit the new world, they did not find many people, and they formed their own conclusions.

Mann writes that North America not only had people before Columbus, it was once as populated as Europe in the pre-1492 era. He says it is only in the last few decades that humans have devised the tools to better probe the past to glean this data.

Mann said it is beginning to look like New England could not have been readily colonized any time sooner because it was too densely populated for settlers to assimilate. By the time the Pilgrims came, however, disease had killed off the population. The new immigrants were constantly discovering skeletons as if they had landed in a cemetery.

A book titled the *History of America Before Columbus, According to Documents and Approved Authors Volume I*, compiled by Peter De Roo (1839-1926), was published by Lippincott, Philadelphia in 1900. As a public domain book, it was recently scanned by the Google project and is available to all online. It offers many theories of the time before Columbus.

It opens up our eyes to even more wonders of America and its ancient past. It shows evidence that primeval man may very well have lived on this continent along with fully developed humans. Now, if that is the case, then the notions learned in our early history books that not too much was happening before 1492 is quite suspect.

One thing we do know is that US history books often begin with Leif Ericson, who is believed to have travelled to this land in the year 1000. Rasmus B. Anderson wrote a book, published in 1874, known as: *America Not Discovered by Columbus*. In this book, Anderson pointed out the accomplishments of the Norsemen and the Vikings for being the first Europeans in America.

We certainly do not know too much about this, regardless since there was little recorded history in those times. But, with today's tools, the theories of how it was in early America, even before anybody "sailed in," are much more plausible.

And so, based on the work of some great people, we now have reason to believe that America (North and South) wasn't exactly a *New World*. Instead; it was a very old one;

whose inhabitants had been here for quite a while, and had built a vast infrastructure of cities, orchards, canals and causeways along with gardens, buildings, homes, roads and pathways.

Many in the Mormon Faith still hold on to the belief that two of the lost tribes of Israel found their way to America and were here when the colonists arrived. They viewed the American Indians as having come from one of the two lost tribes of Israel even before Jesus Christ's time.

They see one of the twelve tribes in America and the other lost tribe in Polynesia. There is debate on this even today within the Mormon people. It is within the realm of possibility based on recent work. There is even speculation that St. Thomas the Apostle spent time in America.

No one has seriously suggested that Christ, during his visible mission on earth, ever visited our continent; but America was part of the world, over which He sent his apostles to teach His doctrine of salvation.

The question of His apostles' actual preaching in America has been in discussion for quite some time but most of US, who do not study such matters as a life mission, would naturally be unaware of these efforts. Many of US would discount some of the religious theories as unbelievable without more proof.

Quite interestingly; despite speculation about major populations being in North and South America at the time of Columbus, traces in North America are much rarer. Many of the population groups in the southern hemisphere built great edifices with grand architectures scattered through the land.

But, in all the rest of America—our America—aside from the miserable huts (tepees etc.) of the nomadic Indians, not a single memorial has been found to give evidence to national history for several centuries past—i.e. pre Columbus.

Additionally, no modem student of American antiquity fails to notice the close and striking resemblances between several leading particulars of Christian faith, morals, and ceremonies and those of the ancient American religions.

And, so, the question remains, "Was America Christianized from Asia?" The legacy surely appears that America has been a Christian nation for a long time. Despite this, I would not expect that even Alex Trebek will find that answer for any of US any time soon.

Chapter 7   America Post Columbus and Pre- Revolution

Columbus, Vespucci, de León , & Cabot

After the first voyage of Christopher Columbus in 1492, the Navigator Columbus and his small cast got credit for being the "Old Worlders," who had discovered the "New World." But did Columbus really discover the American mainland? If he did not, is it really such a big deal?

Historians seem to agree that on his first two voyages, Columbus discovered Cuba, Puerto Rico, Jamaica, the Bahamas, and some other islands. It was not until his third try in 1498, that he reached the mainland U.S. Thus, the claim that Amerigo Vespucci, a Spanish seaman, had reached the continent the year before Columbus may very well be valid.

Considering that the U.S. is part of the Americas and not the Columbias, leads one to conclude that the Amerigo Vespucci claim had enough merit when the naming was going on that the Spaniard got to give US his name.

Some historians argue that neither Columbus nor Vespucci discovered America. They say it was Juan Ponce de León who, who was Puerto Rico's first governor. This is ironic since Columbus is credited with founding Puerto Rico.

Certain historians have de Leon pegged as the first documented European to set foot on mainland American soil when he arrived with an expedition in Florida in 1513. As you know, he is also purported to have discovered the

Fountain of Youth, the legendary spring that, so they say,
restores the youth of anyone who drinks of its waters. Yet,
since de León, is surely in his grave today, the waters, even if
helpful, are not eternal.

Reasonable people have concluded that since there may not
really be a Fountain of Youth, de León may not have
discovered it. But, he surely discovered a nice state with
some real nice warm weather on the mainland. Florida of
course continues today to be an exceptional vacation spot.

Don't write the name "de León" down on your pad in
permanent ink yet as the first guy to walk on the US
mainland from the Old World. There are yet other historians
who suggest that he was in fact preceded by John Cabot to
the US mainland in 1497.

I am so glad that this is not a history book and we are not
here to argue these points. One indisputable fact that we can
take from this is that neither de León, nor Cabot, nor
Columbus nor Vespucci, are at fault for the current failings of
the U.S. representative government since they predate even
the "Founding Fathers." I am sure they would all be happy
getting honorable mention in this book about their roles in
the discovery of our great country.

The Jamestown Settlement

The first documented major group of settlers from the Old
World arrived on April 26, 1607. After a few weeks, they
built the Jamestown Settlement Colony. It was established on
the mainland of North America in Virginia. .

The passengers were a group of 104 English men and boys
who began the settlement on the banks of Virginia's James
River. The fleet consisted of the three ships, named Susan
Constant, Discovery, and Godspeed. The captain's name was
Christopher Newport. The ships took off from London and

landed after five months in Puerto Rico. Later they took off for the mainland.

The Virginia Company of London sponsored their trip. The company stockholders hoped to make a profit from the resources of the New World. Unfortunately, even though there appeared to be ample time to prepare for the first winter the community suffered terrible hardships from disease and starvation in its early years, but it managed to endure. Thus it became America's first permanent English colony.

Early on the colonists, who were not very good agrarians or hunters received help from the Indian Tribes near the colony. But, the relationship soured and things did not go too well.

Within a year of Jamestown's founding, the Virginia Company brought Polish and German émigrés to help improve the settlement. It was then that the first women were brought to America. It was more than ten years later, in 1619, that the first documented Africans were brought to Jamestown. At the time, there was no formal notion of slavery but slavery did begin in Virginia in 1660.

The Mayflower and the Pilgrims

The Pilgrims were among the first immigrants to seek freedom in America. In the absence of religious freedom in their native England, the Pilgrims were willing to endure great trials and diffilculties in a new land in order to gain the religious freedom they cherished and to raise their children properly.

Though she was not one of the first colonists, Anne Bradstreet was born Anne Dudley, and she lived from 1612 – 1672. She was the first poet and first female writer in the British North American colonies to be published. She emigrated to America in 1630 with her parents. Here is one of her works which captures some of the hope from colonial days. She aptly calls it perspective:

"If we had no winter, the spring would not be so pleasant: if we do not sometimes taste adversity, prosperity would not be so welcome."

Most of us are tuned into the story of the Mayflower and the Pilgrims and the first Thanksgiving. The Mayflower was the ship that carried mostly English Puritans and Separatists, collectively known today as the Pilgrims from England to America. They left from a spot near the Mayflower Steps in Plymouth, England, and landed in Massachusetts, in 1620. There were 102 passengers and a crew of 25–30.

This is one of the big stories of the founding of America over 100 years after Columbus. This voyage is a story of major accomplishments yet it is also a tragic story about deaths and survival as there were no hotels when the Pilgrims came to America. They immigrants had to endure harshest New World winter environment in the Northeastern US. The voyage, as well as the signing of the Mayflower Compact was one of the greatest moments in the story of America.

The Mayflower Compact was the original governing document written by the Separatists on the ship after it landed in Plymouth Rock. As many of US may recall from learning early US history as youngsters, Plymouth Rock is the traditional site of disembarkation of William Bradford and the rest of the Mayflower Pilgrims who founded the Plymouth Colony.

One of the most written about experiences of the Pilgrims was sharing a Thanksgiving harvest with the American Indians. Only 44 of the 102 original passengers survived that winter. It was the kindness of the local Native Americans (Indians) that saved them from a frosty death. They displayed remarkable courage when the Mayflower sailed back the following spring. Not one Pilgrim was on the ship. None had deserted their New World in Plymouth.

The first governor, who had been elected under the Mayflower Compact did not survive the winter and William Bradford, was elected governor. In May of 1621, he performed the colony's first marriage ceremony. Life was beginning again for the Pilgrims.

By the way, the second marriage soon after was between John Alden and Patricia Mullins, both of whom had come over on the Mayflower. There are many nice stories written about this couple.

The First Thanksgiving

By the fall of 1621, the Pilgrims were very thankful for their opportunities throughout the year. They had a bountiful harvest and William Bradford, a major hero in this colony, decided they would celebrate with Chief Ousamequin and about ninety other Indians.

They enjoyed the First American Thanksgiving, which at the time was basically an enactment of the great English tradition of Harvest Festival. They enjoyed a bounty over several days of items such as venison, goose, duck, turkey, fish, and of course, cornbread, a new staple from their first bountiful corn harvest. This was such a wonderful an experience that it was repeated each year at harvest time, and it is still celebrated throughout the US in November each year.

Some other settlers

Though close to London in the British Isles, the Scotch and Irish did not come to America until the early 1700s, and the Welch did not venture over en masse until near the end of the eighteenth century.

There is also evidence that early expeditions from the British Isles (Wales, etc.) had come to America as early as the Twelfth Century. When the Scotch and Irish came to the New World in the 1700s, they settled mostly in Pennsylvania before many moved south and west to other colonies. Some went as far north as New Hampshire.

A few hundred years before the Revolution

So that we all have a good idea on how the great American experiment with democracy and constitutional representation began, let's take a look at how the states were organized originally and how they ultimately were able to form a government.

Just like the discovery of America, this is not a fully clean story as historians continue to argue about what is actually what. For example, two of the original states were governed by a notion called self-government but later they were classified along with Massachusetts in a category known as "Corporate." But, the thirteen colonies, regardless of these classifications, were ultimately the geographical land bodies that became the first Unites States of America.

The thirteen colonies of England were founded 100 + years after Columbus, with Virginia the first colony in 1607 and Georgia the last in 1733.

Among the things we can be sure about as we look back to these colonial days, nobody from 1607 to 1733 created the current confidence problem in U.S. representative government, and they did not create a huge national debt for US, though our current "honorable representatives" might like to suggest otherwise.

These thirteen colonies were organized into two to three varieties depending on your historical perspective. The original three forms were known as (1) the Charter form, (2)

Royal form, and (3) Proprietary form. Later these were combined into two forms, known as the Corporation (formerly Charter), and the Provincial (formerly either the Royal or Proprietary).

So, the individual colonies, did not each have the same exact form of government but ultimately they all reported to the Crown of England. The Corporation form included Massachusetts, Rhode Island, and Connecticut, though Rhode Island and Connecticut were also, "self-governing."

The provincial forms included the former proprietary colonies of Maryland, Pennsylvania, and Delaware as well as the former Royal Colonies of Georgia, New Hampshire, New Jersey, New York, North Carolina, South Carolina, and Virginia. By the way, these colonies stretched from Main to Georgia and that is the whole Eastern US seacoast other than Florida, which for the longest time was under Spanish dominion.

Even during this period, there was confusion and pressure as to which form a particular colony would take. For example, some of the Royal colonies became Proprietary colonies and vice versa and thus the notion of the term Provincial came to describe what today in our political system would be called the flip-flopping colonies... though their flipping and flopping was hardly voluntary.

The governmental form was similar

Though not exactly, Most of these colonies had the same form of government consisting of a governor, appointed by the English Crown or by the proprietor(s). Additionally, they each had a council that also was appointed by the Crown. The most important body to the colonists was an assembly, which was known as the house of representatives.

Even while America was attached as a colony of England, this body was elected by the people. These three bodies took on a governmental shape very similar to the king and the two houses of Parliament as existed in England.

Thus, in many ways the government of the colonies resembled the British government, and you can bet that was its intent. Though the English argued that this was a representative democracy, it is easy to see the failings in this notion when the "Crown" appointed the most important ruling bodies - the Council and the Governor.

The Governor

The Governor directly represented the Crown or the proprietor, who had already paid "allegiance" to the Crown with some type of tribute. Being the proprietor of a colony required a large stipend in cash or in kind.

Now, with that the case, it meant that the Governor did not represent the people though it was his mission. His loyalty was clearly to the Crown and / or the proprietor. To be successful, however, in governing the people, he owed a duty to the people over whom he was placed. Therefore, smart governors knew that it was nice, though not necessary that the people liked him.

As you can easily conclude, the interests of the two parties were so conflicting as to keep the Governor in a constant turmoil. Perhaps this is where the temperament of the politician as we now know them today, would have served best. But, the notion of the politician as we know it, would not arrive for a few more hundred years.

The Governor had immense power in his territory. He could convene, discontinue, postpone or even dissolve the legislature, and he had veto power over all of its would-be laws. He controlled the state militia, and he was the grand miffintiff, who appointed the important officials, such as judges, justices of the peace, sheriffs, and any others of authority.

The one thing the Governor could not touch however, was the public purse, and this soon became a cause of lament for the British.

Though history suggests there were many kind and benevolent Governors, there were also those who took advantage of the fruits of the spoils system and they even sold some of the offices at their disposal to the rich in the community, thus affecting their own personal purse in a positive way. Unfortunately many of these men, and there were no women at the time, cared little for the welfare of the colonists.

The Council

Typically there were twelve men in the Council, though in Massachusetts there were twenty-eight. In Maryland, there were only three. Council members needed to posses certain attributes to retain their positions.

For example, they had to be residents of the colony in which they served, and they needed to be men of station and wealth. The Crown or the proprietor appointed the council so the normal conflicts arose and they were settled in the normal way -- in favor of the Crown or the proprietor. Council had three major functions:

- Advise the governor
- Provide the "upper house" of the legislature (Lords)
- Serve as the highest court in that particular colony

In Massachusetts, after 1691, the council was elected by a joint ballot of the legislature, called the General Court. In the other colonies it was by appointment of the Crown or the proprietors.

The House of Representatives

Then, there was the lower house which was elected by the people and whose mission in life was to represent and theoretically support the people. It was the body of the legislature that actually made the laws.

The innate power to make laws is a big deal in any form of government. So, the people did not get to elect the governor, nor the council (also served as judges) but the subjects of the crown actually were permitted their own house of representation to the Colony and ultimately to the Crown through the Council or the Governor.

Now, that's fair, right? Unfortunately, something happened on the way to real fairness. The laws/acts passed by this lower house could be vetoed by whim of the governor, or be set aside by the Crown within a certain time after their passage for any reason whatsoever.

Is Alf a friend or foe?

In other words, if Alf, the furry non-Muppet character circa 1986, were to materialize as a friend of the Crown, and he did not like some legislation about cats that was introduced, just by having the ear of the Crown or the proprietor or the council, the legislation to protect cats could be defeated.

Just by Alf's whispering, the people's voice could be overturned. This would occur simply because of Alf or perhaps it was really a guy named Gordon Shumway (Alf's pseudonym). Additionally, the Tanner family (human family home where Alf lived in the sitcom) would have no standing in the matter. You get my point.

The assembly had something that the Crown really did not want to give up but it already had. The lower legislature had the power of taxation. In retrospect, the Crown must have viewed this as a major faux pas.

Since the Assembly had the right of taxation and the Crown did not, the normal and natural governance of the colonies seemingly was in control of the colonists -- other than the veto power etc. of the other loyal bodies.

Historians might even claim that the colonies were self-governing, and they should have had no concern for their liberties as long as they and they alone could retain this sole right of taxing themselves. We'll see how this notion plays out later in this section.

For the British, this did become a big problem. Not having any say in controlling the purse strings (tax coffers) of the colonies was a big issue that kept getting bigger as American wallets, made of the finest British leather, got fatter and fatter. The poor Brits had not given themselves an easy way of siphoning off a few pence for the Crown. A faux pas indeed!

This representative system of government, though obviously flawed, was common to all the colonies, but It did not enter the sphere of influence in Georgia until 1752. The notion began in Virginia in 1619; as noted previously it made it to Massachusetts in 1634, and it hit Maryland in 1639.

The system of representative government was allowed by the Crown, but not required, by the early charters. After it had begun almost spontaneously in a number of colonies, it became a big part of a number of the charters. The people loved it. People love having control of their own destiny still today.

The problem with Colonial suffrage

The one little piece of the fight for democracy puzzle that we have intentionally left out so far was that there was no colony in which universal suffrage was to be found. How about that? It was a piece of democracy in which certain people had to first be anointed.

If you were not anointed, you did not get to vote. Sounds like cause for a revolution -- but we are moving too quickly. The notion of "who was able to vote" gave back a bit more power to the Crown than otherwise might have been noticed. Theoretically, the Crown could stack the deck in the House of Representatives so that some crooked people in the Assembly, and not the people in general would control the purse.

The people of the colonies had lots of concerns and they had many reasons to fear. Most importantly, they feared for their lives. For example, there were these guys known as Native Americans, colloquially described as "Indians" during colonial times, since originally the settlers thought they had discovered India.

These folks were not as some may think—a western U.S. phenomenon and only a major nemesis of cowboys. In fact, at the time, there was no western U.S.

The "Indians," many of whom had died from disease over the hundred or so years preceding the colonists, were not very happy that uninvited guests were in their territory, and so they protected what they saw as theirs, and thus, there were conflicts with the settlers.

The colonists therefore needed as much help as they could get to guard against the Indians and the wild animals and any other fears, real or imaginary. The British Government

Officials and the British Army provided reassurances and for a time it seemed the British did all this work for free.

Moreover, the colonists also wanted the right to attend their own churches so they could talk to their maker without interference and they wanted to have a safe trip each Sunday both forth and back. Their affiliation with the British provided these assurances.

The Towns

Knowing that to be alone in this semi-wilderness was at best an at-risk notion, they settled in small, compact communities, or townships. They called them simply towns. In these times, the town was a legal corporation, a political unit more or less, and in the big scheme of colonial life, it was represented in the General Court or another governing body. The Town itself where colonists lived thus had political standing.

It could be argued that this whole notion (if we take the Crown from the Picture) was a representative democracy of the purest type. The people met (adult males) and discussed the issues of the day; they created taxes for the common good, and they created laws to make it simpler to put the bad guys away. How could anything be better?

Colonialism and its pluses and minuses is not the matter of focus for this book but it helps in understanding why the colonists revolted. In this section, so far, we recounted a number of things you already know from the beginning of colonialism to the period of time right before the revolution.

In all of the notions that we just discussed, I am unaware of any that suggest that the public representatives of the time before the revolution until at least the year 1750, were working for anything other than a better town or community. Yes, there was taxation, but, there was also some form of representation, though not perfect. There was resentment by

the colonists in tithing for the Crown but there were some
benefits delivered for the taxation. After 1750, however it
seemed to get a lot worse.

Of course, that is not how it is today and as we move forward
through this chapter, we hope to identify the roots of the
change and carry that into the representative pandemic from
which today we suffer. If you were alive in 1750, then you
know what I am talking about but if you came shortly after,
you may have to take my word about a number of these very
important events.

Today we know the Democrats say blue and the Republicans
say red, and 47% of the people feel one way and 47% feel the
other way. Besides them, there are about six percent in the
middle who are for something else. If we were to put a few
names on that something else, on a perennial basis, the
names in the past might be spelled, "Ron Paul" or "Dennis
Kucinich."

The latter six percent of American voters are known today by
the media as undecided. A good part of them are
Independent thinkers or so they would like to describe
themselves. The 1750 crowd never knew it was going to get
like it is or I am sure these great minds would have done
something about it then to prevent it today.

The Colonial "Democracies" were NOT like the state
governments or the Federal Government that we have today.
The "voice of the people" was often artificially limited—at
times just to property-owning white men. Suffrage was not a
big deal since men and mostly rich men were more tuned-in
than anyone else. Women were simply denied the right to
vote, and there were few discussions about that.

On top of all the natural potential for corruption before 1750,
the structure made it real easy. The colonial governors in
some cases did have autocratic powers, and could act
accordingly, despite the democratic aspect. If they decided to

take more power than they were entitled, nobody was powerful enough to answer back.

Some of these governors, as noted previously, were appointed by the Crown back in England. Even those that were not Crown appointees could not be overruled by the people's representative legislatures, even if they so desired.

Chapter 8   England Dominated the New World

To the victor belong the spoils

As the most successful imperialist nation of the day, Britain won control over American lands during the 17th and 18th centuries, and lost to the Americans in the late 18th century. Its control of the seas and its notion of colonial representative government were major factors in its ultimate success. The English nation of yore had a keen ability to recognize a good deal when it had one coming its way.

The European countries such as England, Holland (Dutch Republic), Spain, France, and Portugal developed colonies in the Western Hemisphere for many reasons, but primarily the reason was to bring in more revenue for the home state.

Though the English were late arrivals, they ultimately took all the spoils. The colonies were a great source of raw materials for trade (e.g. furs and precious metals) and they served as ready markets for finished products.

The Spanish, French, and Dutch had small settlements in what is now the continental US for a long time before the English got fully involved. But, none of the settlements were of major consequence.

As the thirteen colonies began to grow with immigrants pouring in from a number of different countries, these settlers, who more and more thought of themselves as Americans, regardless of their origin, liked the English system much better than the authoritarian systems of the other countries.

When England made its moves to capture these colonies as well as Florida, which was not one of the original thirteen colonies and which was hitherto dominated by the Spanish, they did so with ease. The settlers in many ways were happy to move to the more representative system of government, though as noted previously, it was not perfect. Florida could have been the fourteenth colony, but instead it did not sign up. Eventually Florida became the 27th state of the Union.

The success it had in the continual conflicts between the European countries and England -- especially the conflicts with the French, culminating in the French and Indian War (1754–1763) positioned the English to dominate the New World. The French and Indian War was the North American front for a war going on in Europe at the time known as the Seven Years War, in which most of the European powers and England were battling.

France Was the Big Loser

The North American name for the war comes from the two major enemies of the British in America, namely the French and the various American Indian tribes. England emerged the big winner in this war, resulting in its conquest of all of what had been labeled New France (French claimed land east of the Mississippi), in addition to Spanish Florida.

The French were big losers on both fronts in this war— Europe and America. In fact the combination of the French and Indian War and the Seven Year War in Europe ended France's position as a major colonial power in the Americas.

Their losses were huge and the French were left with little more than French Guiana, Guadeloupe, Martinique, Saint-Dominguez, Saint Pierre, and Miquelon. To pay off the

Spanish for its support in the war and Spain's loss of Florida, the French ceded control of French Louisiana (West of the Mississippi).

Perhaps more devastating to France was its demise as the leading power in Europe. It sustained such heavy losses in the war that it was not until the French Revolution that France again became a major force in Europe.

American leaders understood the British Government

Getting back on point, nothing that the English or the French or the Dutch Republic or the Portuguese or Spanish did during this pre-revolutionary period caused the current lack of faith in representative government as exists today in the United States. This lack of confidence in the motivation of duly elected representatives who represent special interests and themselves today rather than their constituencies was not a phenomenon of the 18th century.

In fact, as noted, the ultimate takeover of the colonies by the British in many ways was welcomed by the settlers because the British offered the concept of self-government, whereas their European counterparts were autocratic and authoritarian in dealing with the residents of the New World.

This notion of self-government and representative government marked the colonies' early political development and this notion continues to exist today, though admittedly today in the U.S. it is in need of a bit of rebuilding. That, my friends, is why you are reading this book.

All good things must come to an end, or so it seems. The rise of self-government in the colonies was a direct result of the fact that many of the English colonies were created as private corporate enterprises and as proprietary ventures. Additionally, a good number of the English colonists were knowledgeable of government and had in fact participated in government at home. So, they carried this tradition with them to America. They knew a good deal from a bad deal.

As noted previously, England was a bit late to the colonial party. It was not until the 17th century that the English Parliament, the legislative branch, began to stretch its own powers at the direct expense of the English Crown. These internal English "constitutional" struggles were not lost on the early Americans.

In fact, most of the English in America supported the Parliament and the notion of representative government. In the British colonies, this was marked within the three original types of colonies, which we examined earlier in this Chapter as the Royal colonies, Proprietary colonies, and Charter colonies.

Part III: The Revolution

Chapter 9   The Seeds of Revolution

The Beginning of the End

The beginning of the end of this love affair of the colonists with English-style government came about when the English government began to appear to the colonists as big bullies, and not grand protectors. The British began to impose direct controls and taxes on the settlers. The French and Indian War had given England control of the thirteen colonies plus other American territories. They had yet to flex their muscles.

And so, it seems that finally, somebody in England said that it was time to collect from the colonists. England had forgotten that their conquering of the other European powers in America was partly because the Americans liked how they were being treated by the Brits. Increasing taxes and controlling actions in America without the colonist's permission was strictly taboo. The British simply did not get it! Americans would not put up with crap! There, I said it!

It seems that the British snatched defeat from the jaws of victory as they seemingly could not stand their own success and they began to behave badly from an American colonial standpoint. We still might be British subjects if the Crown had not gotten so greedy.

In the 1750's some historical estimates suggest that the 13 colonies had about 5 million people. The "benevolent" King of England at the time (Not King Charles and Queen Camilla), King George III had concerns about how to protect so many people from invaders, be they American Indians or other European powers.

He chose to do so with a British army of 10,000 men stationed in America for the "protection of the colonists." Though some objected to a standing English army in the Americas, many others did not have an issue. But, then, King George III decided he did not really want the Crown to pick up the tab for all of the soldiers so he figured the colonists should pony up to pay the bill. The colonists obviously thought otherwise especially since they were not asked. Britain had already been extracting its "due" from the colonies, and the due bill was about to expand.

Illegal Taxation – Stamp Act, etc.

England did not want to admit publicly that its resources had been stretched in all of the wars it had just won. The burden of providing the colonists with the protection they expected became a bit more than the British wanted to handle.

Their own government, which the colonists were faithfully operating under, had not provided a means for England to grab funds directly from the colonists without permission. For its own reasons, England, the most powerful nation in the world chose not to ask the colonists. Instead, they decided to "take."

King George saw himself as the ultimate ruler and so he imposed a tax on the colonists in what was known as the Stamp Act of 1765. Just a few years after defeating the American Indians and the French across the globe, the British could not wait for the lower house in the colonies to tax themselves for the support of the British standing army.

Instead, without authority, they simply imposed the tax. This tax was to be paid by having tax stamps placed on newspapers, licenses, calendars, playing cards, dice and other items that were frequently purchased in the colonies.

These were today's equivalent of smart phones, and iPhones, and i-pads and pods, and the finest e-games of the century. The British decided to whack Americans with a big tax if they chose to enjoy themselves.

Think of the word "impose" and then think of how you feel when someone else's will is imposed on yours for any reason whatsoever. Think of the Cap and Trade debate, which has quiesced for now, and the major healthcare debates of 2014.

Likewise, the colonists were enraged at the King and the Parliament since they felt the British had violated their own Constitution. Only the lower assemblies as elected by the colonists were permitted to decide which taxes should be levied, how much, when they were to become effective, and who was to get the cash.

The protests began immediately and in 1766 the colonists appeared to have gained a victory as the British government quickly gave in and repealed the Stamp Act. But King George III was not finished. He knew at the time, he was the King, and no other cards mattered.

The Quartering Act

Another nasty little Act that was imposed on the colonists at about the same time was something called the Quartering Act. Colonists despised this act. Instead of having to pay for the 1760 equivalent of a hotel room, under this law, American colonists had to provide housing, candles, bedding, and beverages to the British soldiers stationed in the various colonies. Quartering means "Give them a room and amenities." American men and women were not very happy about this.

Again the British were looking for a means to pay for their
empire defense costs in America following the French and
Indian War and another little war known as Pontiac's War.

A number of American Indian tribes at the time were
understandably upset when the British and French stopped
their war and the British were declared the victors and the
Native Americans were left out of the deal. The Indians had
been fighting on the side of the French and got nothing out of
the surrender deal.

Pontiac's War was named after the Ottawa Tribe Chief
Pontiac, who was the most prominent of the many native
leaders (Indian Chiefs) involved in the conflict. Ultimately
the British finished them off, but they remained unhappy.

In the same vein as the Stamp Act of this same year, various
English Acts presented a big problem. After all, even the
uninvolved without a dog in the fight can easily see that the
whole thing was just an uninvited assertion of British
authority over the colonies.

It completely disregarded the fact that troops had been
financed for the prior 150 years by representative provincial
assemblies rather than by the Parliament and Crown in
London. Americans wanted nothing to do with London
controlling America—at least not so obviously.

Locations, which quartered more than their fair share of
British soldiers, such as New York; resented the Quartering
Act even more-so and they were outwardly defiant. The
problem at this time was that there was no way that the
British were about to go away empty handed.

They began to dig in more and more to protect their
perceived "right" to get at the purse of the colonies through
direct taxation, though in their own laws imposed for a long
time on the colonists, they had excluded themselves from

being legally able to coerce the colonists to pay or else. The colonists were incensed at the betrayal.

The British determination was felt as they exercised their strength in ways that the colonists had never before witnessed. Because of the resistance for example, of the Quartering Act, they almost immediately instituted the Suspending Act.

This was insult to injury as it prohibited the New York Assembly from conducting any further business until the colony complied with the financial requirements of the resented Quartering Act. It was like England had declared war on New York.

When things did not look good, the British always seemed to do something to make matters worse.

For example, they also initiated another act that has been called the Townshend Act in which duties were imposed just as in the Stamp Act. This time the taxes were noted as Townsend duties and were applied to lead, glass, paper, and tea and the tax was payable immediately at colonial ports.

After a reprieve from the Quartering Act, in 1770, the colonists found themselves suffering from an additional quartering clause, which was included in the Intolerable Acts of 1774. The American Revolution was getting closer.

Chapter 10 The Honeymoon Is Over

No taxation without representation

The British government's honeymoon with the American
colonists was well over but many colonists felt that it would
be better to just act like it was OK. Yes, there were appeasers
even back in early America. Think of the situation in which
Britain found itself.

Unlike the Dutch and the Spanish and the French, their
ruling style was not authoritarian and they had given the
colonists the right to decide to whom they paid tribute. After
all that fighting with American Indians and French and
others, the British felt they had a right to something out of the
deal. Where were their spoils? Since they had not asked for
any up-front, Americans were not about to give. And the
Brits, desperately in need of funds, thought they were
powerful enough not to have to ask.

Perhaps with diplomacy, the British Parliament could have
convinced the lower assemblies of the colonies to see it their
way. They also could have used some pressures from the
governor or the council and court system to gain the will of
the colonists so that they would agree as a group to be taxed
to support the protection funding which would keep the
British Army nice and cuddly at night.

One thing is for sure, the way it went down, the Americans
were not ready for an imposition and the British were not
ready to make America a loss-leader "possession."

Parliament was not about to give up. They showed their resiliency to play another round by finding other means of taxing the colonists. Their next try was an import tax on everything. The colonists did more than offer objections.

Checkmate for the colonists when they boycotted all imports from England. After a few minor scuffles and 18 months of time, Parliament dropped the tax on everything but tea and then the British ships had to sail away from Boston Harbor.

In 1773, the British were back and at it again hoping that knowingly or unknowingly they could get the colonists to buy teas with the tax buried in the price. Shiploads of tea from India were of lower cost and they sold it so low that even with the tax included, many of the colonists, who enjoyed the English tea customs from the old world, could not resist purchasing it.

It actually was a good deal but it would have been a better deal without Mother England grabbing an unauthorized cut of the proceeds. And, so there were many colonists who hated England's actions who resisted and finally chose to take action as patriots to stop the sailors from unloading the tea.

This is just a little reminder of the fact at this point in the story, the royal governor of Massachusetts, who happened to be Thomas Hutchinson, reported to the Crown and not to the people. So, with the people, he had no standing on the matter.

Hutchinson decided to use his power to muster the British Troops and have the ships unloaded under their protection.

As most Americans well know the story, the Bostonians disguised themselves as Indians, snuck onto the ships and dumped about 340 tea chests into the sea. It was the Boston Tea Party and quite a party indeed.

Figure 10-1 Boston Tea Party

"The Destruction of Tea at Boston Harbor." 1773. Copy of lithograph by Sarony & Major, 1846. -- National Archives and Records Administration

This is another lesson in representative government. "No Taxation without Representation." And it certainly demonstrates how clever the constituency can become when made angry of taxes imposed by a body not representing the people. Shall we all take lessons?

In the past most Americans from grade school through high school learned the principles upon which this country was built and along with that the notion of representation.

Unfortunately, because progressive socialists now control education, and most of our government infrastructure, our children may not know what we are talking about when we discuss this part of history.

Looking back at the Boston Tea Party we can ask ourselves again questions about why Americans, after 200 years are so upset again!

The question to be answered is: "Who is it that our elected officials represent - a combination of special interests and themselves or the people alone?

It seems that in recent times this answer is rarely, "the people" and if it is; it is never alone! The British eventually learned its lesson well. Americans must teach our teachers and our leaders well, once and for all.

U.S., state, and local legislators need to relearn this lesson or The U.S. may be looking at some more Tea in Boston and other areas of the mainland some time soon. In 2014 as we have seen Tea Parties in the US are making a comeback.

My party, the Democrats, have chosen to denigrate the moms and the pops and people like you who express outrage and the tyranny of our central government. They call us all TEA Party. Yet, I am a Democrat by registration. What do they know other than hate for anybody not thinking the collective way.

Why not just let the people decide who has the better message? Why cheat and defame opponents simply because we do not want the country turned over to the socialist progressive Marxists.

Just as the tea tax upset the settlers, the tea party that was held with prepaid British tea made the British furious. Parliament and the King were embarrassed that a colony could impose its will on the Great Britain. They would not stand still on that matter or on the matter of getting their share by taxing the colonies.

Not really to be taken lightly, the British brought their ships back into Boston harbor and they imposed a blockade on trade until the colonists agreed to pay for the spoiled tea.

With the port of Boston being a major point of commerce in Massachusetts at the time, the colonists had little choice but to give in or face financial ruin. But, their message was well delivered even if not well taken. The British were firing up again, the strongest of those who had emigrated from their shores for similar reasons. Americans are a tough lot indeed. Such Americans would not stand still.

The Intolerable Acts

The activity of the British known as the "Intolerable Acts" was so intolerable that it led to the colonists calling the first Continental Congress of the thirteen colonies. In other words, the USA, on its own, without even being the USA at the time, were getting ready to talk turkey long after the Pilgrims.

And, so, the colonies, knowing their representatives could be shot or otherwise held accountable by the British for treason of the Crown, chose to convene in Philadelphia's Carpenters Hall on September 5, 1774. Consider all of the delegates in this meeting as having begun the fight for your freedom.

They risked life and limb for sure, and the British were expected to be vindictive in victory or defeat. So, these colonists, the original patriots, had deep concerns for the welfare of their country and their families.

They finished their work on October 26, 1774. It had been a meeting of 56 delegates from 12 of the 13 colonies. Major historical figures such as John Adams, his cousin Samuel Adams, Patrick Henry, and George Washington were present when this first meeting of the united colonies was held.

Only Georgia, the newest colony at the time, was absent from the meeting as its English-controlled Governor ordered its delegates not to attend.

The Congress met until late October with its major function to affirm the right of the colonies to life, liberty and property and to assure that they would meet again the following year.

Among their work was a letter to the King of England demanding an end to the blockade, and the Congress also approved resolutions for the people of Massachusetts to arm themselves, and to stop trading with Britain. These were gutsy calls.

Declaration of Rights and Grievances

Two principal accomplishments of the Congress were the formation of a Continental Association as well as the Declaration of Rights and Grievances, a historical document included with this book.

The text of the Declaration is shown in Appendix A and the text of the Articles of Association is shown in Appendix B.

This patriotic association (Articles of Association) set up a boycott against importing British goods to the colonies. The teeth of this boycott was its enforcement by community groups and small committees. All of these patriots feared that the English would take their lives for such treason against the British Crown. Yet, they were brave enough to carry on.

The Declaration of Rights and Grievances was the formalization of the letter to King George and it called on the Crown to disband its army, cease and desist in the enforcement of its "Intolerable Acts," adhere to the right of no taxation without representation, and to recognize the right to liberty of the American people as protected by the common law of England.

Figure 4-2 The First Continental Congress - Carpenter's Hall
Philadelphia

The Declaration also called on the King to restore the
benefits of the existing English statutes at the time of their
colonization. Just as these protected the English in England
so also, according to the Declaration should they protect the
English Colonists in America?

This was a major operation on the part of the colonists by
rejecting the "Intolerable Acts" and it specified the only
acceptable basis for a continued relationship between
England and America. Though polite, it was a forceful
document.

Article Four of this work was authored by John Adams. This
article is fundamental to the notion of representation as we

are learning in this book. It states that representation of the
people in their legislature is a fundamental English right,
essential to free government.

Moreover, it acknowledges that colonists could not be and
were not represented in Parliament (England), and thus it
concluded that that body of the Parliament had no control
over them.

It went on to inform the King that only by consent of the
colonies—which America cheerfully granted—did
Parliament have a right to regulate trade.

In a powerful assertion, it concluded that such regulation by
the Crown must not have as its purpose the raising of any
kind of revenue. In other words, the message clearly was that
with no representation there would never be taxation. These
words were delivered plain and simple. The patriots were
strong willed and brave Americans.

This was not the beginning of the revolution per se and
America had not yet declared independence, but one could
sense that the winds of war for freedom's sake were in
motion.

There was some real hope that the formal written plea to the
King would work but, just in case, the colonists put together
a plan to elect delegates to a Second Continental Congress to
deal with the possibility that the King would simply dismiss
their concerns.

King George III for his part was enraged at what he viewed
as an "illegal" and treasonous document sent by the colonists
and he was not moved to corrective action. After all, he was
the King of the most powerful nation on earth.

The response to a potential revolution was in the offing as the
colonists suspected. Brave as ever men would ever be, the
colonists were ready to take on the Brits to preserve our

America. That is why we celebrate the Fourth of July. Bravo to our patriots who fell in battle to preserve our freedom and liberty.

Chapter 11   The Beginning of the American Revolution

Friends do not wage war with friends?

In preparation for a potential war with the Crown, the colonists began to train and gather arms and ammunition. They were brave indeed to take such action.

Anybody who spent one day at the firing range in the military of the US knows that all soldiers must fire a weapon at least once to understand the force with which a rifle or a pistol or a revolver sends its metal projectile forward. Eventually, the troop gets qualified but the major issue is not qualification.

The spookiest time for a Sergeant on the range is when a new group of nobodies shows up to learn how to become soldiers. The sergeant must assure that the troops always assume there is a round in the chamber and that they carry their weapons accordingly way up or way down to the ground so nobody gets hurt by a mistake.

They biggest problem for any troop on the first day on the range is adapting to the hellish sound of a round, once chambered, and then fired at a target. This preparation during the revolution made the American troops stronger in battle against the British professional army than even the British expected.

This was well noticed by British General Sir Thomas Gage, the Commander in Chief of the British forces and he became very concerned. Feeling that this was a plot of treason against the Crown, he planned to take action.

On the night of April 18, 1775, his troops seized some of the supplies and, according to some accounts; they planned to arrest two of the militia's leaders, Sam Adams and John Hancock.

Other accounts suggest that Gage didn't order troops to arrest John Hancock and Samuel Adams in Lexington on their way to Concord and as we have learned, such historian disputes almost never fully are resolved.

After Gage's papers were reflected in history, it is clear that a number of patriots thought that the capture of colonial leaders was probably the British column's mission, and they prepared accordingly. But, the facts indicate that was not really Gage's plan. Nonetheless, you can feel the type of tension that was growing between American patriots and the British army.

Paul Revere

Paul Revere had been a hero in the pre-revolution period in his ability to bring needed communication among the colonies about very important matters. Thanks to his warnings that the "British were coming," as well as those of William Dawes, Joseph Warren, and others, the militia was waiting for the British and thus the American Revolution began the next day.

Paul Revere and the other patriots rode from Boston to Concord through the dark on the eve of April 19, 1775, to warn as many families and country folk as they could of the danger about to come.

The next day war broke out in the battles of Lexington and Concord. The revolution had begun. The unprepared and disorganized British ultimately had to retreat. The Minutemen prevailed and put the British on the chase. History will never forget that day.

Ralph Waldo Emerson, in his beloved Concord Hymn described the first shot fired by the patriots at the North Bridge as the "shot heard 'round the world." The clear irony of this shot however comes about because nobody knew then, nor is it known today; who it was who actually fired that first shot of the American Revolution.

It is as if from then 'til now, we moved from not being able to find a bullet, to not being able to find a huge Boeing 777. Who knows why? For the colonists, the mission was freedom, and the fact that a shot was fired, began the war. Whoever knows anything about the missing plane, I suspect will keep their silence.

No taxation without representation, the rationale for freedom, was a major cause of Americans joining in for the fight for liberty. Today, without bloodshed, the battle of the Whigs and the Tories continues in the halls of Congress while neither seems to care about the will of the people. You are reading this book because you care.

Unlike the late 1700's this new group of "representatives" does understand the value of public opinion and so these esteemed representatives in the U.S. in the latter part of the 20th century and past the first decade of the 21st seem much more ready to manipulate public opinion than to work to fulfill the public will.

The Second Continental Congress (May 10, 1775, to March 1, 1781)

The Second Continental Congress met for the first time on May 10, 1775, during the war, on a day, which incidentally was the same date as the American capture of Fort Ticonderoga.

The American Revolutionary War continued with battle after battle. George Washington was appointed Commander of the troops even before the Second Continental Congress. The militias had gotten the colonists through the first battles of the war with England.

Now, with Washington leading an Army of the United Colonists, the superiority of numbers represented by the more than 5 million colonists was expected by the colonists to mathematically eliminate the Old World British from having its way in America. But, the British were well armed and well prepared, and they rarely chose to stand down against what they perceived to be a weaker foe.

The more skill Washington gave the American forces, along with the more effective leadership he provided, the more it reduced the American casualties and it helped give the troops the stomach to see the Revolutionary War to its ultimate victory.

Americans thought so much of his work in this regard that after the war, they elected him the first President, and they were more than willing to make George Washington, America's first and only King. Washington of course would have none of the pomp and circumstance.

It's time to remind the readers again that this is not a history book and so there is lots missing from the fantastic story of the American Revolution. Information is readily available on the Internet as well as in many wonderful books that give accounts right from the journals and diaries of the soldiers themselves on both sides.

The purpose again of this book is to show how hard our founders worked for our freedom; that freedom does not come easy; and that it can be lost if it is not tended to. And so after finishing our discussion of the war, we go through the founding documents in chapters that follow, so that we can help all Americans know their rights, and how precious they are.

That's why all Americans must pay attention to our government to stand against every hint of corruption. We cannot afford to ever lose our precious hard-fought freedom. Standing up for freedom is an act of bravery, even today!

If you like this story about how Americans obtained their freedom, and this has given you a new interest in those subjects that may not have been quite as interesting in high school, I repeat that your need for knowledge can be easily met on the Internet. The Internet can also direct you to some wonderful books on the subject, including those used in K-12, colleges, and universities.

Putting Freedom in Perspective

During the trauma of the revolution, the bravery and direct suffering of the colonists to insure for Americans for all time the rights to life, liberty, and the pursuit of happiness surely puts our freedom in perspective. Many of these brave souls died to preserve our right of representation, and it is that right that is under attack again today, though in a much more subtle and muted way.

As noted above, while the American Revolutionary War was in progress, on May 10, 1775, as directed by the First Constitutional Congress, members of the Second Continental Congress met at the State House in Philadelphia. Again there were major historical figures in their membership including John Hancock from Massachusetts, Thomas Jefferson of Virginia, and Benjamin Franklin from Pennsylvania.

The New England battles were still fresh in the minds of the representatives and the colonial militia was still outside of Boston working to drive the British from the area. The Second Continental Congress gave the preceding events an air of legitimacy and established the militia as the Continental Army to defend the thirteen states from the only known enemy of the day, England.

With Washington anointed as the Commander in Chief of the Continental Army, the colonists clearly meant business.

As upbeat as the delegates were to the Second Continental Congress, many expected, and at least hoped, at the outset, that the issues between colonies and mother country would be healed. This was not a congress whose mission it was to sanctify a revolution.

Additionally, even though the delegates themselves believed they had no legal right to govern, since they were all still part of the dominion of the Crown, they went ahead and did so anyway since there was little choice, and they knew that weakness would provide nothing they needed.

They did have the ability to ask the "states" to provide money, supplies and men for the war effort, but just as the request was without authority, the answer if positive was purely voluntary. The states were free to accept, reject or modify these requests. They asked and for the most part they received what was needed from the states. That is why there is an America today.

This Congress knew that to make the war a success, it needed a stronger central authority. If you remember the last big 4th of July fireworks display you saw. It memorializes July 4, 1776, when the Declaration of Independence was drafted, signed by John Hancock, and sent to the printers.

The Second Continental Congress put forth the work to create the United States of America (though no states at the time were actually ratified) as an independent country. In summary, the matters of work put forth by this Congress are noted below:

Matters of the 2nd Congress

The Congress, having met on May 10, 1775, accomplished many tasks related to the new government and related to the growing revolutionary war with England from the time that it convened to its conclusion on March 1, 1781. Among these are the following:

"State" Governments: The Congress adopted a resolution that urged the colonies to form their own independent governments to replace the all-but fully defunct royal governments. By the time the Second Continental Congress met, the American Revolutionary War had already started with the Battles of Lexington and Concord. These battles were fought on April 19, 1775, in Middlesex County, Province of Massachusetts Bay, within the towns of Lexington, Concord, Lincoln, Menotomy (present-day Arlington), and Cambridge, near Boston.

Figure 4-3 Second Continental Congress

Second Continental Congress at the State House in Philadelphia

After this part of the war, patriots expelled royal officials from all the colonies, and took control through the establishment of Provincial Congresses. Once the "state" governments were seized by the colonists, there were no colonies anymore and the term state in the unofficial sense (not ratified) began to be used to refer to the original thirteen colonies. These became the original thirteen states.

However, by the time state ratification came, they had been operating independently of Britain for some time. For example, Delaware was the first state to ratify on December 7, 1787, and on May 29, 1790, Rhode Island became the last of the original thirteen to become a state. During the time between lots was happening. The Revolutionary War was fought and won; the Articles of Confederation were ratified, and the Constitution was drafted, presented and ratified.

Military: On June 14, 1775, Congress voted to create and assume control of the Continental Army and it appointed George Washington, a congressman from Virginia as commanding general. It was originally formed from military units from the Boston vicinity.

War Justification: Hoping to avoid a major escalation of hostilities with England, Congress approved petitions such as Dickinson's Olive Branch Petition, a statement of abiding loyalty to the king, but disapproval of the actions of his ministers and Parliament. Congress also approved a much stronger statement titled: the Declaration of the Causes and the Necessity of Taking up Arms on July 6, 1775. This second document suggested that if America's rights are not restored, independence will be sought.

War Financing: This Congress issued certificates and borrowed from colonial and foreign sources. Financing was a major problem which continued for much of the war.

Independence: By July 2, 1776, the Congress was accepting that colonial rights were not going to be granted and it passed Richard Henry Lee's resolution of June 1776 that promoted the notion of independence. Lee's resolution of independence was adopted by Congress (12 colonies --

New York abstained). Jefferson's Declaration of Independence was completed after many revisions with the help of Ben Franklin and others on July 4, 1776.

John Hancock, President of Congress and Secretary Charles Thomson signed the original document and sent it to the Printing Shop of Charles Dunlap, just a few blocks away. The formal signing of this Declaration of Independence, on a huge parchment, was effected by 50 delegates on August 2, 1776. Some signed this original document later. Several hundred copies were sent to various governments across the world, reflecting the seriousness of the matter. The United States was henceforth open for business.

Independence Humor: President John Hancock signed the declaration's parchment, laid down his pen (quill) and said to the body in a very serious tone: "We must all hang together." Benjamin Franklin, upon hearing his comment replied: "Yes, we must, indeed, all hang together, or most assuredly we shall all hang separately."

The text of the full Declaration of Independence is included in this book as Appendix C. You may enjoy reading now before you continue.

Diplomatic Channels: The Congress needed world recognition and allies for its independence undertaking. They dispatched Silas Deane to France and later with the help of Arthur Lee and Benjamin Franklin; they concluded the Franco-American Alliance (1778).

Laws: The Congress still did not have authority to pass binding legislation on the states but did approve a number of non-binding resolutions. The technique was to ask the states to provide resources, including fighting men, for the war effort. Thankfully, in most cases, the states agreed, or we might be looking at Prince Charles as our next king..

To gain the authority needed to win the war, the Congress sought to make itself a stronger central authority. The July

1776 proposal called the Articles of Confederation, shown in Appendix D, was intended to do just that. Upon introduction, however, the ambivalence of some of the delegates sparked a lengthy debate before the articles were adopted in November 1777. Ratification of the Articles by the states was not completed until 1781. As they say in Scranton, PA, the rest is "history."

Chapter 12   The American Revolution Summary– Causes, Events, and Chronology

A New Nation Is Born

The French and Indian War was very expensive to wage, and it cost Britain a lot of money. Britain felt that it was helping the colonists by fighting the war and so it wanted the American colonies to help pay for it. That is how the big issues between the colonists and King George began. It was a fight over money.

And, so as discussed in detail in prior chapters, after the war, in the 1760's the British passed new taxes forcing the colonists to pay additional money for sugar, tea, and other things. The colonists were incensed. Eventually, it got so bad in Boston that they threw crates of British Tea into Boston Harbor. The colonists were "mad as hell and were not going to take it anymore." In 1774, they held their First Continental Congress at Carpenter's Hall, Philadelphia to talk things over.

The colonists' resistance started peacefully with petitions and pamphlets and moved to intimidation, boycotts, and inter-colonial meetings. Many events as discussed above exacerbated the friction. These include the Boston Massacre, the Boston Tea Party, and the Coercive Acts. These destroyed the one-time good relations between Britain and its American colonies.

Attempts through the Sugar Act, the Stamp Act, and the Townshend Acts to raise money rather than simply control trade met with deep resistance in the colonies. Such taxation was something new: Parliament had previously passed measures to regulate trade in the colonies, but it had never before directly taxed the colonies to raise revenue

The severe tensions increased and the division escalated further after Parliament passed the Coercive Acts and so the First Continental Congress took the initial steps toward independence from Britain. Before the colonies gained real independence, however, they had to fight a long and bitter war.

The patriots at the first Congress talked about plans to make Britain treat the colonies more fairly. Britain was the most powerful nation on earth at the time and it largely ignored these ideas and then sent its troops to control the colonists. The colonists had local militias at the time but chose to begin to recruit men from all of the states to handle this threat from England.

And, so the American Revolution began with the shot heard round the world in the battles of Lexington and Concord. In 1776, the colonists knew their world had become intolerable by the rapid British intrusion into American lives.

So, they wrote the Declaration of Independence in which it declared the American colonies were free from Britain's rule. At the same time, it kicked out the royal governors in the states and replaced them with patriots.

Thomas Jefferson wrote most of the Declaration of Independence. Here is the beginning of this historical work. The full Declaration is in Appendix C. It is surely inspiring:

When in the Course of human events, it becomes necessary for one people to dissolve the political bands which have connected them with another, and to

assume among the powers of the earth, the separate and equal station to which the Laws of Nature and of Nature's God entitle them, a decent respect to the opinions of mankind requires that they should declare the causes which impel them to the separation.

We hold these truths to be self-evident, that all men are created equal, that they are endowed by their Creator [1] Genesis 1:26-28 with certain unalienable Rights, that among these are Life, Liberty and the pursuit of Happiness.

Thomas Paine, a great patriot wrote this short piece called Crisis about the events to come:

The Crisis

by Thomas Paine, December 23, 1776

"THESE are the times that try men's souls. The summer soldier and the sunshine patriot will, in this crisis, shrink from the service of their country; but he that stands by it now, deserves the love and thanks of man and woman. Tyranny, like hell, is not easily conquered; yet we have this consolation with us, that the harder the conflict, the more glorious the triumph. What we obtain too cheap, we esteem too lightly: it is dearness only that gives every thing its value. Heaven knows how to put a proper price upon its goods; and it would be strange indeed if so celestial an article as FREEDOM should not be highly rated. Britain, with an army to enforce her tyranny, has declared that she has a right (not only to TAX) but "to BIND us in ALL CASES WHATSOEVER" and if being bound in that manner, is not slavery, then is there not such a thing as slavery upon earth. Even the expression is impious; for so unlimited a power can belong only to God...."

Not everybody liked being independent

Not everybody was in favor of independence. Some liked
being tethered to King George III. They were the Loyalists.
Those wanting independence were known as the patriots. As
the war began, the people took sides. The Loyalists were not
bothered by the patriots unless they spoke against the patriots
or got in the way of planned initiatives.

Florida was not one of the thirteen original colonies / states.
Consequently most of its people were Loyalists and they
stayed loyal to Britain for a number of reasons including their
idea that the British protected them from the attacks of the
French, the Spanish, and American Indians.

Since slavery was the order of the day, the loyalists also
feared that enslaved Africans might attack them. Britain
spent a lot of money helping Florida and it bought for the
Crown its loyalty.

Though the trigger for the war was the imposition of British
taxes and trade regulations, the American Revolution was
more than that. It was the first time in recorded history that a
group of people under the control of a government fought for
their independence from their own government.

The principles of independence that motivated the colonists
to risk their lives and their sacred honor were universal
principles such as rule of law, constitutional rights, and
popular sovereignty. Many citizens in our current time have
forgotten how difficult freedom was to obtain. Many others
fear that if we give freedom up for expediency any time soon,
we will never get it back.

Specifics about the Revolutionary War

The British had many advantages in the war, such as a trained Army and Navy. They also had many loyalists who supported the British Empire. Colonists at the time viewed slaves as property and among other things, they did not like the notion proposed by Lord Dunmore to free slaves who joined the royal army.

Independent of the slavery issue, the patriots were inspired by Thomas Paine's pamphlet called Common Sense. In clear, simple language this short literary work explained the advantages of and the need for immediate independence. You may read this work by Paine for free: http://www.ushistory.org/PAINE/commonsense/singlehtm l.htm

There were lots of events in the war and it lasted until 1783.

At the conclusion of this summary of the cause and the action in the Revolutionary War, you will see a comprehensive chronology of the war and the creation of America in table form. It should help in your understanding all that happened in this War of Independence. It has been provided by Ushistroy.Org.

You will enjoy the great snapshot this gives of all the major events that occurred during the war—including the signing of the Declaration of Independence and the ratification of the Constitution. Once the Revolution began, it was obvious that it would take a definite smashing defeat for the American patriots to ever abandon their quest for freedom and independence.

As we all know, American colonists known as patriots won the war for all of US. Most historians credit the bravery and willingness to risk it all of the colonists, the excellent leadership of George Washington; the aid of such European nations as France; and the many tactical errors by British commanders as the significant factors that contributed to the American victory.

The British strategy called for crushing the rebellion in the North first and they almost succeeded but for the bravery of the patriots. Several times the British nearly defeated the Continental Army. This took its toll on the morale of the fighters.

Major victories at Trenton and Princeton, N.J., in late 1776 and early 1777 restored patriot hopes, and then another victory at Saratoga, N.Y. halted a major British advance from Canada, and eventually France, certainly not a friend of England's at the time, and looking for its own opportunities in the New World, intervened on behalf of the Patriots and contributed very positively in the win. .

Then, in 1778, fighting moved to the South and again Britain was successful. They captured Georgia and Charleston, S.C. and defeated an American army at Camden, S.C. However, as things were getting dire, a band of patriots began to harass loyalists and they disrupted the supply lines.

Thus, Britain failed to achieve control over the southern countryside before they were compelled to advance northward to Yorktown, Va. In the war's last major battle, in 1781, an American and French force defeated the British at Yorktown. It was all over but the agreements for peace.

At the time of the Revolution, there were about five million colonists in the New World. Not all were patriots of course. The peace came with a high price. Some of the unintended consequences of the war include the following:

About 7,200 Americans died during the battles of the Revolution. Another 10,000 died fighting the elements suffering from disease or exposure. Another 8,500 or so died in British prisons.

At least a quarter of the slaves in South Carolina and Georgia freed themselves during the Revolution. The Northern states chose to outlaw slavery outright or they adopted gradual emancipation plans.

The states were no longer under British control and so they each adopted written constitutions guaranteeing freedom of speech and religious freedom. They also increased the legislature's size and powers, made taxation more progressive, and reformed inheritance laws.

The following timeline gives a blow by blow snapshot of the war. Once can purchase books at major booksellers that expand this timeline into several volumes of books.

Timeline of the Revolutionary War Courtesy of Ushistrory.Org

1754	The French and Indian War ending in 1763 June 19-July 11; The Albany Congress
1763	Oct. 7 Proclamation of 1763
1764	April 5 The Sugar Act September 1 The Currency Act
1765	March 22 The Stamp Act March 24 The Quartering Act of 1765 May 29 Patrick Henry's speech -- If this be treason, make the most of it!" May 30 The Virginia Stamp Act Resolutions Oct. 7-25 The Stamp Act Congress
1766	March 18 The Declaratory Act
1767	June 29 The Townshend Revenue Act
1768	August 1 Boston Non-Importation Agreement

1770	March 5 The Boston Massacre
1772	June 9 The Gaspee Affair
1773	May 10 The Tea Act Dec. 16 The Boston Tea Party
1774	March 31 Boston Port Act, one of the "Intolerable Acts" May 20 Administration of Justice Act, one of the "Intolerable Acts" May 20 Massachusetts Government Act, one of the "Intolerable Acts" June 2 Quartering Act of 1774, one of the "Intolerable Acts" June 22 Quebec Act, one of the "Intolerable Acts" Sept. 5-Oct. 26 The First Continental Congress meets in Phila. issues Declaration and Resolves Oct. 10 Battle of Point Pleasant, Virginia Oct. 20 The Association (prohibition of trade with Great Britain) Oct. 24 Galloway's Plan rejected
1775	March 23 Patrick Henry's speech "Give me liberty or give me death" Apr. 18 The Rides of Paul Revere and William Dawes Apr. 19 Minutemen and redcoats clash at Lexington and Concord-- "The shot heard 'round the world." May 10 Ethan Allen and the Green Mountain Boys seize Fort Ticonderoga May 10 The Second Continental Congress meets in Philadelphia June 15 George Washington named Commander in Chief June 17 Battle of Bunker Hill: The British drive the Americans from Breed's Hill July 3 Washington assumes command of the Continental Army

	Nov. 10-21 Ninety Six, SC, Patriots sieged Nov. 13 The patriots under Montgomery occupy Montreal in Canada Dec. 11 Virginia and NC patriots rout Loyalist troops and burn Norfolk Dec. 22 Col. Thomson with 1,500 rangers and militia capture Loyalists at Great Canebrake, SC Dec. 23-30 Snow Campaign, in SC Patriots are impeded by 15" of snow Dec. 30-31 American forces under Benedict Arnold fail to seize Quebec
1776	Jan. 1 Daniel Morgan taken prisoner in attempt to take Quebec City Jan. 15 Paine's "Common Sense" published Feb. 27 The patriots drive the Loyalists from Moore's Creek Bridge, North Carolina March 3 The Continental fleet captures New Providence Island in the Bahamas March 17 The British evacuate Boston; British Navy moves to Halifax, Canada June 8 Patriots fail to take Three Rivers, Quebec June 12 The Virginia Declaration of Rights June 28 Sullivan's Island, SC, failed British naval attack June 29 The First Virginia Constitution June 28 Patriots decisively defeat the British Navy at Fort Moultrie, South Carolina July 1 British agents instigate Cherokee attack along the entire southern frontier July 1-4 Congress debates and revises the Declaration of Independence. July 4 Congress adopts the Declaration of Independence; it's sent to the printer July 8 The Declaration of Independence is read publicly July 15 Lyndley's Fort, SC, Patriots fend off attack by Indians and Tories dressed as

Indians

Aug. 1 Ambushed by Cherokees, Patriots are saved by a mounted charge at Seneca, SC

Aug. 2 Delegates begin to sign The Declaration of Independence

Aug. 10 Tugaloo River, SC, Andrew Pickens defeats Cherokees

Aug. 12 Andrew Pickens' detachment surrounded by 185 Cherokee Indians, forms a ring and fires outward. It is known as the "Ring Fight."

Aug. 12 Col. Williamson and Andrew Pickens defeat Cherokee Indians and burn Tamassy, an Indian town

Aug. 27 Redcoats defeat the George Washington's army in the Battle of Long Island. Washington's army escapes at night.

Sept. 15 The British occupy New York City

Sept. 16 Generals George Washington, Nathanael Greene, and Israel Putnam triumphantly hold their ground at the Battle of Harlem Heights

Sept. 19 Col. Williamson's patriots attacked by Cherokees at Coweecho River, NC

Oct. 11 Benedict Arnold defeated at the Battle of Valcour Island (Lake Champlain), but delayed British advance

Oct. 28 The Americans retreat from White Plains, New York. British casualties (~300) higher than American (~200).

Nov. 16 The Hessians (German auxiliaries contracted for military service by the British government) capture Fort Washington, NY

Nov. 20 Lord Cornwallis captures Fort Lee from Nathanael Greene

Dec. 26 Washington crosses the Delaware and captures Trenton from Hessians

1777	Jan. 3 Washington victorious at Princeton
	Jan. 6-May 28 Washington winters Morristown, NJ
	Apr. 27 Benedict Arnold's troops force a British retreat at Ridgefield, Connecticut.
	May 20 Treaty of DeWitt's Corner, SC: Cherokees lose most of their land east of the mountains
	June 14 Flag Resolution
	July 5 St. Clair surrenders Fort Ticonderoga to the British
	July 27 Lafayette arrives in Philadelphia
	Aug. 6 The Redcoats, with Iroquois support, force the patriots back at Oriskany, NY, but then have to evacuate
	Aug. 16 American Militia under General Stark victorious at the Battle of Bennington, VT (actually fought in Walloomsac, New York, several miles to the west)
	Aug. 23 British withdraw from Fort Stanwix, NY, upon hearing of Benedict Arnold's approach
	Aug. 25 British General Howe lands at Head of Elk, Maryland
	Sept. 11 The British win the Battle of Brandywine, Pennsylvania
	Sept. 16 Rain-out at the Battle of the Clouds, Pennsylvania
	Sept. 19 Burgoyne checked by Americans under Gates at Freeman's Farm, NY. This is part of the "Battles of Saratoga."
	Sept. 21 Paoli Massacre, PA
	Sept. 26 British under Howe occupy Philadelphia Oct. 4 Americans driven off at the Battle of Germantown
	Oct. 7 Burgoyne loses second battle of Freeman's Farm, NY (at Bemis Heights). This is part of the "Battles of Saratoga."
	Oct. 17 Burgoyne surrenders to American

	General Gates at Saratoga, NY Oct. 22 Hessian attack on Fort Mercer, NJ repulsed Nov. 16 British capture Fort Mifflin, Pennsylvania Dec. 5-7 Americans repulse British at Whitemarsh, Pennsylvania Dec. 19 Washington's army retires to winter quarters at Valley Forge
1778	Feb. 6 The United States and France sign the French Alliance March 7 British General William Howe replaced by Henry Clinton May 20 Battle of Barren Hill, Pennsylvania. Lafayette with 500 men and about 50 Oneida Indians successfully evade British onslaught June 18 British abandon Philadelphia and return to New York June 19 Washington's army leaves Valley Forge June 28 The Battle of Monmouth Court House ends in a draw July 4 George Rogers Clark captures Kaskaskia, a French village south of St. Louis Aug. 8 French and American forces besiege Newport, RI Dec. 29 The redcoats occupy Savannah
1779	Feb. 3 Maj. Gen. Moultrie defeats British detachment at Port Royal Island, SC Feb. 14 Patriots Andrew Pickens and Elijah Clarke beat Loyalists at Kettle Creek, GA Feb. 23-24 American George Rogers Clark captures Vincennes (in what is now Indiana) on the Wabash in the Western campaign March 3 British Lt. Col. Jacques Marcus Prevost defeats Americans under Gen. John Ashe at Brier Creek, GA May 11-13 Maj. General Augustin Prévost (brother of Jacques, see above) breaks his siege when American forces under Maj.

	Gen. Lincoln approaches June 20 Stono River, SC, Maj. Gen. Lincoln inflicts extensive British casualties in indecisive battle June 21 Spain declares war on Great Britain July 8 Fairfield, CT, burned by British July 11 Norwalk, CT, burned by British July 15-16 American "Mad" Anthony Wayne captures Stony Point, NY Aug. 19 "Light Horse" Harry Lee attacks Paulus Hook, NJ Aug. 29 Newtown, NY, after two massacres, American forces burn Indian villages Sept. 23 John Paul Jones, aboard the Bonhomme Richard, captures British man-of-war Serapis near English coast Sept. 28 The Tappan Massacre ("No Flint" Grey kills 30 Americans by bayonet) Oct. 9 American attempt to recapture Savannah, GA fails Nov.-June 23, 1780 Washington's 2nd winter at Morristown, NJ (the harshest winter of the 18th century)
1780	May 12 British capture Charleston, SC May 29 British crush Americans at Waxhaw Creek, SC June 20 Patriots rout Tories at Ramseur's Mill, NC July 11 French troops arrive at Newport, RI, to aid the American cause Aug. 6 Patriots defeat Tories at Hanging Rock, SC Aug. 16 British rout Americans at Camden, SC Sept. 23 John André arrested, leading to the exposure of Benedict Arnold's plans to cede West Point to the British Oct. 7 King's Mountain, SC: battle lasts 65 minutes. American troops led by Isaac

	Shelby and John Sevier defeat Maj. Patrick Ferguson and one-third of General Cornwallis's army Oct. 14 Washington names Nathanael Greene commander of the Southern Army
1781	Jan. 1 Mutiny of unpaid Pennsylvania soldiers Jan. 17 Patriot Morgan overwhelmingly defeats British Col. Tarleton at Cowpens, SC Feb. 1 The Battle of Cowan's Ford, Huntersville, NC March 2 Articles of Confederation adopted March 15 British win costly victory at Guilford Courthouse, NC April 25 Greene defeated at Hobkirk's Hill, SC May 15 British Major Andrew Maxwell cedes Fort Granby, SC to patriot Lieutenant Colonel Henry Lee June 6 Americans recapture Augusta, GA June 18 British hold off Americans at Ninety Six, SC July 6 "Mad" Anthony Wayne repulsed at Green Springs Farm, VA Sept. 8 Greene defeated at Eutaw Springs, SC Sept. 15 French fleet drives British naval force from Chesapeake Bay Oct. 19 Cornwallis surrounded on land and sea by Americans and French and surrenders at Yorktown, VA
1782	March 20 Lord North resigns as British prime minister July 11 British evacuate Savannah, GA Nov. 30 British and Americans sign preliminary Articles of Peace Dec. 14 British leave Charleston, SC

1783	April 19 Congress ratifies preliminary peace treaty Sept. 3 The United States and Great Britain sign the Treaty of Paris Nov. 25 British troops leave New York City Dec. 23 Washington resigns as Commander
1787	Sept. 17 U.S. Constitution signed
1788	June 21 U.S. Constitution adopted, when New Hampshire ratifies it

Chapter 13   The End of the Revolutionary War

Cornwallis Surrenders

Washington made significant progress prosecuting the War of independence. When the Continental Army arrived in Yorktown on September 26, 1783, the French Fleet, was in firm control of the bay. The French, operating under the Franco-American Alliance, had offered substantial assistance to the new United Sates.

They had Cornwallis pinned in. With about 20,000 troops from state militias combined with troops from France, the American forces had stymied the British who were being led by General Lord Charles Cornwallis. Cornwallis's troops were taking heavy casualties from a constant bombardment.

Cornwallis was the 2nd General in Command in the Americas, and to put it frankly, when reinforcements from New York, sent by the top General Henry Clinton, did not arrive in time to be of use, he knew he was licked and he surrendered on October 19, 1781. This was the de-facto end of the war though skirmishes continued for several years.

Figure 4-4 Surrender of Cornwallis

Surrender Of Cornwallis - The End of the American Revolution.

In December 1783, George Washington made the end of the American Revolution official when he resigned his commission to Congress. The revolution had ended. America had achieved its independence and its representative democracy was about to get even stronger.

Revolutionary War Videos

To continue your study about the Revolutionary War, the Internet is a great source of free information. If you are intrigued about the American Revolution and would like to sit back and listen to some historical tunes or watch some great videos, take your browser and type the following search phrases. There is a wealth of information at your fingertips.

- Revolutionary war
- Revolutionary war videos
- Revolutionary war tunes
- Schoolhouse Rock Kings.

The lyrics to some great patriotic songs are on the
Schoolhouse Rock site if you want to print them and sing
along. When you play this video on YouTube, look on the
right hand frame and you will find a number of other
Schoolhouse Rock productions such as "The Shot Heard
Round the World." It's both a fun and uplifting experience
and even before you read the rest of this book, it can be a nice
learning experience. Enjoy!

End of War Summary

The government in the colonies was formed very much like
the government in England. The Governor, the Council and
the Representatives of the people made up the three branches.
The Governor and the Council had their allegiance to the
Colonial Proprietor or the Crown. Only the representatives
could levy taxes.

When the French and Indian War and the Pontiac Wars
concluded, the English Crown was looking to America to pay
it back for its war costs and to pay it back for the 10,000-
strong English standing army residing on American soil.
Instead of doing things by their own book of laws, the
English were impatient and began to directly tax the colonists
but this was forbidden by the English Constitution and the
Americans were subjects of the Crown, just as those living in
London.

Beginning with the Stamp Act and moving to the Intolerable
Acts, it was a cat and mouse game of English taxes, Colonist
complaints, England concessions—until the taxes were too
many to take away. The English had the strongest Navy in
the world but they had just 10,000 soldiers compared to the
5,000,000 colonists.

Soon the Colonists were sick of the taxes and longed for their
freedom. The thirteen colonies formed the First Continental
Congress and sent King George a note of demands called the

Declaration of Rights and Grievances, hoping he would lighten up. Instead the King dug in. At the Second Continental Congress the war had already begun and the delegates fashioned the Declaration of Independence as well as the Articles of Confederation upon which the Constitution was built.

George Washington was appointed commander in chief and he and the army of the new U.S. won many battles and finally in 1783, the British General Cornwallis surrendered to Washington. The U.S. came into being and was commissioned as a free country and for years the country was bound by its Articles of Confederation until the drafting and ratification of the Constitution.

The Government of the United States

America's founding documents tell a tale of the character and temperament of the men who are now known as the Founding Fathers. They represented the best that America had to offer. When the Articles of Confederation was introduced, it sparked lengthy debate before adoption in November 1777. This was the beginning of the government of the United States of America. The forming of that government of the people for the people, and by the people is fully treated as the subject matter of Part III, beginning with Chapter 14.

Part IV Meaning of Founding Documents

Chapter 14 The Forming of the United States Government

Representation at All Levels

One of the first documents on the way to the Declaration of Independence and the Constitution was the *Declaration of Rights and Grievances,* It was a product of the First Continental Congress, as shown in Appendix A and discussed in prior chapters. It was the first formal request of the "United States" to England for a return to representative government.

Though nothing close to a constitutional democracy, the Colonists under English rule enjoyed representation in the lower house of the colonial governments. There was no union of colonies or states at the time and had the English kept to themselves and not levied taxes directly on the colonists, Americans today would be much more interested if Camilla is really ever going to be the Queen.

With a careful reading of the Declaration of Rights and Grievances, one can get a quick sense of what the colonists wanted from the Crown. It was simply, "no taxation without representation," and all of the many positions this plea represented. As the thought of a revolution became more of a reality for the Patriots, independence and freedom and liberty become even more important than the tax burden.

This early declaration was the first major document of the new government of the United States, though it occurred at a time when the states were not actively seeking independence from the Crown.

The expressed purpose of the First Continental Congress held in 1774 was:

> *"That a Committee be appointed to state the rights of the Colonies in general, the several instances in which these rights are violated or infringed, and the means most proper to be pursued for obtaining a restoration of them."*

The committee was constructed and the declaration was drafted and it was read on September 22nd and the draft of the grievances was read on the 24th. The members of the First Congress debated the drafts on October 12 and 13, and after a final draft was produced, it was agreed on Friday, October 14, 1774.

Several days later on October 20, the Congress passed the Articles of Association. It was addressed to King George III. In essence, it was a formal agreement of the colonies themselves to work together as an association of states with common purpose. It was basically a union of protest and boycott as many of the articles outlined the specific actions that the colonists were to take regarding the export and import of goods.

As you read these articles in Appendix B, you can't help but notice the elegance and forethought in the draft. We are a fortunate lot indeed to have had such fine and capable, and yes, honorable men, representing America in those days.

Since life had not improved and the British, after initially backing off from its impositions, began to double down, continuing to impose its will on the colonists, The Second Continental Congress began on May 10, 1775 and it went on until March 1, 1781. During the war, the meeting location was moved from Philadelphia several times to other locations to protect the lives of the representatives.

The delegates of each of the 13 colonies gathered initially in Philadelphia to discuss their next steps in dealing with England. This Congress met at the State House in Philadelphia as the American Revolution had already begun in earnest with the shot heard round the world still ringing in their ears.

The militia was still engaged in Boston while the Congress was using its powers to formally establish the militia as the Continental Army of the United States with George Washington as the top general known at the time as the Commander in Chief. This marked another stage in the formation of the government of the US. The government would continue to evolve and after Independence was gained, Washington would again become Commander in Chief when he was elected First President of the United States.

Sixty-five representatives originally appointed by the legislatures of thirteen British North American colonies accomplished a body of work that is historical in nature. At the time, it formed the basis for the new government. The Declaration of Independence, with text shown in Appendix C was the first well-known historical document produced by this Second Congress. The second was the Articles of Confederation, text shown in Appendix D. This was the precursor document to the United States Constitution, the text of which is shown in Appendix E.

As noted previously, the Second Continental Congress was begun during the American Revolutionary War. It served as the de facto U.S. national government. This Congress assumed power and raised armies, directed strategy, appointed diplomats, and it made the government formal.

At the same time, it produced numerous important documents, including three of the most fundamental and historical documents to American freedom—The Declaration of Independence, The Articles of Confederation, and The Constitution.

United States Declaration of Independence

Some dates, one can never forget. The Declaration of Independence was written by Thomas Jefferson, and it was put forth and approved for printing on July 4, 1776. It did exactly what it purported to do in its title. It declared independence from Great Britain.

It was not Pennsylvania, or Massachusetts or Virginia that declared this independence and this is a key point. Instead, it was all of the thirteen colonies in unison, known to themselves as states at the time. They had chosen to assemble and join in a union to create a new federal government that would be known as the United States of America.

Once independence was declared, America began to legally operate fully independent of the Crown with its own government. Considering that the colonists were in revolt and war had commenced, it is an understatement to suggest that the colonists were not operating independently prior to the Declaration. The Declaration formalized their union of independence.

The states were declared to be free and independent and "all political connection between them and the State of Great Britain, is and ought to be totally dissolved." The formal title of the document ratified on July 4, 1776 is the "**Unanimous Declaration of the thirteen United States of America**," but to Americans it is known simply as the *Declaration of Independence*. This was the formal end of the thirteen colonies.

In addition to declaring independence, this document gave justification for the separation from the Crown in sufficient detail that the King and Parliament could not misunderstand its purpose and from whence it came. Since the colonies were no more, historians consider this Declaration as the founding document of the United States of America. In his Gettysburg Address of 1863, at the beginning of his address, President Lincoln memorialized the founding of the United States in these words:

> *Four score and seven years ago our fathers brought forth on this continent, a new nation, conceived in liberty, and dedicated to the proposition that all men are created equal.*

As we know from our knowledge of American History and from the recount of the Revolutionary War provided in past chapters, there were a number of battles until the Americans prevailed in the war with England. After the *Declaration of Independence*, the Second Continental Congress stayed in session passing laws and drafting documents that ultimately would define the new nation as the United States of America. The next major document in the formation of the government of the United States to be examined in this book is known as *The Articles of Confederation*.

Articles of Confederation

Just as the Declaration of Independence is short for a longer title, the "*Articles of Confederation and Perpetual Union*" has been shortened over time to be simply The Articles of Confederation. Some say that the Articles of Confederation represent the United States of America's first Constitution. This document was the work of the Second Continental Congress, who drafted it in 1777. The Articles established a "firm league of friendship" between and among the 13 states.

After having been subjected to the wiles of the strong central government of the British prior to the War of Independence, these Articles reflect a sense of the wariness by the states of a government that would not provide them with their God-given rights.

The Articles are the agreed-upon remedy for the concerns of states' rights and for individual rights. Ever fearful that a government of the future (such as the current regime or one hence) might not have the right measure of concern for our individual needs if it were given too much power, and that abuses such as the Intolerable Acts, might again be the result, the Articles purposely established a "constitution."

This document vested the largest share of power to the individual states. When the Constitution was built and later enacted, it reflected the same notion of states' rights and individual rights, as the Articles, and the last claimant on the rights list was the federal government in Washington.

Under the Articles of Confederation, each of the states retained its "sovereignty, freedom and independence." The preamble of the US Constitution drafted in 1787 and ratified later by the individual states one at a time, sets its purpose as "in order to form a more perfect union."

The founders of our government recognized that there were flaws in the Articles of Confederation that would more easily permit a tyranny to take place. And, so their best, "more perfect" work, the Constitution, was its way of correcting those flaws and correcting the notion of a constitutional representative democracy (aka, a Republic) for the United States.

There was a permanent institution called the Congress formed in the Articles as a national legislature comprised of representatives of the states. The Congress was responsible for conducting foreign affairs, declaring war or peace, maintaining an army and navy and a variety of other lesser functions.

The Articles did not call for the separation of powers with an executive, legislative, and judicial branch. The Articles did not permit the delegates to collect taxes, regulate interstate commerce and enforce laws. Under the Articles of Confederation these important functions could only be performed if the states agreed.

Though the Articles had shortcomings, the document provided the guidelines for the United States government and it was the only real law of the land until the Constitution was adopted and ratified.

Eventually, the shortcomings were addressed and this lead to the U.S. Constitution. The beauty of the Articles of Confederation was that it provided a workable framework during those years in which the 13 states were struggling to achieve their independent status.

Considering that the Constitution itself is under fire today by those who would like it constructed in ways that were not intended by the Founding Fathers, from November 15,1777, when adopted by the Congress, the Articles of Confederation did their job to keep the Country in good stead. Nothing in life worth having is easy.

On March1, 1781, the Articles became operational when the last of the thirteen states signed the document. Then came the work for the Constitution.

Chapter 15   The Constitution, An Awesome Document

Introduction to the Constitution

The Articles were an imperfect constitution for the newly formed union. The phrase "a more perfect union" in the Preamble notes the imperfections in the document and it introduces the rationale for the drawing of the Constitution.

The U.S. Constitution (and its subsequent 27 amendments) has survived for over two-hundred years testifying to its perfection as the basis for the constitutional representative democracy of the United States as we will further discuss in the Civics Lessons in coming chapters.

From the National Archives:

http://www.archives.gov/national-archives-experience/charters/constitution.html

I like how this text from the national archives reads so instead of trying to rephrase this, I simply include it below to explain the purpose of the work behind the Constitution.

The Federal Convention convened in the State House (Independence Hall) in Philadelphia on May 14, 1787, to revise the Articles of Confederation. Because the delegations from only two states were at first present, the members adjourned from day to day until a quorum of seven states was obtained on May 25. Through discussion and debate it became clear by mid-June that, rather than amend the existing Articles, the Convention would draft an entirely new frame of government.

All through the summer, in closed sessions, the delegates debated, and redrafted the articles of the new Constitution. Among the chief points at issue were how much power to allow the central government, how many representatives in Congress to allow each state, and how these representatives should be elected--directly by the people or by the state legislators. The work of many minds, the Constitution stands as a model of cooperative statesmanship and the art of compromise.

The Law of the Land

As noted previously, the Constitution of the United States comprises the primary law of the U.S. Federal Government. In simple terms it is the law of the land and all other laws must conform to the statutes with this original document and its amendments (changes).

It also describes the three chief branches of the Federal Government and their jurisdictions as well as the separation of the powers. In addition, it lays out the basic rights of citizens of the United States. The Constitution of the United States is the oldest federal constitution in existence and was framed by a convention of delegates from twelve of the thirteen original states in Philadelphia in May 1787.

The Constitution is the landmark legal document of the United States and all other laws are tested against its specifications. Many other constitutions, such as the Constitution of Mexico, for example are based on this work.

The full Constitution is included in Appendix E. The Bill of Rights (first ten amendments) and the other 17 amendments are in Appendix F, and those Amendments that were submitted but not passed are shown in Appendix G. To give the reader an appreciation or a reminder of just how significant the Articles and the Amendments of this document really are, I am including this brief summary below:

Preamble

We the People of the United States, in Order to form a more perfect Union, establish Justice, insure domestic Tranquility, provide for the common defense, promote the general Welfare, and secure the Blessings of Liberty to ourselves and our Posterity, do ordain and establish this Constitution for the United States of America.

Article I: The Legislative Branch: Consists of 10 sections and defines:

(1) All Legislative powers, (2) Composition of the House of Representatives, (3) Composition of the Senate, (4) Holding Elections, (5) Congress sets its own rules by House, (6) Compensation for Senators), (7) Revenue Bills originate in House, (8) Congress can lay and collect taxes, (9) Defines states rights and taxes (10) State treaties.

Section 9, Clause 8 of the Constitution is of particular interest to this writer. In later chapters we discuss the automatic conferring of the title, the *Honorable*. Please look at what the founding fathers thought of such titles:

Section 9 Clause 8: No Title of Nobility shall be granted by the United States: And no Person holding any Office of Profit or Trust under them, shall, without the Consent of the Congress, accept of any present, Emolument, Office, or Title, of any kind whatever, from any King, Prince, or foreign State.

One of the first constitutional loopholes was the notion of the giver being the King, Prince, or a foreign state. There is nothing here unfortunately about taking the title ("Honorable") for oneself or having it granted via obscure rules of etiquette that have never passed the test of law.

Article II: The Executive Branch: Consists of 4 sections and defines:

(1) Executive Power and President, (2) President as Commander in Chief, (3) State of the Union & Information Requirements, (4) Rules of Executive Branch impeachment

Article III: The Judicial Branch: Consists of 3 sections and defines:

(1) Judicial Power, (2) Laws and Trial by Jury, (3) Treason

Article IV: Relations Between States: Consists of 4 sections and defines:

(1)Faith and Credit of State Laws, (2) Privileges apply to all in all states, (3) New States May be Admitted tot he Union, (4) Federal guarantee to defend states.

Article V: The Amendment Process: Consists of 1 section and defines the Amendment Process for adding / deleting from the Constitution.

Article VI: General Provisions, Supremacy of the Constitution: Consists of 1 section and defines the debt process and the requirement to support the Constitution

Article VII: Ratification Process: Consists of 1 section and it outlines the process for ratifying the Constitution.

27 Amendments to the Constitution

The Bill of Rights

Amendment I: Freedom of speech, religion, press, petition, assembly.
Amendment II: Right to bear arms and militia.
Amendment III: Quartering of soldiers.
Amendment IV: Warrants and searches.

Amendment V: Individual debt and double jeopardy.
Amendment VI: Speedy trial, witnesses and accusations.
Amendment VII: Right for a jury trial.
Amendment VIII: Bail and fines.
Amendment IX: Existence of other rights for the people
Amendment X: Power reserved to the states and people.

Later Amendments

Amendment XI: Suits against states.
Amendment XII: Election of executive branch.
Amendment XIII: Prohibition of slavery.
Amendment XIV: Privileges or immunities, due process, elections and debt: Consists of 5 sections and defines: (1) Citizenship (2) Apportionment of representatives among the states, (3) Rules for being a Senator or Representative, (4) Validity of the public debt, (5) Congressional Enforcement of this Article.
Amendment XV: Race and the right to vote.
Amendment XVI: Income tax.
Amendment XVII: Senator election and number.
Amendment XVIII: Prohibition on sale of alcohol
Amendment XIX: Gender and the right to vote.
Amendment XX: "Lame duck" session of Congress eliminated.
Amendment XXI: Repeal of Amendment XVIII (Prohibition).
Amendment XXII: Limit of Presidential terms.
Amendment XXIII: Election rules for the District of Columbia
Amendment XXIV: Taxes and the right to vote.
Amendment XXV: Rules of Presidential succession.
Amendment XXVI: Age and the right to vote.
Amendment XXVII: Pay raises and Congress

Amendments Never Ratified

Besides the above summary of the constitutional body of law, six other amendments have been proposed to the constitution that have not been ratified and thus do not represent the law of the land. The entire text of these amendments is included in Appendix F.

What Does This Mean?

Here we are in Chapter 15 of a book about America 4 Dummmies. We have examined the founding and the revolution and the articles and precepts in the Constitution as the primary law of the land. This more or less completes the historical section of this book, though there will be citations in later parts of the book referencing the founding documents.

We will have a civics lesson and then we will be examining representation or the lack thereof in subsequent chapters. So far, we have more than hinted at the major culprits to the dilemma, which is a major theme of any book about America—Taxation Without Representation.

Taxation was a major problem for the colonists and the representatives of the Second Congress, even during the war did not have taxing authority. There was never a welfare state. Every buck that a colonist earned could theoretically be kept since the state's mission was not to provide for the welfare of others. The Constitution does not provide for redistribution of income.

No Bucks Required

Actually colonists did not ever get to spend bucks per se. The thirteen colonies retained the British monetary units for years: pounds, shillings, pence. Besides barter, the colonists also used foreign coins made of precious metals (gold, silver).

These were in circulation in the colonies and their values were determined by the several colonial legislatures. The dollar coin (or buck as we call it) was used even before the Declaration of Independence.

The Congress had authorized the issuance of dollar denominated coins and currency. The term 'dollar' was a natural since the most commonly used coins at that time was something called the Spanish colonial 8 reales dollar coins. Since Britain would not permit the colonies to mint their own coins, these fit the bill fine. They were also known as Spanish Milled Dollars.

Figure 5-1 Colonial Currency

Types of New England currency, including a Massachusetts bill of 1690, earliest paper money issued in America. It's not your eyes.

Several different systems of money were proposed for the early United States. The dollar eventually was approved by Congress in 1786. The first US dollar bill was not printed as legal tender, however, until 1862.

Though there is nothing in the Constitution about income redistribution, a basic tenet of our current welfare system, the Constitution is the document that we can credit or blame for giving the government the right to tax the people of their wealth. The Constitution is also the current body of law that gives us our constitutional democracy and thus with this democracy we have a representative government.

Americans who read this paragraph should like the founders even more. The founders did not include an income tax in the Constitution and thus it was illegal for Congress to collect

such a tax. However, on February 3, 1913, hard as it is to
believe, the people of the US in 36 states approved the 16th
Amendment to the Constitution providing the government
with permission to levy an Income Tax on the people and on
corporations. And shortly after that came the IRS.

The founders of the country had no idea that even with the
three branches of government representing the people and
serving as a system of checks and balances, there would be
thieving and conniving representatives in all branches and
levels of government who now have the authority to take as
much as 1/2 of the income of a middle class American and
even more if that American is self employed.

Chapter 16   Introduction to the Federalist Papers Part I

Should Americans read The Federalist Papers?

Most readers already know that America is in peril; yet many Americans choose not to believe this is the case. For those who see it as it is, tyranny in our highest federal offices, it would help to reread the Declaration of Independence and the Constitution, included in this book, and then to crawl into the pure minds of our Founders, who never expected corruption to interfere with the many checks and balances they had prepared for America and had written into the Constitution and the Bill of Rights.

To help US in our cause, we need the Federalist Papers today more than ever. In this way, we can all understand the basis of our freedoms in the Constitution. Perhaps we need the anti-Federalist papers even more so that we can fully understand the cracks in our liberty.

Fixing cracks is much easier when you know where they are. With the president or dictator scare that Americans have been experiencing since 2009, we need to patch our government the first chance we get in the future.

Reading the Federalist Papers

I finally read the Federalist Papers after having put them on my list several years ago. I finished paper # 85 several months ago, and then I set about organizing them into a small footprint and an affordable reprint so all Americans could learn as I did. My edition of the Federalist Papers along with parts of this two-part introduction is included in a book titled: *The Federalist Papers by Hamilton, Jay, and Madison.* Like this book, it is available at www.bookhawkers.com. The founders wrote the 85 papers. I corrected some typos and chopped up their huge paragraphs into smaller ones to make the papers much easier to read.

There is a lot of work required for all of US to be able to enjoy freedom through the ages. My purpose in writing these two chapters is to help frame an argument to the American people for why it is critical for all of US to read The Federalist Papers and our founding documents.

Ironically, most of my life, I had never even heard of the Federalist Papers. I presume the same is the case for many other Americans. It is time we all correct that for our national well-being.

From grade school through high school through college, the papers were never on any teacher's agenda. In addition to civics and history classes in grade school, high school and college, like most Americans, I had long ago read the Declaration of Independence, the Articles of Confederation, and the Constitution. These gave me insights into the founding of the country and what the US is all about. Consequently, I believed that I had a fundamental understanding of how America was supposed to work. From these readings, I actually thought I knew it all pretty well.

I was wrong about that. It is not that my perceptions from what I had learned through the founding documents were wrong; it is that they were incomplete. I first tuned-in to the fact that the Federalist Papers existed and had great value about seven years ago, when I wrote my first patriotic / political book titled, *Taxation without Representation.* This book has been updated and is in its second edition. Just as the hard copy of this book, along with other patriotic / political books, it is available at www.bookhawkers.com.

Having read about the Federalist Papers and now having read them, and having read some dissenting views on the topic, I am convinced that we Americans need to understand the Federalist Papers today as much as the people of America in the late 1780's when the Constitution was being debated.

According to the late Richard B. Morris, a 20th century historian—the Federalist Papers serve as an *"incomparable exposition of the Constitution, a classic in political science unsurpassed in both breadth and depth by the product of any later American writer."* Morris is well known by historians for his pioneering work in colonial American legal history and the early history of American labor.

Thomas Jefferson called *The Federalist Papers* the best commentary on the principles of government, which ever was written. Over 200 years after the writing of these articles and essays, most commentators — liberal and conservative alike — still agree.

It is time that all Americans begin to read these works, and with dispatch, because we as a people no longer know if our President is serving US or breaking the law to serve his personal ideology.

Though it is difficult to read the Federalist Papers since they use the English language distinctly from the 1700's, with words and sentence structures, of which most of US are not accustomed, it is still a worthwhile endeavor. It certainly won't hurt US; that is for sure. The way the papers are composed is exactly how the educated spoke in the eighteenth century.

Consequently for those of us living in the 21st century, the papers appear archaic and can be difficult to follow. Nothing worthwhile in life is easy. I can assure you that after reading several of these papers, they do become easier to comprehend. In any case, they are a fine challenge for the human mind. How could these old-timers have been so smart? Yet, they were!

Our language is simpler today and it may be tough for some to traverse these papers, and their long sentences, while remaining awake. Nonetheless, they are phenomenal learning pieces and all of US can and should take the time to read the originals and gain insights about the US, and how our government is supposed to function. Along with other founding documents, the entire 85 papers are included in the book previously mentioned.

Without changing its composition, I corrected spelling errors, and I broke up many long paragraphs to make the works much more readable. This work, though corrected and more readable, is unabridged because I did not shorten any of the Papers. They are all intact.

Understand the Founders' Intentions

I call your attention to the fact that the current administration in Washington is failing in its adherence to the Constitution, and that is why it is so critical now that we understand the precepts of the Constitution by reading the Federalist Papers. These papers show the Founders' intentions on the clauses and the amendments in the Bill of rights.

We all need a solid footing from which we can select our new legislators. Many view the current crop as mostly self-absorbed politicians, who have abandoned US and, who instead operate on behalf of their political parties, their lobbyists, and their cronies.

We the People have been left behind. When we hear that the administration is lawless, without understanding the basic precepts of the Supreme Law of the land, we are stuck with no benchmark for the truth. The US Constitution is that benchmark, and the Federalist Papers are the citizens' gateway to fully understanding its meaning.

Constitution & the Philadelphia Convention

A number of states had sent detailed written plans for the Constitution along with their delegates to the Constitutional Convention in Philadelphia. The Convention began on May 25, 1787 and lasted until September 17, 1787. It was convened at the State House in Philadelphia. Most of us know the State House today as Independence Hall.

After three months of work, James Madison, a prolific writer, put out his rough draft of the Constitution. Madison's "Virginia Plan" as it was called, became the basis upon which the Constitution was developed. After about another month of tweaking, the final work was completed.

On September 17, 1787, the state delegates approved the Constitution in its final form, completed their work and sent the document back to the individual states to be ratified. They then adjourned the convention.

Convincing the Public

The commencing of the Federalist Papers began shortly thereafter. The writing of the papers was commissioned by Alexander Hamilton, who knew he could not write them all. He and James Madison, and John Jay together wrote The Federalist Papers to defend and explain the newly drafted Federal Constitution, and to promote its ratification in the state of New York.

All of the papers were written as essays, such as this two-part introduction, but when published they became articles in NY newspapers / magazines. Because New York at the time and to this day is a huge and prosperous state, their being published in NY was very important to the ratification of the Constitution. Thus for the writers, it was the major object of their attention at the time.

Along the way, John Jay became ill after writing just four of the papers. When he became well, he came back to write one more. The other eighty essays were written by Hamilton and Madison.

These articles were published without tribute in New York City newspapers, and I would bet the newspapers sold better when one of them were included. From October 1787 to August 1788, all eighty-five articles appeared under the pseudonym "Publius," in various NY media outlets. Publius was the perfect pseudonym as he was the legendary founder of the Roman Republic and "friend of the people."

At the same time, those who had deep concerns about the value of the Constitution separately wrote what today are known as the Anti-Federalist Papers. It is good to review them also as their focus was the potential for tyranny in the governing structure. These offerings are as patriotic as the Federalist Papers with which they vehemently disagreed.

Ironically in the 21st century, for the first time in my lifetime, we are now seeing the tyranny, which was the subject of the Anti-Federalist papers. It is coming from both our Congress and from our chief executive.

It surely would be nice if it were not so. Understanding what is the law and what is not the law of the land is therefore more important than ever for Americans, and that is why I commenced this work.

As noted, the original essays were written for the common man of the day. In New York, three popular print media outlets chose to publish and profit from them. These were the Independent Journal; the New-York Packet; and the Daily Advertiser. The idea was that such men would have an influence on their representatives after the convention, which had approved the Constitution.

Before the Constitution took effect, the US had been using a government formed under the Articles of Confederation. Most scholars of the day noted that the Articles had become ineffective in handling the affairs of an independent and growing nation.

Some, who were labeled as Anti-Federalists, believed that a mere tweaking of the Articles of Confederation was all that was needed to make them right. However, at the convention, the state's delegates changed the government almost completely by offering the new Constitution and its precepts as the way to move forward.

And, so, Hamilton in his kickoff message in the last Federalist Paper # 85, written almost a year after the Constitution had been completed, offered this simple caution to the country:

A nation without a national government is, in my view, an awful spectacle. "--Alexander Hamilton, The Federalist Papers, No. 85."

US Constitution – Worth Explaining and Defending

Not too long after the Revolutionary War, the Founders realized that the government established by the Articles of Confederation was not working perfectly. In fact, that is an understatement. It became obvious to most patriots that America needed a new form of government. It had to be strong enough to maintain national unity over a large geographic area, but it also had to be balanced so as not to become so strong that it would become a tyranny on the people.

The guiding formula for the operation of the US government from the revolution onward came from the Declaration of Independence (June 1776), and the Articles of Confederation (Ratified by Maryland, the 13th state in January, 1781). Besides these imperfect documents, in order to form a more perfect union, the framers researched many other different forms of government.

Their main sources of ideas in altering the American plan of government included works from Ancient Greece and Rome, English history, as well as major European philosophers such as John Locke, Jean Jacques Rousseau, and Baron de Montesquieu. These philosophers are quoted many times in the essays put forth in the Federalist Papers.

Despite their best effort, the framers were unable to find an exact model to suit the needs of what they viewed as America's unique situation. To solve the problem of an imperfect foundation for the government as expressed in the "Articles of Confederation," when the states' delegates met in May 1787, their intention was to use the Articles and the result of their research and their collective thoughts, to form a government to meet the new country's needs.

Additionally, they were prepared to interject their own ideas based on their governing experience from the time shortly after the Revolution. It helps to remember that Washington could have been King if he had chosen but instead he refused. Our first President was elected in 1789, just two years after our Constitution was initially approved.

Washington loved the Constitution and never chose to violate it even in its infancy stages. He knew he was the most powerful man in American long before he became President but he loved the notion of America and worked for our greater good.

Though charged with merely creating an enhancement to the Articles of Confederation, the framers went much further and as noted previously, they created a new form of government that was to operate under the newly minted United States Constitution.

In forming the original government known as the Union— based on the Articles of Confederation, all of the thirteen original states were required to ratify the plan. For the Constitution, it was deemed that before it took effect, it would need to be ratified / approved by at least nine of the thirteen colonies, which by then had become known as "states." They were then all part of America, though theoretically at least, our first President under the Constitution, George Washington had yet to be elected.

The rationale as I see it (that not all states needed to concur) is because the country was already a country from the time all thirteen states had signed up to be part of the USA. The Articles of Confederation was a great work and it got the government moving in the right direction, but as the Federalist Papers prove, it needed improvement.

Who was running the country from 1776 after the Revolution until 1789 when Washington was elected? Well, this may come as a surprise but John Hanson, a Revolutionary War patriot, was the first US President, and there were seven others presidents before Washington.

The Founders reset the government with the Constitution and began to count presidents from that point on. Yet, America had eight presidents before Washington. The most well known of the eight presidents; was John Hancock. At the time, Washington was in Congress.

Thomas Jefferson, James Madison, Thomas Paine, John Adams, Alexander Hamilton, and to an extent George Washington are the major figures responsible for the writing and putting of the Constitution into its final form. When the state delegates signed the Constitution on September 17, 1787, they all knew ratification would not be easy.

Many were bitterly opposed to the proposed new system of government. Even today, one can search the Web and get many hits about the Anti-Federalist Papers. They were written in the spirit of debate, not tyranny. Their point was to provide less power to the central government. Their concern was that the Constitution did not 100% assure that a tyrant could never become King of the US. Many alert citizens are concerned about the same thing today.

Shortly after its approval at the Convention, A public debate erupted in each of the states over whether the new Constitution should be accepted. This was a crucial debate on the future of the United States.

The Federalist Papers, written by Alexander Hamilton, John Jay, and James Madison answered the debated questions as posed by the opposition in great detail while copious detractors wrote their own essays / articles in rebuttal. Many were published in the press so to offer other thoughts on such an important issue. Today's press, unfortunately are corrupt. They favor the socialist progressives and they do not operate on behalf of the people's interests.

At the time they wrote the papers, the three "Publius" authors were focused just on the state of New York, and they did not submit their works to other states for publishing or review.

Yet, these patriotic and historical articles / essays made their way across all thirteen states and ultimately were a major reason why the Constitution was ratified, one state at a time.

Chapter 17   Introduction to the Federalist Papers Part II

New York was the battleground state.

Nowhere was the furor over the proposed Constitution in the few states of the US more intense than in New York. Governor George Clinton was very concerned that the state's influence would be compromised at the Convention. The legislature selected State Supreme Court Judge Robert Yates and John Lansing, Speaker of the NY Assembly; to attend the convention. Both were well known Anti-Federalists. Their selection was seen by many as a way for New York to be able to outvote Alexander Hamilton.

When the notion of a new government and not a revision of the Articles of Confederation became the obvious intention of the majority of delegates, even before it was completed, Anti-Federalists Yates and Lansing pulled up their tents and went back to NY in disgust. Neither wanted anything to do with the new Constitution as it was shaping up in Philadelphia. After four months of effort, and within days after it was signed, the Constitution therefore became the subject of widespread criticism in the New York press.

There were those, such as Yates and Lansing, whose opposition to the new document was based on their view that the Constitution diminished the rights that Americans had won in the Revolution. The Federalist Papers presented a view that this was not true while the Anti-Federalist Papers, also displayed in popular newspapers of the day, presented a

view that the Constitution was bad for America and offered
its specific notions.

Alexander Hamilton, one of America's finest patriots,
became fearful that the cause for the Constitution might be
lost in his home state of New York. This was his purpose in
putting together the Federalist Papers. The Anti-Federalists
saw Hamilton's effort as "selling" his ideas and to this day,
various Anti-Federalist writers still mock it as one of the
greatest marketing stunts of all time.

When anybody tries to convince anybody else of something,
it can be mocked as salesmanship. Without Hamilton's
determined sales approach however, today our country might
be a monarchy or a dictatorship, or worse.

Hamilton was a brilliant lawyer, and an accomplished writer.
He loved the notions built into the new Constitution. It was
no surprise that he came forward almost immediately after
the signing to defend the new Constitution. Earlier, when he
took off for Philadelphia to attend the Convention, nobody
really knew that he was to become the only New Yorker to
have signed the Constitution.

As noted, the other New York delegates were not happy
about the model for the new government, and so they angrily
left the Convention before it was completed. Yet, the
delegates from most of the thirteen states at the convention,
none of which, other than perhaps Virginia, were as powerful
as New York, chose to pass the Constitution on to
ratification. They were convinced that the rights of the people
were not being abandoned, and they did not really care what
New Yorkers thought.

Hamilton himself was very much in favor of strengthening
the central government. Thankfully, all of his ideas were not
adopted. His original notion of a Constitution would have
called for a president elected for life with the power to

appoint state governors. As much as I admire Hamilton, that sounds a lot like the current president's wishes.

As much as conservatives may admire Hamilton in his deeds, his thoughts, such as this were a different matter. Hamilton soon backed away from these ideas, and concluded that the Constitution, as written mostly by Madison, and not with all of the Hamiltonian precepts for which he had originally lobbied, was the best one possible.

Hamilton published his first "Federalist" essay in the New York Independent Journal on October 27, 1787. For historical accuracy, I report that Hamilton soon recruited two others, namely James Madison and John Jay, to contribute essays to the series. As previously noted, He, John Jay, and James Madison signed each of the articles with the Roman name "Publius." (The use of pseudonyms by writers on public affairs was a common practice.)

James Madison, sometimes called the Father of the Constitution, had played a major role during the Philadelphia Convention. As a delegate from Virginia, he participated actively in the debates. He also kept detailed notes of the proceedings and drafted much of the Constitution.

Unlike Hamilton and Madison, John Jay of New York had not been a delegate to the Constitutional Convention. A judge and diplomat, he was serving as secretary of foreign affairs in the national government when enlisted by Hamilton to write his essays.

Between October 1787 and August 1788, "Publius" wrote 85 essays as articles in several New York newspapers. Hamilton wrote over 60 percent of these essays and helped with the writing of others. Madison wrote about a third of them with Jay composing the rest (5).

The essays had an immediate impact on the ratification debate in New York and in the other states. When you read them, you will see how convincing they are.

The demand for reprints was so great that one New York newspaper publisher printed the essays together in two volumes entitled The Federalist, A Collection of Essays, Written in Favor of the New Constitution, By a Citizen of New York. By this time the identity of "Publius," never a well-kept secret, was pretty well known.

The "Federalist" book, edited by Kelly, provides this two-part introduction in addition to the full 85 articles as written by the Founders and our nation's precious founding documents. These include the Declaration of Independence and the Constitution. As you know from reading so far, it introduces an amazing set of essays that only great American patriots could have written. God Bless America. Thank you Kate Smith!

The Federalist, also called The Federalist Papers, has served two very different purposes in American history. The 85 essays succeeded in helping to persuade doubtful New Yorkers (as well as the public in the other states), despite the well written efforts of the Anti-Federalists, to ratify the Constitution.

Today, The Federalist Papers help US to more clearly understand what the writers of the Constitution had in mind when they drafted this amazing document more than 200 years ago.

Important questions re USA: our democratic republic

Where did the idea of the US government structure come from? Have you ever wondered how our government came to be? Have you ever wondered why there is a Constitution and why that is important to our being a nation of free people with liberty and justice for all? Why are there certain precepts written into our Constitution and not written into the Constitutions of other "democracies" in other countries?

The Federalist Papers explain the climate of our new nation by exploring all of the persuasive arguments for adopting the new Constitution and the need of a strong federal government that provides the final power to the people.

The tenets of the Federalist Papers are just as pertinent today as they were at the beginning of our nation. To understand what and who we are as Americans... not just as individuals but as a society, a citizenry... it's necessary to understand the intent of our Founding Fathers.

When you do that by reading the Federalist Papers in this package, or any other, or by downloading the free versions to your own stationery or portable unit, you are on your way to understanding this great republic. Together with other founding documents, the changes in the world—technology, etc. can still be seen through the eyes of the Founders. This reading will open your eyes, and it is especially necessary today to open all of our eyes to prevent our government from stealing our lives.

The Federalist Papers are a very important tool for understanding the meaning of our Constitution and they demonstrate that its relevance is based on something much deeper. The authors of the essays knew that the principles of our founding would not always be unquestioned. So, in the papers, they gave us the strongest defense of those principles as part of the immediate political struggle for ratification.

The Federalist Papers not only illuminate the meaning of the Constitution's text; they also explain how our Constitution embodies the core principles of the Declaration of

Independence and why it must be preserved, especially in the face of present struggle.

Over 100 years ago, according to most historians including Matthew Spalding of the Heritage Foundation, "progressive thinkers sought to 're-found' America according to ideas alien to Washington, Adams, Jefferson, Hamilton and Madison."

"Repudiating the Founders' belief in the existence of self-evident truths, progressives saw only relative values. Similarly, they claimed, man enjoys no permanent rights endowed by God, only changing rights held at the indulgence of government."

The progressives have yet to destroy America though they are trying very hard to do so. Despite our contemporary challenges, we still enjoy a great measure of the original constitutional freedoms as delivered kindly by the Founders.

More importantly, through this work, the Founders have left US with their teaching and their example, showing us the way to restore our Constitution to its rightful place in America.

Our Constitution is built to endure unless good men choose to act as godless men. It will endure only if our leaders understand why it is defensible, and we can convince them or find others to defend it. There is no better argument in favor of the Constitution than *The Federalist Papers*.

We the People, when we learn or begin to fully understand what our rights have always been; will become convinced that each of us has the right to demand that our legislators adhere to our demands. If they choose not to do so, regardless of to which party they belong, it is time to call them home and bring on a patriotic representative who espouses freedom, to serve US.

Americans too often forget the work of our Founders in establishing our freedoms. We all know how our forefathers in WWI and in WWII fought to preserve freedoms—life, liberty, and the pursuit of happiness. These are the freedoms established through the revolution, which have been preserved by many wars at a great cost of human life.

The Founders did not want this country to endure the malfeasance from which it now suffers. The same type of bad policies that motivated them to come to America and establish the USA as a new country should now motivate all Americans to understand our founding, and our inherent right to liberty, freedom, and justice—before it is too late.

The Founders were surely not from America. They came from other countries to have a better life and to form a new country that would be better for all the American people for years to come.

Like you, I absolutely love America and the more I read about our history, the more impressed I am about these wonderful patriots who, with quill pens and huge brains forged documents to guide US forever.

Though presidents may possess pens and phones, and they may think that their opinions, rather than laws matter the most, when they create their own laws and choose not to enforce the laws of the nation, their actions are unconstitutional. It is forbidden.

This is exactly why Americans must read the Federalist Papers and understand the Constitution to know how wrong-headed this thinking is. This is exactly what the Founders cautioned US about. One man's pen and a phone cannot be how our country's government work is accomplished or we have no Constitution, and thus, we have no rights!

I think it is logical to conclude that the Founders and the framers did a great job or else few freedom-lovers would be here today. Can you imagine how long it took for them to write down their great thoughts in the implements of their day? How good are you at printing legibly with a quill pen and a bottle of ink?

I admit that until I read the Federalist Papers, I did not know what was on their minds and what their options were as they created the short document for US freedom known as the Constitution. Apparently at least one high government official of today, once a constitutional professor, does not fully understand the intention of founding documents; or he simply chooses to ignore them—at great peril to Americans.

It is imperative that all Americans reintroduce ourselves to the meaning of freedom and liberty and how it is preserved in our great Constitution. We must always assure that neither a single president, nor conspiring members of our Congress ever grow powerful enough to steal our freedom from US. Americans must pay attention or bad things can and will happen.

The reality is that when compared against the thoughts of the Founders, as placed in the Constitution and explained in the Federalist Papers, an individual president is nothing and cannot change our structure of government, even if he chooses to make attempts. Eventually, such a president will fail.

The Founders provided the basis so that what we do is up to US, and not the government. Presidents are not Kings. America has the best government in the world. We have no reason to change it. But, we must stay alert and continually vote scoundrels out of office so they do not change America in a fundamental way.

Because the Founders anticipated that there might be presidents such as the current executive, and his historical friends, FDR, and Wilson, along with other socialist progressives, who place government ahead of God, they put clauses into the Constitution and the Bill of Rights to protect US.

We must know about these in order to be protected. The Founders worried mostly about a tyranny brought forth by a government gone bad—more than anything else. Therefore, they created the best Constitution ever. They wrote down the rules of behavior, and they gave the power to the people, not the government.

Presidents most certainly know the rules, even if they choose not to abide by them. Despite having taken an oath of office in which they swear that they will defend all of the laws in the spirit of the Constitution, when a divided Congress chooses not to reign in presidential power, the result is tyranny.

All Americans worry about how to make this administration adhere to the precepts emblazoned in our Constitution. Americans are not prepared to relinquish freedom and liberty just so that an elected president can behave as a King.

Let me say it again in different words. The idea of the Constitution is to protect regular Americans from government tyranny more than any single other element. That's why the Founders gave Americans the right to bear Arms—just in case the government gets off kilter and stops deferring to the people.

The right to bear arms has nothing to do with hunting. The idea is that if our government ever becomes tyrannical, and this curse cannot be solved by elections, the people have the right, in the Constitution, to disband the current regime by the force of arms. The next right is to quickly form a new government of the people. In our 200 + years, thankfully, we have not needed to do this. Yet, it is our constitutional right.

While the Founders were trying to convince the public, one state at a time, to accept the precepts of the Constitution, as discussed previously, Alexander Hamilton, James Madison, and John Jay put their rationale to paper. In this way, the public would understand how important freedom is and how the Constitution was built to help assure freedom and liberty for as long as the people pay attention.

Subsequent generations must also subscribe to the notion of the Constitution as the Supreme Law of the Land in order for freedom and liberty to last. And, we too must pay attention.

The notion of democracy and a free republic does not come easy. The press (media) is supposed to keep the country on its best behavior but in recent times our press has become corrupt and they lie to protect the favored political factions in America.

The socialist progressives lie and the corrupt mainstream press swears to it. And, thus, we must all think for ourselves and not depend on the lies of the media for our information.

The press in the US is respectfully called the mainstream media. Unfortunately, decades ago, yet still in my lifetime, they gave up on honesty. Now, they are part of the problem, not the solution. The mainstream media is in bed with the economic and political powers, which they are supposed to watch for the people.

They are charged in the Constitution to keep a vigilant eye on the political process. The Founders had no idea that the press could be bought by rich operatives with liberal progressive Marxist leanings. It is time to wake up America!

Unfortunately, gullible Americans recently have become cheerleaders for the socialist progressive cause. Thus, they no longer insist that the US Press is honest. Instead, they enjoy the corrupt coverage of their politicians because they have been convinced that it helps them in material ways.

It wasn't supposed to be like this and it must change. Understanding the Constitution through the Federalist Papers is a great way to understand the fundamentals of liberty and freedom, and the need for an honest press.

If it were not for the bloggers who mostly tell the truth today, along with Talk Radio, and parts of some news outlets, Americans might conclude that we would be better served by inviting Mr. Putin to come on down and just take US over.

At least he has the underpinnings of a strong and courageous man, though none of his personal underpinnings are those about which our country was founded. If we must be controlled by a King, Putin would more than likely make a better King than our current executive.

Because of our Constitution, Americans should not ever need the likes of Vladimir Putin or Joseph Stalin to become our dictator or King. That is anathema to the freedoms for which many of our ancestors have fought and died.

We also should not have to worry about our leaders choosing to run our country in the same fashion as Vladimir Putin. Vladimir Lenin, or Joseph Stalin ran Communist Russia. It is against the most basic Law of the Land, The US Constitution.

Americans have the power through national elections at this moment in history, to simply throw out all tyrants and bring in people who are more sympathetic to America, the American people and American beliefs. Don't forget that the Constitution also permits US to impeach bad government officials—who we once elected in good faith.

I for one hope—that we do something very soon. This man's hope is for change. Big change! The socialist changes that we have been experiencing must be reversed. We risk becoming serfs to an oppressive government much sooner than later.

I hope this two-part introduction and the Federalist Papers, (Chapters 16 & 17), helps you and all American citizens to begin to understand our roles in keeping American strong. Without all of US; and that includes both you and I, corruption and lawlessness will win. When this happens, America and its children will lose.

I therefore beg you all to start your fight against tyranny by reading the Federalist Papers beginning today. Never let your guard down. Pay attention as if your life depends on it. It does!

"America- if we cannot define Liberty, we cannot defend it. If we cannot define tyranny, we cannot defeat it. If you wish to be ignorant and free, you wish for what never was and never will be." KrisAnne Hall www.conservativeactionalerts.com/author/krisanne-hall

Summary of Founding Document Chapters

In Part IV of this book we took a look, not only at the Constitution but also at the earlier original documents and declarations.

This brief walk through all these documents gives us a general perspective of how the government got to be as it is, and that's necessary as we discuss its structure in the civics lessons. It also helps as we look at things that are wrong with the government and ways that we can improve them as we read subsequent chapters.

As you read the Constitution in Appendix E, and I urge you to do this to be as informed as possible about the basic law of the land, make note that there is no article or section or clause that provides an upper limit to what government can take in taxes.

The idea of course was that taxation would be reasonable. The founders always expected Americans to reap what they would sow. Socialist progressives in our government today, however, have a different notion about that. This is not your father's America.

Putting politicians in control of the money supply in all three levels of government is certainly one of the weakest notions in the Constitution. Though the idea of nobility is expressly verboten by the Constitution, there is nothing that suggests that the representatives of the people could not behave nobly if they chose to do so. .

History proves that the Founding Fathers were very noble and so they expected that those who followed them to office would also be noble. They may be honorable (See coming Chapter 31 for some humor on the hizzonners), but few are noble.

We can blame taxation on the Constitution and the fact that it the document is just over 30 original pages for some of its shortcomings. Of course if all men were honest, 30 pages would be more than enough.

States also have constitutions and cities have charters, and all of these bodies can levy taxes and create more laws. So, it is no wonder, as this country has grown, the whole system has gotten unwieldy. Maybe we can start again but our primary reason to do so would be to rid the government of scoundrels and pilferers known as politicians.

Maybe we can simply vote them out of office. Surely this will be an option we examine as we explore how to deal with an unresponsive government after we cover civics in the next section.

Part V: Civics Lesson for Dummmies!

Chapter 18   The Study of Civics

What is Civics?

In a book titled, America 4 Dummmies, it is most
appropriate to have a chapter or more that discusses the
notion of Civics.

History buffs well know that Thomas Jefferson was a great
believer in an educated population. He was not interested in a
government of the dummmies, for the dummmies, and by the
dummmies.

In 1816, about forty years after the American Revolution,
when the youngest of US were not even born (Irish humor),
Jefferson wrote: "If a nation expects to be ignorant and
free…it expects what never was and never will be." Jefferson
saw education as the bedrock of democracy. Many scholars
credit Thomas Jefferson as being our earliest and strongest
champion of public education.

Yet, education about America; its appropriate founding; its
structural integrity, assuring the minority a voice regardless of
what the majority trumpets, its built-in notions so that crooks
can not readily become our leaders, and its reliance on
rugged individualism, if not simple individualism, in order to
assure freedom from a tyrannical government; are among the

missing lessons for today's under fifty-crowd. They cannot help it if their generations are the dummmies that today we must write for. Though we can chalk some up to laziness, it is totally the fault of a too trusting public.

The public has some skin in the game as it finds US losing more liberties and more freedoms every day. John Q. trusts government too much. Consequently, regular people, who lack the fundamental knowledge of America can and have been manipulated to serve our socialist progressive Marxist government's end game, which is not for the benefit of the people.

Government over the years since Jefferson has become its own entity requiring constant feeding from a too-adoring public.

Nobody can replace the civics stuff that Americans missed in the classroom by having an education system dominated by unions rather than educators and wise people. The less the people know, the more likely those who think they know it all will exploit US and they will hurt US even long after we wake up to Cry Uncle!

Considering the US spends twice per capita on education than any other country, why do we create so many dummmies? What can the ideological left's answer be to solve the educational ills of our country. Should we collect more taxes and spend more money on the same unions and teachers?

How do they explain away the lack of knowledge on the part of citizens to the foundational precepts of our nation? They simply do not explain and instead pretend that it has always been this way. In fact, the left is accomplishing its objectives of dummming down Americans quite handily. Many Americans are too brainwashed to complain.

Their goal is to be able to keep the direction of the dummming down—down. The Common Core at the Federal level is another power grab to prepare Americans for the coming of socialism with control of education by the central government. When the federal government makes the tests, and provides the cash to the school districts, the teachers will be using national, not state or local education plans to meet the Fed targets. Expect even dummmer graduates as the worst thing for a communist state is an informed public. The truth is the greatest enemy of the state.

The tests and the curriculum to follow are put together by leftists and it is intended to slip in more Blame America First propaganda. I regret that the truth about America, as would be discussed in a real civics course will be kept from Americans by an ideology that hates America first! Indoctrination of our youth by the Federal Department of Education with the Common Core as its tool will make it worse.

Consider the twelve year old who came home from school in March 2014, and called a radio talk show because he was angry at the day's lesson. He had just learned that Christopher Columbus was an evil, money-hungry, greedy, Native American-killing person. He never considered that his teacher might be lying or did not know the facts herself.

So, he was mad at Columbus until his parents took him to a PC and spent an hour of research showing the young man that Columbus was a hero.

In 2010, Sandy Hingston got it 100% right when writing for Philadelphia Magazine. She noted that:

> *"Children today seem, well,'dumber' than they used to. They don't know the most basic stuff: who fought against whom in World War II, how many pints are in a quart, and in Jake's case, the days of the week. (He's shaky on the months, too.) They may be*

> *taking every AP and Honors course their schools offer, but they can't tell you who invented pasteurization."*

Like many of their parents, children are even less tuned in to what their own country is about. They are beyond the notion of dummmer regarding the country, as are most of their younger parents. Until recently, most did not care. They are simply dummm, and the ideological socialist progressive left likes it that way because the dummmer the American, the easier they will be to control when left coast nirvana is reached and they are dependent on the government for all their needs.

The US Department of Education, which is so far left, parts of it lie in the deep Pacific Ocean (left coast), at the national level has been trying to overtake state's rights on education. Washington bureaucrats think they know it all. Their objective is to degrade the founders as slave traders and elitists who cared nothing about the people. In this way, they can be assured that those of you, who have registered as American dummmies, will sign away your lives and become dependent on them, instead of yourselves.

The founding documents have placed huge chains on the Marxists, socialist progressives, and communists and they know they are there. They do not like it one bit. This is the best reason for you to want to be very familiar with these documents.

Why do they hate our fundamental laws and the words of the founders so much? Because they stop them from taking over this country and turning it into a Banana Republic, with them in control. Many of these anti-Americans are in our Congress today but they will not tell you their true ideology. They lie instead. You have to hear them speak to know who they really are.

They hate the constraints provided by America's founders, especially those in the Constitution, and so they want US all to give up our freedoms willingly by the force of lies and other propaganda. They want US to give them the right to tear down all of our Constitutional protections including right to life, liberty, freedom, and the pursuit of happiness. Our rights only matter to US.

Then what? They think we are dummm enough to do what they want because their spiel is so good. That is why so subtly they have taken civics out of our schools. They do not want Americans to love America. It gets in their way and it may stop them from taking over the country completely in the coming years.

For years, these same people have been trying to take over America in so many other different ways. Their newest and greatest weapon is the "lie." Gullible Americans, who are now known as low-information voters, buy into their lies and never question their words. They sop it all up and believe every word as if it is the truth. But, it is not the truth.

Once they get regular Americans to trust them, it is their best weapon and it works well for them. They quickly learn that they have no problem getting people who pay little attention to governmental affairs to believe their lies. They are so good at lying; their noses do not grow.

The lies grow, however, and the next thing, as in all other countries where this has been attempted, the people suffer. There is no big wave of egalitarianism. Instead, there is a takeover of the government by those who hate the common people and who detest the poor rabble that have a tough time getting by. In most countries, where this occurs, many people are killed simply for their possessions. Quite frankly, that is why many Americans will not give up their guns.

Unbelievably, the corrupt politicians in this country have the chutzpah and the charm to make the people, even the lowliest, whose only asset is their ability to breathe, to follow them right to their own deaths.

It hasn't happened just yet but more signs are readable every day. Such leaders do not love America or Americans. They want to overthrow US and take over and control US. The more we know about our foundational laws, the less likely we will ever permit them to have their way at our expense.

And, so they see the only solution to the chains the founding documents have placed upon them; is to discredit the founding of America and the founders. They try to tell US all that the founders are old fogies--believers in the Republic and freedom—and they are fools. They try to tell us that the neo-communists are the good guys because they like sex and porn, and dirty lyric music, and so they are like US and we are like them.

Is that really so?

Would we have been better served as pawns of King George III than to be Americans?

Why not give it up to an ideology that will help us understand the meaning of the word subjugation. Why not do it tomorrow? Why wait if lack of freedom and lack of liberty, and no option for a pursuit of happiness is such a splendid idea for an end to you and to America? If you believe that, they would argue, why not take the trip today?

Of course, I did not write this book for dummmies for anybody interested in staying dummm. I expect that any of you who read just a few pages will pick up something good that will inspire you to move towards an even better understanding of America and a better, more purposeful life. Hopefully, you will get mad as hell, and you won't take it anymore.

Additionally, my goal is to have Americans, such as you, reading this book because you choose to do so—to learn more about why it is such as great deal being an American—regardless of what lies you might hear someplace else.

So, on our way to more good stuff, let's drop off the map of excitement for a bit and start learning about things we must know to be good citizens. Being good citizens in America, of course starts with believing in America. Believing in America starts with understanding America. And, understanding America starts, as in all good courses, with a comprehensive yet brief (if that can be) definition of important terms. So, let's run through some definitions for the greater good.

In the important definitions that we put forth in this chapter and in Chapter 19, we use the work of Aristotle, and a little work from Plato to help present positions about our government that are true and are believable, and are well founded in a history, documenting life long before the founders. Let's start with the definition of civics. It will take a while for US to begin defining other important terms in Chapter 19.

Civics in a nutshell

Civics, in a nutshell, is the study of the great practical and theoretical aspects of citizenship including its rights and duties, and the duties of citizens to each other as members of the body politic (the electorate, country) and to the government of the nation. There are many things that can be included in a civics lesson including the study of laws and the study of the structure and function of government.

In civics, we pay close attention to the role of the citizen within the context of the country as opposed to the operation and oversight of government. Yet, for an American to be a good citizen, one must first understand how government functions. For the most part, that is the thrust of our civics lesson. That is the thrust of the book you are reading, which, of course is titled, America 4 Dummmies!

Would you believe it if I told you that it was right after the Obama election in late November 2008, that Michelle Healy of USA TODAY, a rag paper not well known for conservative thought, was compelled to write an article titled: Americans don't know civics. Her rationale for writing the piece was that Americans were dummmies in all matters civics. Here is how she begins her article. It made me stand back to "listen:"

> From high-school dropouts to college graduates to elected officials, Americans are "alarmingly uninformed" about the USA's history, founding principles and economy — knowledge needed to participate wisely in civic life, says a report scheduled to be released Thursday. The study, the third in a series by the non-profit Intercollegiate Studies Institute, finds that half of U.S. adults can name all three branches of government, and 54% know that the power to declare war belongs to Congress. Almost 40% incorrectly said that it belongs to the president.

Healy also has done research about how Americans perceive civics. She noted that though 56% could name Paula Abdul as a judge on American Idol, only 21% knew that the phrase "government of the people, by the people, for the people" comes from Lincoln's Gettysburg Address. Lastly, and amazingly, just 54% were able to identify a basic description of the free enterprise system.

Check this for a proper grade for Americans:

In the survey cited by Healy, a whopping 71% of those tested earned an F in civics. Are all Americans dummm on civics or are we simply underserved by those who are paid to teach US? The average score was 49%. The report notes that from ages 25 to 34, there was an average score of 46%; ages 45 to 64 had a 52% average. The elected class—164 respondents—were deemed unworthy of holding office. They came in at a diminutive 44%. Is this a case of the dummm governing the less dummm?

We vote for these people. Yet, even elected officials know nothing about America. Those with degrees did a bit better but overall the verdict is that Americans have not been taught much about America in our public schools, colleges, or universities. It is too widespread for it not to be intentional.

It does not serve socialist progressive Marxists (US government leaders) to help the population understand that we actually have rights. Ask yourself if you have met anybody on the street recently who cares about any of this. Perhaps many people are afraid to talk about it in public. Is this America or has Rod Serling been fooling with some cosmic atoms.

John Taylor Gatto was the New York State Teacher of the year for 1989, 1990, and 1991. That is quite a record. He is very concerned for America. He was cited as the best there is in his profession. Since then, Gatto has written numerous books and given speeches about the *dumbing down of America*. Has he been part of the solution or part of the problem?

In his acceptance speech in 1991, he speculated that if instead of being hired to enlarge children's power, he may have been hired to diminish it. He noted that as he looked at his career objectively, he began to realize that

> *" the bells and confinement, the crazy sequences, the age-segregation, the lack of privacy, the constant surveillance, and all the rest of the national curriculum of schooling were designed exactly as if someone had set out to prevent children from*

*learning how to think, and act, to coax them into
addiction and dependent behavior."*

Upon further examination he concluded that

*"… All of these lessons are prime training for
permanent underclasses, people deprived forever
of finding the center of their own special genius."* He
began to view the notion of school as a *"twelve-year
jail sentence, where bad habits are the only
curriculum truly learned. I teach school, and win
awards doing it. I should know."*

Gatto is not the only one coming to such frightening
conclusions.

Noted education expert, analyst and author, Samuel
Blumenfeld sees the deliberate dummming down of
American children by their education system as very well
planned, and well executed. He writes:

*"Anyone who has had any lingering hope that what
the educators have been doing is a result of error,
accident, or stupidity will be shocked by the way
American social engineers have systematically
gone about destroying the intellect of millions of
American children for the purpose of leading the
American people into a socialist world government
controlled by behavioral and social scientists."*

The public and private education systems for American
youth, as a topic, is way too large for any one book,
especially one, such as this, designed to strengthen patriotism
by retelling the facts about our great country. Yet a short look
at the dummming down of America as we have covered
above is necessary and appropriate because its cause is the
same as the lack of understanding of civics in our culture
today. It is why we have more people dumm about America
today, than at any point in our history.

It is simply not politically correct to teach Americans that we have a right to anything, including life, liberty, and the pursuit of happiness, and so the teaching textbooks and the teachers themselves simply do not do so. Teachers are dummmed down by the unions and leftist administrators, and the students consequently are dummed down by the teachers and the left-sided textbooks.

Besides not being able to learn we have rights, It is also not politically correct for Americans to believe they have rights. It is not politically correct to challenge the government, the unions, or teachers about how our children are not learning the needed lessons in schools.

Try arguing with a teacher about any subject today. Our only connection with teachers is that we pay twice more for what they do than they would make in any other country on earth.

Yet, despite not being told too often about them, we do have certain rights that are inalienable and others that we get from keeping the government from stealing them. Before the socialists in government today succeed in destroying the Constitution, a huge treasure chest of rights and freedoms are available for the American people.

But, the left does not like US to know that so please do not take your rights for granted. Pay attention and when you see their grubby little fingers trying to steal any of your rights, step on their fingers with pride.

The lack of knowledge of civics in America is a direct result of Americans no longer being taught to be patriotic by learning about the founding, our great Constitution, and what it takes to remain a free country. The socialists in tandem with the corrupt media, whose true role as the fourth estate is to fill in our knowledge gaps, have negatively impacted what Americans are permitted to learn.

Americans all over the country however, are slowly waking up to the negatives of government control and across this great land, we are fighting back.

There is some hope for the future if we can believe what we see. Former Supreme Court Justice Sandra Day O'Connor, a formidable proponent of our constitutional republic, has taken up the civics torch as the co-chair of the Campaign for the Civic Mission of Schools. O'Connor writes:

> *"The better educated our citizens are, the better equipped they will be to preserve the system of government we have…And we have to start with the education of our nation's young people. Knowledge about our government is not handed down through the gene pool. Every generation has to learn it, and we have some work to do."*

Amen! Now, that is a refreshing thought!

At birth, Individuals do not automatically become responsible participating citizens. We must all be educated for citizenship. This determination to educate young Americans about their rights and responsibilities as citizens is known as the civic mission of schools.

Yet, we are doing very poorly as a nation in assuring that our population cannot be hoodwinked by the corrupt politicians du jour. One of the easiest ways to be sucked in by the chicanery of the unprincipled is to be unaware of one's rights.

Each state's constitution or library of public education establishment statutes and codes, acknowledges the civic mission of schools. It is there but it is being ignored today. Instead, the dummming down of Americans continues at a blistering pace.

You see; another movement in our country, the "Hate America First! Crowd" continues to make progress slowly yet deliberately towards a form of communistic government. Because of our lack of civic knowledge, the people are not just allowing it to happen but many are even clamoring for more of it.

Dependent Americans are becoming more dependent and they are demanding more welfare benefits. These have become an entitlement and a reward just for being a dummm American. But, those rewards are meager, and when anybody wants more, even if they think they are willing to work for it, there will be no opportunities.

In recent years, civic learning has been increasingly pushed aside. In some states it simply does not exist. The Federal Education Department is not interested in creating patriotic Americans and it discourages civics by omitting it in its plans.

I do not mean to suggest that the Feds are not hollowly suggesting civics is important for they feel right now since America is not fully socialist yet, they must. For example, in 2012, Arne Duncan, President Obama's Education Head offered these comments:

> *"The need to revitalize and reimagine civic education is urgent. But that urgent need brings a great opportunity —the chance to improve civic education in ways that will resonate for years."*

Arne, with all due respect for your position, there is no civic education currently going on so how can it be improved? I suspect it can be improved in ways none of us would imagine.

Having watched the government's interpretation of improvement for many years, Duncan's words are empty and not very reassuring. Meanwhile the US Department of Education is doing its best to hurt America. Where's the beef?

Until the 1960s, three courses in Civics and Government were common in American high schools, and two of them ("Civics" and "Problems of Democracy") explored the role of citizens and encouraged students to discuss current issues. Today across all the states such courses are very rare and Duncan is not suggesting we bring them back.

As a socialist, the education chief does not really want the problem solved. What remains, after all these years, is just one course on "American Government" that usually spends little time on how people can – or why they should – participate as citizens. Is this intentional? Does Heinz have 57 varieties?

As of 2011, only 19 states include civic learning in their state assessment / accountability systems, generally as part of an overall social studies assessment, including history, geography, state history and economics. I would not expect it to improve until there is a fundamental change in the top echelons of our government.

Chapter 19   Various Government Structures

Civics definitions for dummmies

In this book, in each chapter so far, we have discussed the importance of honest representative government. We have also lightly introduced the notion of taxation without representation as our elected leaders fail to accomplish their duties in representing the people.

In this civics lesson for dummmies so far, we have discussed the problems we are experiencing today with an uneducated, and thus dummm population. Soon, we will examine our form of representative democracy and we will explore other forms and variations so we can all know that the US form of government is about as good as it can get. The founders were not dummmies.

This continuation of our civics lesson into this chapter and beyond is presented as a substantive part of this book written for dummies. The objective is to leave this book with an understanding of the fundamental facts about America that makes our country so exceptional.

It is intended to give all Americans who are willing to learn, the opportunity to understand the basic tenets of the US representative constitutional democracy (aka constitutional republic). For a deeper appreciation of the notion of the US government and its underlying political principles, there is an excellent free course available on the Internet and I encourage you to visit the Cyberland University of North America at the following URL:

http://www.proconservative.net/CUNAPolSci201HOutline.shtml.

Dr. Almon Leroy Way, Jr. University President & Professor of Political Science in his free Internet course titled Political Science 201H - The American Political System: Politics & Government in the USA captures the details of politics and government in America. It is an excellent reference for just about any facet of American Government and Politics that you would like to examine. My hat is off to Dr. Way for a wonderful work and a thank you for sharing it for no charge with us all. Below, you will find the course description taken from the Web Site:

COURSE DESCRIPTION:
A free, self-study, non-credit course in American Government and Politics designed to benefit (1) the general reader interested in politics, government, law, and public affairs, (2) the advanced high-school student enrolled in an American Government, Advanced Civics, Modern Problems, Problems of Democracy, or Political Science course, and (3) the university or college student enrolled in or planning to enroll in a Political Science or International Relations course or in a History, Geography, Sociology, Economics, or Business course with substantial political content.

Another great source of free continuing education on the Constitution is a course titled Constitution 101: The Meaning and History of the Constitution, presented as a public service by Hillsdale College
https://online.hillsdale.edu/constitution101/info

This not-for-credit online course follows closely the outline of the full-semester course required of all Hillsdale undergraduates as part of the College's Core Curriculum. Lectures and other Materials are archived to view at your convenience.

You may also read any online version of the Federalist Papers. In the founders words, The Federalist Papers tell us all why the Constitution is the greatest document for freedom and liberty ever written. This is another great learning opportunity. Of course, you can also purchase the hard copy of this book and other patriotic books by your author. Just visit www.bookhawkers.com

Can Aristotle and Plato help US?

They sure can! It would help to recall that even before the founders, many philosophers, had taken on the notion of government and what the best form of government might be. So, let's begin this with a quote from Aristotle, one of the greatest Ancient Greek Philosophers, who was also a logician, and a scientist:

> *"The most perfect political community is one in which the middle class is in control, and outnumbers both of the other classes."*

In all times before America, such as Ancient Greece, and in Europe during colonial times, the political and the social classes were much more obvious, They do not exist formally in America but surely, there is the notion of a class contrast with regard to those with wealth and those in poverty. These extremes are quite obvious.

Aristotle wanted to see as many people in the middle tier as possible so that there were few poor and they could move upward; and there were few rich and they could not overpower the people.

Let's go through this section beginning with a few definitions, which will help us learn the form and structure of our government from the time of our founding. Aristotle understood these notions well. He along with Plato spent many hours pondering the finest form of government.

Constitution—Aristotle uses the complex word, Politeia, in his writings and musings on government. It translates directly into the word, Constitution. To him, it also means constitutional government. Aristotle likes the notion of a Constitution or primal body of laws regardless of which form of government may be used. With a Constitution, it is less likely that the government would go awry. With a Constitution, Americans are less likely to ever see a time when a book titled "America Gone Wild" will be written about US!

He believes that constitutional governments are bound to govern with everyone's best interest in mind. Everybody knows the rules from the start, and this helps get the "game" right. He sees a government with a constitution as a compromise between the demands of both the rich and the poor.

Kingship / Monarchy—Aristotle loves the notion of an intelligent thoughtful King as the sole ruler. In this scenario, he sees the people benefitting from the king's beneficence and munificence. He sees such a king as an exceptional individual who governs with everyone's best interests in mind.

Aristotle, being the wise man that he is, admits that that finding such an outstanding leader is difficult, but he loves to believe that it may be a possibility, nonetheless. In Colonial times, if he were alive, Aristotle would have seen George Washington as a candidate to be the ideal king.

When the king rules for himself and not the people, Aristotle sees this as pure tyranny

Aristocracy—Just as he admires a kingship, Aristotle also has high regard for a government of aristocrats / elites. In this, he is not thinking of the hoity-toity, or the hoi polloi.

Instead he sees aristocracy as "the rule of the best." Plato goes even further and refers to an aristocracy as "rule by the virtuous."

Aristotle recognizes that when an aristocracy goes bad it becomes an oligarchy. In an oligarchy, a few important people of not so virtuous character rule for the few and not for the good of all the people. He sees an aristocracy as superior to an oligarchy because it values everyone's interests.

Oligarchy—Aristotle uses oligarchy literally "the rule of the few," to refer to a government controlled by a few people who are always wealthy and looking to achieve more wealth. Aristotle sees oligarchy as a bad form of government. For example, big "C" Communism is a form of oligarchy.

Aristocracy v oligarchy—The term oligarchy always has a negative or derogatory connotation in both modern day and classical usage. Some see the US government today, formed as a constitutional republic, having denigrated into an oligarchy in which rich powerful ideologues control the people.

The worst attributes of an oligarchy are that as a ruling faction, it governs solely in its own interests, disregarding those of the poor. There is a deep contrast with the term aristocracy, which in contemporary times sometimes has a derogatory connotation (nobility), but never is it seen negative in classical times. In classical times, the most intelligent people with virtue as a guide work through governmental processes for the good of the people.

Democracy—Aristotle sees little value in a pure democracy, which means literally, "the rule of the people." With over 300 million citizens, it would be tough for all of US in this huge country to run the government. Aristotle's concern is that democracy is a type of government in which the poor masses have control and they choose to use it to serve their own selfish ends.

The poor are so many that they rule the day in a democracy, and so there is heavy taxation and exploitation of the rich, among other things, making the productive class if you will, less ambitious. Such governments do not last long.

Aristotle does not take issues with the idea of a government of the people, for the people, and by the people as is our great nation because he sees a major buffer to forms of majority rule such as democracy, in the use of a politeia, or constitution. Thus, a constitution makes a democracy OK in his eyes. It also subtly changes a democracy into a republic.

Republic-- a state in which supreme power is held by the people and their elected representatives, and which has an elected or nominated president rather than a monarch with a birth right. This sounds a lot like a democracy. However, a Republic always has a constitution or a basic set of laws which prevent the majority from oppressing the minority and keeping them from being part of the government.

In a republic, the minority has a voice. However, in a democracy, the majority can impose its will on the minority, and bring the minority to submission. In a republic (the US form of government), the majority cannot take away certain inalienable rights such as life, liberty, and the pursuit of happiness.

Minorities cannot be rounded up for example, and put in prison because they do not agree with the political thinking of the regime.

Most philosophers see a well functioning republic as the most ideal form of government. To repeat, the US is a constitutional representative democracy, which is by definition, a republic.

Tyranny—The rule of an individual interested solely in his own benefit. A perverse form of kingship and/or dictatorship, tyranny is unpopular and is usually overthrown. In Aristotle's opinion, it is the worst type of government. Tyranny can exist as an issue in all forms of government when leaders become too powerful. In such cases, throughout the history of man, the people eventually have enough and they revolt and form a new government.

Many Americans see today's president's unconstitutional use of executive orders and regulations as pure and simple tyranny. The president is operating without authority.

Demagoguery—As noted, Aristotle does not like the notion of a pure democracy in which the people held all the power and are constraint free. He sees this as mob rule. The worst type of democracy, in Aristotle's opinion, is when mob rule is carried to an extreme.

In demagoguery, everyone's voice is equal, and the rule of the majority has greater authority than the law. As a result, the apparent will of the people supersedes law. Invariably, a charismatic leader, or demagogue, takes control and becomes a tyrant. Because he speaks with the voice of the people, and because the voice of the people is sovereign, the demagogue is free to do what he wants.

Again many see this happening in America today and fear that our republic is on the verge of collapse.

Constitutional Democracy and Other Political Regimes—a bit more detail

The United States of America has been formed as a "constitutional representative democracy."By definition, a constitutional representative democracy is a republic. Democracy can be defined as government by the people or by their elected representatives. Add a constitution, and some representation instead of direct control, and the flavor changes to a republic.

We have discussed the notion of a "direct democracy" or as it is sometimes called, a "pure democracy" in numerous chapters so far to assure that we understand it. It is a system in which all the people of a country or entity, who choose to participate, do so directly without elected or appointed representatives. It may, however include the use of stewards whose mission is to do as the people direct.

It might be a great way to get rid of crooked politicians using the principles of initiative, referendum, and recall, but as a total form of government, it is very inefficient. The people would need to give up their daily work to tend to governmental obligations in such a system.

When the people decide to have representatives instead of going it alone, the type of government is referred to as a representative democracy.

Attributes of a direct democracy are included in the notions of Initiative (opportunity to propose legislation), Referendum (opportunity to offer ballot resolutions in elections), and Recall (the ability to vote to have representatives come back home so that an honest person can be chosen.)

These important notions of a direct democracy are not included in the federal government of the United States at this time, but are included in twenty state constitutions. Parts of direct democracy, namely initiative, referendum, and recall, would help if properly done in concert with a representative, constitutional democracy.

The specific makeup of a direct democracy may take on different capabilities depending on the will of the people. Depending on how the system is structured, the members of this assembly might pass executive orders, create laws, elect and dismiss leaders and conduct trials.

When elected officials conduct the people's business in a direct democracy, they are considered executive agents, stewards, or direct representatives and thus are bound to the will of the people. It is not like electing the free thinkers we have today who listen more to the desires of the lobbyists than the represented.

Considering that many citizens of the US are upset with our leaders because of little accountability or so it seems, the notion of leaders being tied to the will of the people at first seems to have substantial merit.

With over 300,000,000 and counting as the population of the US, one can also see how it may be unwieldy for such a system to be fully direct in practice regardless of how attractive it is in theory.

Thus, for a direct democracy to work, intermediary public groups are needed. Theoretically, these groups can be the state legislators but, this too has issues in that the notion of "Honorables" and poor representation of the people's interests is also an ailment of state governments.

The vehicles that are used in a direct democracy - namely, Initiative, Referendum, and Recall all have merit and need to be included soon as amendments to our Constitution for our Federal Government.

When the representatives choose not to do the will of the people, a form of government that inhibits actions directly by the people gets in the way of being able to handle the situation. There is always the wonderful idea that when they are not doing their jobs, we can throw the bums out, and we should. But, today, we the people must hope our representatives will impeach the scoundrels for we may have to wait as much as six years to un-elect them.

With the entanglements that our elected find themselves with the ruling class, waiting two to six years to throw them out can be "taxing" and it makes the system less effective and less responsive than employing some direct democracy notions within our constitutional representative democracy between elections. Having direct democracy tools would also make politicians fear the people more than they do today. .

You see, it is a constitutional representative democracy, aka a republic, that governs the US today. If representatives did not become corrupt over time in office, this form could be very effective.

Chapter 20   Principles of a Constitutional Democracy

Constitutional Democracy v Democracy

Now that we have defined the notion of a democracy, what then makes a constitutional democracy that much different than a "democracy?" A constitutional democracy can be described accurately as a system of government in which the power of government is defined and thus limited, and it is distributed in a body of fundamental written law called a constitution. In our constitutional representative democracy our body of laws is known as The Constitution.

Additionally, the electorate (that's US - the people -- a.k.a. the general voting populace within our political society) is given the effective means of controlling the elected representatives in the government. It also gives US the means to hold them accountable for their decisions and actions while in public office.

> Sidebar: *Unfortunately, in today's America, the electorate is asleep and worse than that, are afraid to engage in political discussions for fear they may upset the foes of all forms of democracy.*

A constitutional democracy thus has two essential ingredients, (1) a constitutional ingredient and (2) a democratic ingredient. Let's examine these two ingredients:

The **constitutional** ingredient of a constitutional democracy is the "*constitutional government.*" As noted above, this means that the founding fathers wrote a constitution so that the elected representatives of this nation could not just go ahead and do what they wanted with complete disregard to the most basic laws of this country—written in its Constitution. In other words, even a US president would be breaking the law if they took any law, such as Obamacare, and changed it to suit her or his needs.

The *democratic* ingredient of a constitutional democracy is *representative democracy* and, it has to do with who holds and thus has the right to exercise authority on behalf of the governed. It also describes how such authority is acquired and retained (elections, impeachments etc.). Additionally it prescribes that the representatives of the people are accountable to the people, and through elections, the people can change the face of the government by changing the face of its representatives. -- i.e. throwing the bums out...

A *constitution* as noted above is a very important document in that it provides the opportunity to protect liberty and freedom beyond the lives of the founders of the government. There is a specific process for constitutional amendments because they are such serious changes in government.

For the United States of America, its Constitution is the *supreme* law of land. Thus, it is of higher importance and takes precedence over all other laws of society. In fact, all other laws, to be valid and enforceable, must be written in accordance with the superior law of the Constitution.

Separation of Powers for Honesty

Our Constitution requires a separation of powers, counting on the notion of countervailing power to keep all three separate branches (executive, legislative, and judicial) of government honest. Separation of powers is thus the structure of the government defined by the Constitution with specific powers to each branch, yet with none of the branches having supreme power.

The founders believed for example that the Congress would not let the President act in an unauthorized manner and vice versa. The court was there to solve conflicts within the branches, though it was not given supreme power.

The Legislators pass the laws and the president gets an opportunity to veto them or sign them into law. The President gets to hire a staff to enforce the laws. The president does not have the right to construct laws of his own. Only the Congress can pass laws. The Supreme Court (nine members) cannot make laws and cannot enforce them. It can affirm them and it can strike them down if they are deemed unconstitutional..

Within the Congress, the House ,with 435 representatives elected by the people based on the population of the states, is the only branch of government permitted to allocate dollars towards funding the laws. Thus, the House is in control of the treasury, or the purse as some like to call it.

The Senate, comprised of 100 Senators, two each from each of the fifty states of the union, is where the voice of the minority is heard. Until recently, 60% of the Senators would have to approve many of the laws / appointments. This is thus not sole majority rule. It gives the minority a voice in the government, as so desired by the founders.

Legislators in the House are elected to two year terms; senators are elected by the people for six years; and the Supreme Court gets to function for a lifetime after being appointed by the President with the consent of the Senate. Notice the notion of countervailing power.

The Constitutional sniff test requires impartial nostrils

Thus, in recent years, a number of cases, in which laws were passed about matters of great importance such as abortion, have been appealed to the Supreme Court of the U.S. This is right now deemed by practice, not by the founders as the court of last resort. This court determines whether laws pass the constitutional sniff test.

However, constitutional scholars believe that the Supreme Court has taken on more power than granted and it has begun to be a partisan to politics. The founders anticipated that the justices would be impartial and would be independent advocates for America. This subtle change, in which ideology has overtaken the freedom and liberty and the power of the people, is of grave concern to the continuance of our constitutional republic.

When the laws do not pass the sniff test or when the political makeup of the court sees things in a different light than the lawmakers, or prior justices, laws created either by the states or by the federal legislature may be affirmed or struck down.

When not upheld, they are no longer in force and thus they cannot be enforced. Many of US in the onlooker category think that the court should not take on more power than the Congress since the Congress is the direct voice of the people.

A proper resolution for the court would be to defer a law at least once, maybe several times, or until they get it right. In this way, the Congress gets to debate it again and vote on it again. This would solve a lot of problems and would dispel the notion that the Supreme Court is the most powerful branch of a government designed with three equal partners. .

Regarding enforcement of the laws, a great example comes from the case of April 16, 2007. The Supreme Court chose to uphold a law that banned a type of late-term abortion, a ruling that many believe portends enormous social, legal and political implications regarding this very divisive issue.

Considering that the nine members of the court itself were sharply divided (5-4) could prove historic. Political analysts suggested at the time that it sent a possible signal of the court's willingness, under Chief Justice John Roberts, to someday revisit the right to abortion which heretofore had been guaranteed in the 1973 Roe v. Wade case.

No branch of government is exempt from following the Constitution. In the U.S., every law enacted by a legislature and every decision or action of an executive office or agency must pass the constitutional test. Not all laws that may be unconstitutional by definition if well examined, however, are challenged in court. The Supreme Court does not go searching for cases. The cases come to the Court.

For a law to be reversed it must be appealed and it can be appealed as many times as needed until it may reach the Supreme Court of the United States. Appeals start at lower courts and progress if accepted by justices at various levels and to the Supreme Court.

If the governmental decision or law or action in question is found by the courts to be contrary to the Constitution, the court system will uphold the Constitution and set aside the unconstitutional verdict or action of the federal or state legislature or of the executive branches.

Unfortunately, many justices of the Supreme Court have decided in recent years to become pawns of government administrations (Clinton, Bush, Obama, etc.), rather than deciding cases for the benefit of the people. After all, these administrations bequeathed upon the appointed justice a wonderful lifelong position.

For example, nobody can ever expect that Justice Elena Kagan, the President's last appointee, will ever vote in a way that Barack Obama's minions have not directed her. Since this is a book of facts, and few opinions, feel free to check this Justice's record.

And so, with Justices of the Supreme Court professing their ideology rather than their adherence to the founding principles, one could logically deduce that the founders be damned if such ideologues could find enough other ideologues to undermine the country. The above is all fact. And so, we the people must pay attention to prevent this from happening.

Back in a historical time, American politicians could be considered honest and even honorable because honesty was at the time a virtue. Justices of the Supreme Court were beyond ideology and thus beyond reproach. At least theoretically, they represented the best interests of the people. Today, that unfortunately is not the case. For those learning about America for the first time, we can get back to those days if we choose, but it will not be easy.

My opinion is that we are at a point in history that the elite in America (not the good elite as in colonial times but the nose in the air, wealthy elite), ruled by those who are not as concerned about America as they are about their own ideologies, have figured out ways to undermine the general population which hitherto has been called "We the People."

They use tricks to attract the low information voter segment of "We the People," aka, dummies, to their side, and their tactics in appealing to such folks has delivered many elections to them. It is unethical and the founders, if consulted, would not approve.

Leftists in control of our government are so convinced that people want to stay dumm and continue in this faux love-fest that they are now moving their agendas into the front lines.

Somehow they are convincing the dummmest of Americans that it was the people's idea in the first place. Not so! Do not give up so easily!

It is very important for all Americans to be smart and to refuse to be dummmed down. When the sales pitch is continual, like the millions of advertising dollars spent on Obamacare, logic suggests it is not good for the people. All of the people know their own intelligence. If you do not respect your own intelligence, talk to your brother or sister or dad or mom or best friends, but don't let these swine suck you into something that hurts America.

For your edification, the text of the entire Constitution of these United States is proudly included in its entirety in many of Lets Go Publish's patriotic books including this book as well as Taxation Without Representation and The Federalist Papers by Hamilton, Jay, and Madison. You can always download the constitution for free by going to www.letsgopublish.com

States Also Have Constitutions

Leftists do not like the Constitution or the Bill of Rights. If the idea of a constitution were so bad, why would it be that each state in our United States of America, would have its own Constitution? The answer is obvious. It is not a bad idea. It is in fact a great idea! It is the only thing in our great republic that assures us all that our rights come before the rights of corrupt politicians.

Each state in the Union of States has its own constitution thus giving the 50 states (or 57 according to our current president) a notion of semi-autonomy meaning partial self-government. These 50 or 57 states comprise the federal union. Why the President thinks there are 57 states is ample proof to me that we have been doing a bad job in America teaching civics for an awful lot of years. Then again, it is possible the President received his civics education in another land mass.

The US Constitution guides the operation of the national government, and establishes its formal power relationships between the three branches of the national government as well as among the 50 semiautonomous states as well as the formal power relationships among the other principal organs, or institutions, of the national government. None of US would want this left to folklore or to memory alone as it is far too important. Thus it is written—and yes, it is law!

The U.S. Constitution is in fact, a single document consisting of the seven original articles drafted by the Federal Constitutional Convention of 1787, which were eventually ratified by the 13 original colonies (states), plus there are 27 amendments that have been added to the document during the 200+ years that have elapsed since original ratification and adoption of the Constitution.

Chapter 21   The Bill of Rights and More

The First Ten Constitutional Amendments

The *Bill of Rights* is what most people think about when we think about the Constitution. In the Bill of Rights, though already covered within the Constitution are noted such fundamental principles as *freedom of the press*, *freedom of speech*, *freedom of religion* and other wonderful freedoms that no people on any planet or continent or country had ever enjoyed until the founders helped Christen America.

When the Constitution was ratified on March 4, 1789, it was because several states that held out would not go along until they knew a bill of rights was coming. Mmany were concerned that they had given up rights that were included in the Articles of Confederation. So, the Congress put together twelve amendments. Ten of them passed and on December 15, 1791, the Bill of Rights (two amendments did not make it) was ratified, making these first ten changes part of the US Constitution.

So, now we say that the first ten constitutional amendments are known collectively as The Bill of Rights. They amplify freedoms for Americans that are included in the Constitution itself yet, the way the left tramples on these lifelines to freedom; one would think they were optional

They are not optional. Any amendment becomes part of the overall law of the land, irrevocable by Congress, the

President, or the Supreme Court. It is tough to overturn something as unconstitutional when it actually is the Constitution.

Despite all the work in assuring freedom for all people, many today choose not to understand their hard earned constitutional freedoms. This permits the knaves in the government, and their backers—the socialist progressive Marxists, enabled by apparent indifference, to handily be taking our rights away.

The *Bill of Rights* may be key, but the Constitution is the lock that prevents government from ruling the people.

The US *constitutional system* consists of the power relationships among the principal branches of government resulting from the constitutional division and distribution of political authority among them by the Constitution itself.

It defines the roles in the governing process played by each of the principal governmental institutions defined within the Constitution. Americans must understand this in order to protect their personal freedoms. I hope that is why you chose to read *America 4 Dummmies!* It is easy to be swayed when your source of news is the popular media. Be careful!

This notion is very important for Americans in that the Constitution provides the following attributes of government on our behalf:

- Divides and distributes the authority of government between the central government over the whole nation and the governments of the member-states of the federal union
- Assigns certain governmental powers to the states, while denying them certain other powers
- Assigns certain powers to the national government and expressly prohibits it from exercising *any*

powers not explicitly granted. ----- In other words, the Federal government cannot by law decide that you cannot use anything. For example, they have unlawfully decreed you cannot use incandescent light bulbs as those invented by Thomas Edison. When the government is permitted to do things like this that violate personal freedom, it is operating outside of its constitutional authority. Since Congress has permitted this and similar erosions of the people's power, some of US, and more very day, suggest we call all of our congressional representatives home and replace them with a set of people who are not afraid to represent the real interests of the people.

- Assigns the powers delegated to the national government to the principal entities of that government (The U.S. House of Representatives, the U.S. Senate, the President of the U.S.A., and the U.S. Courts system, with supreme judicial power reserved for the Supreme Court). Each entity has its own power, a strong incentive, and a legal right to oppose, block, check, and restrain the other entities of government when they get off track.
- Prescribes certain limitations on both the central government and the states by guaranteeing *civil liberties*, i.e., the basic rights and liberties of the individual citizen.

Facets of the constitutionality of the government may be overridden in fact if not in deed. The President has chosen to ignore Congress and not to follow the Constitution. The Congress, choosing to be an inept body in 2014, has enabled the President's power grab though it is unconstitutional.

Power abuse will continue until the people (US) vote out all members of the assembly who are in line with the ideology of a lawless president. The US government must comply with two fundamental legal requirements to remain legitimate

- The government must operate in accordance with the provisions of the Constitution
- The government must not exceed the authority granted to it by the Constitution.

The bottom line unfortunately for all Americans is that our government is no longer legitimate since it complies with neither of these requirements.

As much as we may personally like our representatives, we do not want them taking more power than we are willing to give them. When you read the Constitution, it is clear how insightful the founding fathers were as they built the essential features of constitutionalism into the framework of the US government. The government's compliance with these two basic legal requirements is essential to its legitimacy.

So if we were to summarize the central purpose of constitutionalism, it would begin by sounding like this.

It is to protect ourselves from our too-far-reaching neighbors who become politicians to promote their own welfare.

The notion of limiting governmental power as dictated in the Constitution checks and restrains the persons who hold public office and who exercise political authority.

Thus, it is up to US as a wary and watchful society that our otherwise wonderful government does not get out of control. Hopefully, this book will help us all in this regard. America is not supposed to be a place for dummmies. It is a place where all people are given the opportunity to be the best and the brightest.

Chapter 22   What If the Founders Formed a Different Type of Government?

Washington Could Have Been King

If I said it once, I have said it five times in this book so that you get it. The founding fathers could have made George Washington the King instead of the first President. However, they had already enough of King George III and after awhile, another King George would not have set well with them.

The founders created a Republican Democracy so that people could use their freedom to create that huge middle class of which Aristotle speaks. Most of US are in the shrinking middle class today and it is shrinking before our eyes. That is the source of much angst among the people.

Why does government offer no solutions? I have said man times in this book that they want as many people dependent on the government as can possibly be. I am not kidding and I am consistent. If you want to be a dependent dummmy, welcome aboard the good ship Give-Away! If you want to be a dependent dummy, that makes you a real dummmy! The truth hurts. I wrote this book to help smarten up all chumps.

Thomas Jefferson noted his conclusion in the topic with just these few words right on point: "An elective despotism was not the government we fought for." I cannot recall any history teacher ever telling me that many people wanted

Washington to be the "King of America." Yet, that was a big option after the War.

What if they had given George Washington a kingship with dictatorial powers? Though all of those who have read this same history believe that George Washington would have been a great king, most scholars wonder what would have happened to America after his reign—George II, then George III, and then a revolution? Or what?

What if George decided things about America that were good for George but not good for Americans? What would be the recourse under the law without a law of the land?

In a monarchy, the King has all the power. Thus, a kingship, aka a monarchy with Washington or anybody else as King, was not a good system to choose and it was not chosen by the founders. If you'll pardon me for saying it, in a dictatorship by monarchy, at least for the first King, the people would have been stuck "letting George do it."

Instead of a democracy or a monarchy, complete with a King, the fathers instead could have chosen to form a constitutional oligarchy. There is that word "constitution," again. The basic tenet of all oligarchies is that the few rule the many. All oligarchies are the same though they can be purified somewhat with a constitution.

How about a Constitutional Oligarchy?

A constitutional oligarchy is basically a system in which there is no representation and the few rule the many— under the rules of a Constitution. The good news in this approach is that there is typically a body of law - the Constitution.

The bad news is that laws can be created ad hoc and taxes can be imposed that can negatively affect the people with no recourse but to accept. The rulers in this scenario can choose to accept or follow the laws. They run the show.

In the US, our constitutional republic insists that our leaders follow the laws or face potential consequences. Our current president is prepared to face potential consequences for his actions, yet our representatives are too wimpy to take him on. So, my friends, we must replace them all.

Considering that the major squabble with England was about taxation without representation, it would have been unlikely for the founding fathers to fight a revolution that would not provide for individual rights and liberties through a constitutional and representative form of government.

Our Constitution was written to assure these benefits and to keep the politicians from taking the country in a direction contrary to the will of the people. As we observe the current regime, they seem to have done that anyway.

If it were not that political power, as in the notion that the political class is comprised of politicians, with the assent or tacit acceptance of all three branches, can in fact be wielded against the population, the issues of government today might be as minimal as in the late 18th century after independence was gained.

However, "grabby" politicians separate themselves from the people so they can serve other than their constituents. Unfortunately for America, the Founding Fathers did not have a remedy for lobbyists or real term limitations. They thought we the people would be smart enough to not elect such culprits, who operated against our best interests.

The voters today en masse are way too busy to pay attention and thus are easily duped by the politicos into electing the same bums each time their terms are up. Unless any appeal to reasonableness in the voting booth reaches these voters, who are rightfully called the low information voters, we should unfortunately expect the same results. Our only hope is that one day, these folks will wake up!

For its part, even the Supreme Court today, has its political motivations and sometimes its actions are questionable. Clearly there are those who believe that George Bush would not be President if it were not for Sandra Day O'Connor and the other four Justices of the US Supreme Court. Maybe so! Maybe Not!

And, a new notion of eminent domain was determined by the Supreme Court that permits political agents to confiscate your land and property for the good of someone else.

Many, and I include myself among them, believe this latter idea goes so far beyond the intentions of those who drafted the US Constitution that it is actually humorous - but in a sick way. It needs to be overturned.

So, our Constitutional Democracy—our Republic—is pretty good, but it is far from perfect, mostly because it is controlled and interpreted by human beings who have natural bias. It can be made even better with a bit of direct democracy

Our benign oligarchy can use a dose of direct democracy

You may choose to read more about the forms of government in the other parts of the Civics Lesson. As noted above, our form of government is known as a representative constitutional democracy. Instead of every person having a say in every decision, we elect representatives and we hold them accountable through the Constitution to make sure they don't hijack the government.

When a government is of the rich, for the rich, and by the rich, we would call that an oligarchy--rule by the few over the many. Substitute special interests for "rich," and it means the same. As long as we get no representation from our elected, we really do not have a functioning representative democracy. In practice it is an oligarchy and this is very dangerous.

As long as the oligarchy is benign, there is not much reason to be concerned other than that long before the year 2000, the government was already hijacked and still nobody is calling anybody on it. The great insights of Dr. Michael Savage, a well-known syndicated Radio Talk Show Host suggest that the time to get really worried about your free speech is when the few start sending out the big black cars and one at a time, the many begin to disappear into the gulags.

In the years since 2009 of course, there are a host of unauthorized czars in Washington and they all show up for work wearing questionable integrity and a tailor made government hijacking kit. Watch out! They should have no role in our government—yet they do!

There are parts of a direct democracy that are usable in our republic. As we have previously enumerated, these are Initiative, Referendum, and Recall. Our founding fathers believed they had placed enough checks and balances into the early government so that our constitutional democracy was expected to last.

The founders also that professional politicians, not amateurs such as farmers, and tradesmen, such as our Senators, one from each state, would be the proper way to run the country along with a body of amateurs (the House) and a chief executive known as the president. Originally, Senators were not elected directly by the people but by the state legislatures.

When most people are introduced to the idea of the Senators being elected by the leaders of the state as opposed to the people at large, they are put off and this seems like it is not a good idea. However, in recent times, it would it not be good if a state or several states were able to call back a Senator who is not representing their state well.

Individuals cannot do this but a state such as Arizona would perhaps call John McCain back when he advocates tyranny along with the gang of eight tyrants. Maybe those Senators who voted for Obamacare would get called back to their states.

The notion of permitting a state to select a Senator and therefore have the right to recall a Senator was given up in the Seventeenth Amendment (formal change) to the Constitution. I would like this reversed. The Seventeenth Amendment (Amendment XVII) to the United States Constitution established direct election of United States Senators by popular vote. The people as a group are dysfunctional. That is a fact. If the pied piper ran for the Senate, the people of today would vote him or her into office.

Checks and Balances Aren't Working Today

As they say at realdemocracy.com, "DEMOCRACY WON'T WORK UNLESS YOU FIND THE TRUTH AND KEEP YOURSELF INFORMED." Be a dummmy and stay ignorant of how things really are and you will almost certainly reap the government you deserve.

The checks and balances of the Founding Fathers include (1) the Constitution itself, and (2) the three "equal" branches of government. But the big trick they had up their sleeves was that the (3) representatives in the House were elected, not appointed and there was a huge electorate to make sure that bad representatives would not be reelected. In colonial times, you may recall the representatives were appointed.

In other words, after they had fought and defeated tyranny in the revolutionary war, the founders believed the people for all time would continue to appreciate their freedom and liberty and their right to pursue happiness. They incorrectly believed that the American people would weed out the bad guy politicians so they could not corrupt the government. Corrupted people, through government goodies, continue to bring in corrupted people as representatives. And, so, unfortunately, we get the government we deserve.

These three notions were intended to keep the representatives of the government serving the people, not themselves, and not special interests. If this were the case in practice, however, I would not have been compelled to write this book.

I regret that Americans have stopped paying attention. Most can't even be bothered with the news. And so as our government is faltering, we must look in the mirror for we, the dummmy citizens of the United States of America get the exact government we deserve.

Since the government is beginning to behave as an oligarchy and this was never the intention of the Founding Fathers as they drafted the Constitution, an injection of Direct Democracy might just be what the doctor ordered. It is fully in line with our U.S. Constitution, which vests ultimate sovereignty in the people, to create a mechanism that would permit the people back into our government process.

Through a constitutional amendment, for example, the people could gain the right to initiate national legislation (Initiative), create national referenda (Referendum), or demand the recall of officials (nowadays called scoundrels), who do not represent the people (Recall).

When such an amendment (elements of direct democracy) passes, these activities could be sponsored by various public groups, or through the local and state governments. These three pillars of a direct democracy are presently reserved for those states whose constitutions specify these rights. It would be a relatively minor addition to our political system to engage the public in having a role in setting the political agenda. We're just one amendment away.

Of course it would not help much if at all if the people continue to remain disengaged from our government. Our representatives have hijacked our national government and so the time to act is now. We do get the government we deserve, and so if we choose to act, we will deserve better.

Not all states have constitutions which permit the three prongs of a direct democracy. For example, my home state of Pennsylvania, has no statewide Initiative or Recall rights, but we have Referendum. Philadelphia and Allegheny (Pittsburgh) counties have direct democracy features at the local level, but the state as a whole is without Initiative or Recall. We should change that.

For a number of years, a group of Pennsylvanians called the "PA Taxpayers for Referendum Organization" have been planning legislation to create a state constitutional convention to give PA these important rights. But, they are like a voice crying out in a political desert, and their voice is about dead. But, others have come in their place.

For example, the League of Women Voters are now championing Initiative and Referendum, and the Citizens Alliance of Pennsylvania is looking for all three features including Recall. On their site, the citizens offer this rationale:

Article I, Section 3 of the PA Constitution clearly states, "All power is inherent in the people…they have at all times an inalienable and indefeasible right to alter, reform or abolish their government in such manner as they may think proper."

Unfortunately, the Constitution thereafter provides no mechanism for the people to exercise their "inherent power" over state government. Thus, the people's political will is suppressed; property taxation, for instance, persists even though a significant majority of Pennsylvanians wish for it to be abolished.

A significant majority also wants term limits, lawsuit reform, and a host of other actions that lie dormant under the weight of special interest groups' influence and the inertia of the General Assembly.

This group really helps our democracy as it is involved in assuring that we Pennsylvanians get honest government— or else.

Many notable historical figures have observed that our representative constitutional democracy could be improved with Initiative and Referendum. Their reasons seem to fit the national mood and the national need of today.

Theodore Roosevelt, for example, in his "Charter of Democracy" speech of 1912 said, "I believe in the initiative and referendum which should be used not to destroy representative government, but to correct it whenever it becomes misrepresentative." Amen Teddy!

Abraham Lincoln is well known for his words, "Government is of the people, for the people and by the people." Recall is a way to remove government officials if the government does not act in a responsible way.

Chapter 23   Term Limits by the People

The most important thing for a politician

While running for a federal office in the United States, it seems that the incumbent and the aspiring prospective officials saturate our consciousness day-in and day-out, wheedling us into their self-perpetuating power games with promises of responsiveness, unity, and even candor. Yet, even then, only one primary concern lurks on their minds, that sine qua non of their very daily existence, the next election.

Yet, American citizens in our attempt to eek out a living in the midst of this electioneering do not understand why the politicians are so important, when the forthcoming election could be as distant as two years. Still the impending loss of a job, perhaps due to a plant relocating to China, or one closing in Michigan, is at best a secondary afterthought to the very men and women promising US all change, when we want it, and stability, again when they believe you want it. But, there is no truth to their promises. And, as Mr. W. C. Fields would say: "We are the suckers." Perhaps in our supplications we do not deserve a break.

Unfortunately, the priorities of the political class are one dimensional and your job or my job going to China or just no longer existing isn't their focus. Eventually they get re-elected and go off to Washington for yet another term. The cycle starts again with the eternal candidate alternating between Washington and their well insulated, gated communities far enough from the common people that they don't have to care what we think.

It's Never Them

When they are about to raise your taxes, they are particularly inconspicuous. Being numbed to the excesses and decadent corruption of everyday politics, the low information, gullible electorate think they have no chance, other than the faint chant of "hope" in the background. But it goes no place.

You may not expect communication and straight answers and so you are not disappointed. The elite are unmarked and they appear so sincere, yet, behind it all, can you not feel their disdain for you, a simple American from the un-political class.

You hear about the tax issues on TV or in the paper, not from your elected because your opinion on the matter really doesn't matter. They would rather converse via cellular or generic smart phone, the latest Blackberry or iPhone, with some of the only entities who truly can garner their attention—co-Congressmen , the affluent, the corrupt media, and of course, major campaign donors.

Discussing an important issue with you, while seeming like a charming noble way for a representative to spend an afternoon; is discarded as wanton. It's dismissed simply because it would not tangibly benefit anyone's reelection campaign, which, as we have all learned, begins the day oaths of office are sworn.

They want us to think that any tax increase or otherwise poor legislation is caused by imaginary rival agents or economic forces beyond their control. They will convey this to US with the sole purpose of acquiring our hard earned money. Apparently, they promise, any burdens will fall on some imaginary "other person" and we will remain unscathed.

Horrifically but as expected though, when we get our tax bills from the bureaucracy, we find out that we were that "other" person.

Since the bureaucracy sent us the bill, we blame the bureaucracy, and again let our politicians off the hook, just like our "representative" hoped we would. And again, they live to run for another election, their only professional motivation in life.

Yet, you have entrusted them with your safety and your ability to remain free. Unfortunately for you, it is the grease on their collective palms that means the most to them.

Talk to the Hand

Most individuals feel that their needs and opinions are not taken very seriously by elected representatives who occupy the hallowed chambers of our government buildings. We would call it a communication break-down but there really is no communication.

Despite our inability to get legislators to know our side of important issues, such as taxation, jobs, illegal aliens, etc., and more recently, bailouts, and healthcare (Obamacare), we treat them with too much respect. We intrinsically know that they care only about the desires and opinions of pressure groups, lobbyists, corporate executives and owners, as well as the plain old rich, in both parties.

Only these voices reach our representatives. Yet, time and time again, we let them off the hook. Politicians cut themselves off from their electorate by choice to be spared from accountability. Yet, whenever necessary, they make a resurfacing experience and always in time for the next election. Why are we so nice to them?

You may not see them in action when they work the halls of

Congress but you do see them work the wedding halls when it is the height of the election season. In Congress, the typical representative appears to have some sort of godly mandate, on the basis of which, whatever they put forward must be good for everybody.

However, whether it is a good idea or not, and they rarely are good ideas, you know the idea more than likely came from the whispers of the chosen elite.

Politicians do not serve most of their electorate and they get away with it because again, we the people do not hold them accountable, and we do not break their pattern by showing up on their doorstep with our needs.

It's Time to Fire Them!

What would happen to the placid world of the politician if its constituency took them to task? What might happen to these politicos if the citizens suddenly became extremely active? How would the elected representative handle such a massive increase in constituent contact? Would they become beneficent and magnanimous? Or would they choose the hermitage approach and lock the gates and doors and hope the rabble will go away?

Especially if we think they would never put up with our entreaties, we should deluge them anyway and help power our representative democracy back to working order. In our hearts, we know we would see nothing more than congressional aides coming out of the woodwork to "see if they can help matters." That of course is code for "see if they can shut us up!" And, for their lack of efforts on our behalf, we should do the only humane thing: fire them! Throw the bums out. They've had their day.

The chasm between electors and the elected is widening as we speak. The John Does and the Jane Q. Publics have lost faith in their representatives. Many have become fully disinterested in the political process, though the healthcare "debate" and the fresh air at the "Town Meetings" if they are permitted by the elite to continue, may be just the cure for this malaise.

We must pay attention. We must speak out. We must take action. This disease will not cure itself.

Should you trust your government?

The everyday people in America do not pay enough attention to politicians and this is the root cause of poor government. Yes, we get the government we deserve because we have been coached by a politically correct press that everything is all-right, even if it is not. From accounts in the media, we are to believe that just about everybody is honest, including the dirty, grimy politicians, who are destroying our country.

Our parents and their parents—back to the founding did not trust everybody in government or the country would not have lasted this long. Consequently, government was not so corrupt in those days.

And so, because we are not watching, our lack of attention permits politicians, masquerading as our representatives, to represent other interests. It is an understatement to suggest that representatives are out of touch with the will of the people.

Even the newly elected begin to share the wealth of their constituency with others—friends and cronies and relatives— not more than a day after they begin their "service." They have this need to redistribute income and now they are redistributing healthcare. To do that of course, they must first take it from US—and they have. And we reelect them anyway. We get the government we deserve.

This is a common malady of the often elected and the newly elected are quickly infected. For a politician, corruption is "catchier" than the most contagious flu. Few avoid it as most are afflicted in short order. Elected "representatives" have no problem taking your money and buying votes with it -- even if there is nothing left in the treasury.

Until they got caught by John Q., how many of the "honorables" voted originally to have the non-working and the illegal aliens receive the tax rebate which was a scandal of 2008? We are such dummies and we pay so little attention to these knaves that too many of US are unaware of what they did.

The trick in giving tax rebates to illegal aliens was an attempt to put a down payment on future votes. It was masqueraded as an attempt to help the downtrodden, hapless, illegal foreign national struggling to make ends meet. Not a chance. It was to puff up the elected to demonstrate their magnanimity and vote-worthiness. And, we dummmies fell for it.

For those who like seeing real statistics, check this out: In 2000, according to the IG, the IRS paid $62 million to 62,000 illegal aliens; in 2001, it paid $161 million to 203,000 illegal aliens; in 2004, it paid $778 million to 626,000 illegal aliens; in 2005, it paid $1.063 billion to 810,000 illegal aliens; in 2006, it paid $1.407 billion to 1,016,000 illegal aliens; and in 2007, it paid $1.777 billion to 1,220,000 illegal aliens. Ironically, we cannot find illegal aliens to tax them or deport them but the IRS can find them to deliver a nice check

What if I told you it is still going on and Democrats are still fighting overtures to halt it in its tracks because they might lose some illegal voters. They like doing nice things with your money for potential voters. Remember, the amnesty bill has already passed the Senate. The Treasury Department's Inspector General determined that $4.2 billion was paid in 2010, up from less than $1 billion in 2005. Leading

Democrats, you know who they are, are resisting a bill that would stop future payments.

Meanwhile, it is tough to get current information. But, the IRS maintains that it is without the authority to prevent illegal aliens from getting fraudulent tax refunds. It also offers that it has no legal authority to deny claims, even when they fail to include documents showing the children actually live in the United States. Ironically, this is the same IRS that once employed Lois "'take the 5th" Lerner and whose study of conservative organizations seeking tax exempt status was as precise as a micrometer at best, and illegal at worst.

Besides your money, illegal residents will also take your means of earning a living if it serves their purposes. Corporations have no problem taking your job and giving it to a foreign national, either here in the U.S. or in the worker's home country, in China or India to work in a plant run by a US corporation. Universities have no problem firing American professors and hiring aliens for the cause of diversity.

All of this is done with the blessings of our corrupt representatives. They have just one mission and it is accomplished if they get elected again. The next term of office, not the current one, is all that matters. As long as we keep reelecting them, we get the government we deserve.

The House of Lords

Senators are above it all. They breathe the rarified air reserved for the Gods. If you see a Senator once in your life, it is a memorable event. Perhaps you are among the lucky. Perhaps not! Senators have so many people to represent that they operate as Lords, clearly of the nobility (though nobility is expressly forbidden by the Constitution), and they have no need to ever mingle with the common folk. They can't anyway.

In Pennsylvania, for example, the state in which I live, it is the 6th most populous state in the U.S. with an estimated population of 12,500,000. That means that between the two senators, each gets to work with over six million people. No way no how! The Senators know they do not have to represent the people and so they represent whomever they choose and they still get sent back every six years like it is an entitlement—a sure thing. We get the government we deserve.

The House of Commons

What about our representatives? Why don't we ever see them? Remember that our Constitution clearly specifies the number of senators and representatives. The ratio is fixed at 1 representative for each 30,000 in the electorate. Now, that is still a high ratio but it is workable. Regardless of what is in the Constitution, however, in the year 1911, the representatives themselves broke the Constitutional law setting the ration by passing a new unconstitutional law.

Now, only 435 maximum seats are allocated regardless of the population. This of course has made them all more important and thus worthy of a very large salary and expenses. In 2014, for example without counting his unvouchered expenses, your congressman pocketed $174,000.00. Not bad for a part time job.

With a growing population, the ratio in the House of Representatives right now is about 1 in 700,000. That's an awful lot of hands to shake for one just (whoops—just one person). So, they don't. And, you don't miss them. But, you should! We get the government we deserve.

If you are good at math, you'll be able to tell this puzzle isn't over yet. Take the twenty-some mostly permanent staff members for each of the 435 representatives and multiply that (about 22) by 435 and add that to the 435 representatives. The number approaches 10,000. With the approximate U.S. citizen population just over 300,000,000 (technically illegal aliens have no representation), it can be argued that the ratio of 1 to 30,000 has magically been maintained, if you're happy talking to an aide instead of your representative.

Why they need 22 or 23 staff members is an enigma I will let hang for another day. The point is that we actually need about 9500 more Congressional Representatives to comply with the Constitution. That would certainly make our representatives much more accountable and maybe we would actually be able to reach them and maybe they would even live in our communities.

And, of course they would not be so "important and honorable," which would be good for the people. Moreover, we would not have to pay them as much. It would be a bummer for the Congressman, however, not being quite as important, but so what? Remember, we get the government we deserve.

There are lots of other sound arguments for this notion postured at the Jacksonian party blog at:

http://thejacksonianparty.blogspot.com/2006/04/getting-representation-back-into.html

Should you trust the corrupt media?

You must stay wary about untruths told by the media. Do not believe anything you hear from the media unless you verify it as true. Those in media power today are funded by progressive Marxists and corporations and special interests and they hope that they can keep the system quiet so that their notion of democracy or perhaps socialism or communism prevails.

In their ideal system, we the people are permitted to choose a "representative" offered by one of the dueling parties every two years or so. Meanwhile independent candidates are kept off ballots by chicanery and complicit officials, and a too-willing judiciary.

Additionally, the political duet—the tag team of Republicans and Democrats secretly work together to have the idea of bipartisanism be seen in every way as a positive notion when in fact it really means collusion and no-choice for Americans. Bipartisanship (collusive efforts in Congress) should not be trusted -- no-how, no-way!. Watch out folks!

The best term limits are that when their one term is done, we send them home.

Part VI: Problems in Today's Republic

Chapter 24 A Brave New World—Run by Cowards

The Brave New World

Note:
http://en.wikipedia.org/wiki/Brave_New_World,

Aldous Huxley wrote the <u>Brave New World</u> as a novel in 1932. The book is about the future and its setting is London, 2540 A.D. The novel anticipates that all of the reproductive advancements that today are just notions in a lab someplace, including biological engineering, and sleep-learning, will be commonplace in the future and will be used to change society.

The book talks about drug use as pacifiers to make the people feel better and loudspeakers used to get across the message.   Later Huxley wrote two other books on the topic, an update to Brave New World done thirty years later in which he saw the future coming much sooner and the other, The Island, which took the sterile notions of Brave New World and made them more attractive and more positive. For example, loudspeakers were replaced by pleasing parrots trained to offer uplifting slogans.

Of course, the parrots were talking to the duped dummmies, who were sucked in by the "leaders." That would be today's gullible low information voters who brought all the misery on themselves.

Perhaps we are already there?

Is our current day, "The Brave New World Revisited," is a new deal in which the government hands out pacifiers to keep the citizenry in a state of euphoria? What does such euphoria look like?   For the politician, it is a no-cost notion since they get elected by bribing you with your own money.

Many citizens want there to be "no problems," so much so that they can't or won't listen to hear that there actually is a big problem that requires them to pay for its solution or pay for its lack of solution. In fact, it seems that most folks that you meet today have some kind of fear that big brother is listening and so it is not good to talk politics in public. How many have heard that? How many of you are afraid of your government?

Yet, I am telling you to pay attention and the best way to learn more is to talk about it and keep talking about it. The scum in the government win when the people are quiet. When you are looking for somebody to blame, do not blame your neighbor, your auto mechanic, your doctor, your hospital, your insurance carrier.

Blame the government and the communist leaders who have just about taken over our cowardly new world. Many simply do not believe our Republic is in such danger; but it is nonetheless. And the less we chose to discuss it in public, the more government gets the edge on the people.

The system we have has big problems and the leaders we have are making the problems worse, not better, intentionally. No matter what they say, their intentions are to make things worse, not better so they can be more important when it all collapses. Don't worry, they'll get you nice parrots. And the slogans will be the finest.

Here you are reading this book, which is a very good step, so you must want to change back to the time when America was strong and there were jobs and everybody had a shot at the American Dream.

Such days are more like the founders' imagined. The current notion of hope and change has completely failed. The change is occurring rapidly and it offers no hope for the future unless we change it back. After you finish this book, you will have some ammunition to fight back. Add a little bit of your own personal moxie to that and you and I together can lick this thing.

Those often called the gullible low information voters, or as I call them, big dummmies or dumasses, keep permitting the government to make it worse. Politicians in the current world who speak the truth are rejected because the voting public would rather be served denial and sugar and some pacifying stimuli, rather than face the truth. Huxley was really on to something and it is a scary thought.

Some of us remember that in the 2008 primaries we saw the media at work with sugar packets for those of US who were willing to gobble them up. They were back again in 2012 and we still had not learned our lessons. What will we do in 2014 and 2016?

The corrupt media early on in the 2008 election campaign had picked John McCain and Hillary Clinton as the only viable candidates. They just as quickly switched from Mrs. Clinton to Barack Obama. They glorified Obama and made sure Mrs. Clinton did not get the nomination. They made Hillary Clinton look bad because Obama was the more radical of the two and he would push the socialist agenda. .

The media, the Democrats, and the Independents took the Republican primary from the Republicans without a whimper and they brought their man, Gentleman John McCain in from sure doom to be the primary victor. Somehow, they found a faux conservative in the lot and that's what the Republicans got by going along to get along. Conservatives are not necessarily Republicans, and most of US were quite upset that the progressive socialists had orchestrated McCain's victory.

The utterly corrupt corporate media, the low ratings media I might add, helped voters come to their way of thinking with a constant barrage of propaganda for their guys and against all the others. The sinister part of the deal is that the propaganda, as delivered by the choice news anchors, sounds a lot like hard news, and so the people bought it. We get the government we deserve.

Can we stomach the change we now need?

Both parties spend more and more taxpayer dollars while in office because they get rewarded for spending our money on themselves. They get reelected, and that is the big prize. Even the Republican Party, which supposedly is conservative in nature, were huge spenders of taxpayer dollars during the Bush years. Many of us who are independent in thought wonder "What was that all about?"

No members of either party want to pay for the government spending they authorize with taxes, since such appropriations affect their reelection opportunities. So, rather than cut spending, or cough up the money publicly via tax increases, they borrow from the Chinese.

This of course means that our children or grandchildren or great-grandchildren in the future will have to pick up the tab for their largesse. They call this generational theft—stealing for our own legacy before it is even born.

Aside: For the last forty years, the US has been tricked into thinking we have been slowly cutting spending in in fact, we never do. We use a gimmick called baseling budgeting, which is simply lying to the people and getting away with it. All of our representatives are in on the lie. That's how corrupt the Congress is.

In the Congressional Budget Act of 1974, Congress came up with a way to trick the people into thinking they were doing their jobs prudently. Baseline budgeting is what they call their little cheap trick. It is an accounting gimmick used to develop budgets for future years with built in raises that are called the baseline. It assumes future budgets will equal the current budget times a percentage most often bigger than the inflation rate. It gave politicians a way of spening more money while the people thought they were being frugal.

Fox News Commentator Sean Hannity has a great budgeting plan to bring spending under control. Let's say that the baseline percentage is 8%. That means that every department automatically gets an 8% compounded raise in their budget in year one, year two, year three, year four, etc. etc. etc. It has been going on for forty years. No wonder the budget never balances. The after the 8% (sometimes it is more) Congress may add even more dollars. Let's say that they make the number 15%. That means next years percentage, say 10% is based on this years plus 15% plus 10%.

Hannity calls his plan the "Penny Plan." I think it can work well. Let's say that this year's baseline budget is 8% plus last year's budget. Hannity's plan ignores the 8% increase and actually cuts 1 percent (a penny) from the budget. Democrats of course would cry foul and claim that 9% was cut from the budget. Sometimes knowing their secrets can help us cut them off at the pass.

One of the parties can always get a little more from the rich
by implicitly invoking the subtle principles of class warfare.

Both parties seemed to have no problem borrowing from and
bankrupting Social Security or Medicare or any area that has
a treasury balance. Though all of these treasures were
supposed to be stored in Al Gore's famous "Lock Box," we
know that Al was not minding the store and the Congress
and President pilfered the reserves. .

Nobody talks about making it better because they can make it
better in a flash. They do not want to make it better since big
government suits the goals of both major political parties just
fine. When they get power, they get to control more people.
Consequently, it serves no politician well to talk solutions,
which might limit their gift of taxpayer dollars going directly
to constituents. This of course would limit their reelection
opportunities. It has nothing to do with it being good for the
country or that they are simply great guys.

Inflation is the worst tax possible

Only the well-educated understand that the biggest tax of all
is inflation. This type of spending via almost valueless newly
printed money makes everybody's dollars-worth less and less
and less. The government does not take the dollars but it is
the reason why a loaf of bread is a dollar one day and a buck
and a half the next.

An analysis of the debt and deficit for the last six years,
during this administration, quickly teaches us that the biggest
spenders in US government history now run the government,
and it is getting worse. In addition to real taxes, this regime,
with its team of illegitimate czars, has chosen to use inflation
as its major taxing agent. Inflation is not a graduated tax and
it is the most unfair tax of all to those who can afford it the
least.

Inflation is the worst and heaviest tax on the working poor. It whacks the poor the hardest punch. Each year more Americans have been falling below the poverty line because we pay for government's excessive spending with inflation and not taxes. Taxes are already high enough but somebody has to pay for political pork and you know it won't be the politicians or the elite ruling class.

In 1999 middle class wage earners averaged $56,080 per year. With the latest Census figures from 2012, the number has dipped about $5,000 to 51017. These are real numbers without inflation. It is even worse with inflation. The 51,017 of 2012 is actually worth just 37,242 considering that a 2012 dollar v a 199 dollar is worth just 73 cents. Each year the shrinking middle class has no choice but to fake its standard of living by borrowing more It is the only sensible thing to do when you have inflation. Then, you pay back the debt in dollars that are devalued and thus worth less.

Historians cite the greed of the ruling political class as the final nail which finished the Roman Empire and the same selfish notion is well lined up to finish the American economic empire.

"Free healthcare" may be the final nail in the US coffin. Until the healthcare debates of 2009 and on to the present day, I admit that I did not have overly high hopes that the 47% electorate would opt to change anything as long as they got something from their greed. After all, somebody else is paying?

The vote was so close for Obamacare, and because it was rammed through Congress, it still is in disfavor by the majority of the American public. In more recent times, people are losing their insurance and the Obamacare replacement is substantially more expensive with deductibles that go through the roof. The current administration will not give up Obamacare because it permits government to control the 1/6 of the economy which healthcare entails.

Nobody in formal writing is permitted to use the name of Adolph Hitler because it is so unpalatable to most people. Well, I just did. Why, because the first thing the Nazis did was take over healthcare so they could control the people. Under Adolf Hitler, even abortion became legal in Germany, and Christianity was pushed out of the public schools and out of public life.

Then, they took the guns claiming the problems of violence would be solved by government holding the guns. Then slowly free speech and a free press and other religious beliefs were attacked, By the time it was over, 6 million Jews and ten million Christians were murdered simply because the people thought Hitler had a free lunch to offer.

Why are there so many people today concerned about the ultimate survival of the US as a free country compared to any other issue? Is everybody stupid, or are the IRS and NSA spying on Americans a little creepy. The people think government is too big even without Obamacare and its weight is crushing the nation. The people fear it wants to grow bigger than the monster in the film, "The Blob." Government wants full control of the people and that is why we see all the recent attacks on the Constitution and the Bill of Rights.

Let me ask you, which of the ten Rights in the Bill of Rights do the progressive socialist Marxists who run the current government and who are also in key party leadership positions, want to protect? Are there any?

Is their most important right freedom of the press? Well, they are already limiting the power of the press and they are planning to put state monitors in newsrooms to filter out the news they find objectionable. Is that freedom of speech? No, the left wants bad speech v government curtailed. In fact, the

LA Times will not print any opposing views to "global warming." Leftist university professors have recently suggested jailing talk show hosts who speak ill of the global arming movement.

Bill O'Reilly, a not so conservative show host on Fox, is quoted in late February 2014 regarding Harvard Crimson Paper Editorialist Sandra Korn. Korn suggested heeding the "PC thought police," before Academic freedom and research opinions. O'Reilly writes:

"She wants a shutdown of any opposing points of view. And so do many others on the far left. And the technique in play right now is the smear. If you criticize people of color including the President you're a racist. Call for a stronger border with Mexico you're anti-Hispanic. You oppose gay marriage you are a homophobe. And if you call for responsibility and welfare programs, you are anti-poor."

OK, it is not free speech that the left desires. Perhaps it is religious freedom that they would like to keep within the Bill of Rights? Well, then again maybe not. The Obama Administration has asked the Supreme Court to force Little Sisters of the Poor to pay for condoms, sterilization and chemical abortions. They are threatening Hobby Lobby with stiff fines if they go against their religious consciences.

Ok, if it not religious freedom that they like, then it must be that they like the second amendment, the right to bear arms. If so, however, why would they be trying to take all the people's guns? Go through the other eight amendments in the bill of rights when you have time and you will discover that the left does not want any of these rights to remain as law.

They want the government to have all the rights and the people none. The left runs the country today and the people are not screaming loud enough. It's time to open up the windows and at the top of your voice yell: "I am mad as hell, and I am not going to take it anymore!" Most Democrats are on the far left. I am a Democrat but I am proud to be conservative on the right side of things.

Some think that the current government will not bring the country toppling down to force a socialist dictatorship. Think again! Why not? There are few signs that the administration would not be quite happy with a total collapse of America and all of its freedoms.

Maybe we should characterize this grand re-awakening as "the free lunch is finally over." The administration is presiding over an economy in free-fall with spending through the roof and borrowing at near bankruptcy levels.

America is now a caricature of its once mighty self but there is hope in changing poll numbers that Americans are finally blaming the problems on the political hacks that the people keep sending back to Congress for two more years or four more years or six more years.

Through it all the president, who is well loved and who is forgiven continually by the simplest of Americans (dummmies) for not loving America and for his great penchant for telling lies to the people, has resisted getting the blam, though anybody but a horse's pitut knows it is all his fault. He is the president and these are his policies.

The sun seems to be shining on this folly now as more and more people are crying to throw the bums out. This downslide must end. It won't end, however, until we choose to end it at the ballot box and we Americans forever hold the "honorables" accountable or better yet, we just send them home to get real jobs like the rest of us. This next election, we must pay attention at the polls. All of us should be poll watchers so nobody can steal the election from US.

The question always has been, "do we have the stomach to do what is right?" Your friendly neighborhood politicians, all the way to the lords of the national ring are banking that you and I don't have the guts to do it. This time, I think they are wrong. We get the government we deserve.

Shall we cast off what is left of our independence and join the major political parties and ask for more government control and more dependency? If we do this, we will earn the right to be invited to important reelection functions so that we can loudly applaud our corrupt political leaders.

Maybe We the People can continue to carry around the nominating petitions of long-term corrupt politicians, and perhaps even hand out how-to-vote cards at elections to help these old cronies get back their seats in Washington DC. We surely have the freedom to do this in our great country if we choose.

However, maybe we should take a different approach for the good of our nation. Maybe we should clamp down hard on this big problem with our democracy, speak up, demand action, and if we are not satisfied, let's simply throw the bums out. This is not just rhetoric. It is reality and a formula for survival and a return to greatness for our nation.

Democracy is a relatively new phenomenon in its modern forms. It has developed over the last few centuries to a somewhat acceptable level in perhaps 40 of the world's 200-odd nation states. Judging from the U.S., it must further evolve. It cannot remain fixed in the face of accelerating change in all other aspects of society and the outright threat of takeover by corporate power and influence or as John Edwards correctly characterized it, "corporate greed." On the socialist side of course, there is also union greed. Greed seems to be a common thread where evil is involved.

The elements of direct democracy, which we have lightly discussed in various chapters in this book, are anathema to politicians and government officials at all levels. Initiative, Referendum, and Recall gives the people a direct say in whether the politicians keep their jobs and how they must do their jobs. All three of these tenets could help enliven the political experience for the people and make government at all levels more accountable to the people as it should be.

In all western democracies, including the good ole U.S. of A., there are high levels of dissatisfaction. Thus, there is more and more interest in politics by the yet-to-be-disillusioned young. Innovative notions that can improve the political process, such as the Initiative amendment need to be brought forth, discussed, and adopted.

The mood of the country, voiced often by the young in the past two presidential elections brought forth the current administration and just about all Americans, especially out-of-work millennials are crying out that the hope is gone, and the change so far is frightening.

The American people are getting changes many had never considered possible and every day it seems there are more to digest. Meanwhile not only are things not improving, they are becoming worse than ever before in our history. And, so, there is more and more buyer's remorse out there about the last two elections in particular.

Chapter 25 A Confidence Conspiracy

Look no further than our elected leaders

The Bush years brought great division over the war in Iraq and a very unpopular president, partly from his own doing plus a lot of help from the corrupt, left leaning media. So, now, without Bush, we have even more trillions of dollars of debt, more give-away programs for the rich (Wall street and the Bankers), more crony capitalism to FOBs (Friends of Obama), industries annexed by the government, a big and deadly war in Afghanistan that has not been fought well, problems with Russia for the first time since Reagan, trouble brewing in Iran, North Korea, Syria, and a failure in foreign affairs across the entire globe. But, ironically, nobody blames the President, because he is Obama, or vice versa.

Can you believe that the country that once put a man on the moon now has no space program? The President shut the Space Shuttle program down with no replacement. We now trust the Russians and we pay them $67 million a shot to take our astronauts to the International Space Station.

Maybe Russia will mass troops on its external shell and take it over on one of these launches. But, then again, where could the Russkis find anybody dummm enough to pay them a zillion dollars for a ride to space?

We fired 20,000 scientists from NASA and hired 16,500 IRS agents to spy on us. I would recommend going back to the former deal. Meanwhile as a reach out to Muslims across the world, the President has changed NASA's mission from Space Exploration to Muslim Outreach to applaud the Muslim Americans for their role in the space program over the years and/or to help them become more science and math oriented.

When NASA was shut down in 2010, Chief Administrator, Charles Bolden said in a formal interview that his "foremost" mission as the head of America's space exploration agency is to improve relations with the Muslim World. And, so it shall be after we have disposed of 20 million hero scientists and we continue to pay our friends, the Russians a cool $67 million per launch. If it were not so serious, it would make a great SNL script.

We also have a CIA that is being devitalized, and we seem to have no fear at all of terrorism as the name was even stricken from the federal dictionary. It seems that current officials are now conspiring for heady advice from Alice and the Tin Man, yet they cannot notice America crumbling. Then again, Einstein never really cared if his tie matched. Same thing!

Meanwhile, the semi-capitalist Chinese are preparing their own little game of sock-it-to-US. I fear these are just a few symptoms of a much deeper malaise.

Yet, last time I looked, we still just have just 435 House Members, 100 Senators, one President, and nine Justices of the Supreme Court. They all seem to be prospering but maybe that is because Washington DC is the money sponge of the nation, and they all happen to live there.

In a book titled, America 4 Dummmies, the author needs a license to find things that are easy to read yet, highly impact-driven when read, in order to help get the full message across. When somebody supports your thinking, the value of your thoughts, go up 1000% or more, even if your thoughts were perfectly right on originally.

Belief is in the eye of the reader and the truth is in the pen of the writer. Charley Reese's piece, as presented below is the ticket to help everybody understand the dilemma that still faces US and the US today. He said these things; not me. But, I thought them for sure even before I heard that ole Charley had said them.

I am so glad that I read Charlie Reese's piece when one day it arrived in my email, because he clearly at a time when things were not as bad as today, was frustrated that government could not do a better job for the people. At the time he wrote the article, government actually seemed to try to do well. It was just inept.

Today, government is more inept but now it is convinced that it not only knows everything, but since it has grand pupa status, it has a right to impose its will on US, liberal and conservative alike. The truth is we are all much smarter than the flunkies that man the governmental posts. Yet, they control the IRS, the Marines, the Army, the Navy, and now the DHS, our doctors, our hospitals, our health, and our health insurance companies. Oh, I forgot, plus a Web Site valued at about a buck three eighty. We control only ourselves.

They are pretty darn powerful for sure. Yet, they are still inept. The difference between then and now is that government is actually bragging and propagandizing its notion to control all Americans by redistributing wealth to people that the government now refers to as voters. It could not have gotten any worse. Thankfully, the full takeover has yet to begin.

Charley Reese posted his thoughts on the matter of who is to blame back in the 1980's. This "Reese Rant" was copied

from a web site, www.545assholes.com. Pardon any
vulgarity but that is its name.

Journalist Charley Reese, retired after thirty years with the
Orlando Sentinel but in the middle of his career, got as upset
as Americans are today about the poor state of affairs. He
wrote the first version of this rant against our highest federal
officials while on staff at the Orlando Sentinel. This was
popular then and it is popular now as thousands go to
websites all over the Internet to read this. It makes US all feel
just a little bit better.

In its time, Reese's column was distributed to other
newspapers nationwide by King Features Syndicate. In his
piece, Reese proves that just 545 people, including the
President, Congress, and the Supreme Court are directly,
legally, morally and individually responsible for every one of
the domestic and foreign problems that plague this country.

Reese so loved his own piece that he has improved it a
number of times. On March 7, 1995, for example it was
republished by the Orlando Sentinel under the title, "Looking
for Someone to Blame? Congress Is a Good Place to Start."

I have received permission from the www.545assholes.com
site to copy his essay as it exists today on their site, in its
entirety. This is not the 1995 version. In fact, the one on this
site does not know the date or source of its version. But, Tip
O'Neill from Boston, was a big player when it was written.

One of the challenges about writing a book for dummmies is
to make sure that all of the analogies and missives and
anecdotes that are used clarify the message more than fog it
up.

This outstanding piece by Charley Reese covers the role of
the high federal public offices in a way that is both comical
and very clear. It helps in explaining America to dummies,
more than repeatedly saying, "pay attention," can ever do.

So, we all should thank Charley Reese for his eye opening essay.

"

The 545 People Responsible For All of U.S. Woes
BY Charley Reese

(Date of publication unknown)-- -- -

Politicians are the only people in the world who create problems and then campaign against them.

Have you ever wondered why, if both the Democrats and the Republicans are against deficits, we have deficits? Have you ever wondered why, if all the politicians are against inflation and high taxes, we have inflation and high taxes?

You and I don't propose a federal budget. The president does. You and I don't have the Constitutional authority to vote on appropriations. The House of Representatives does. You and I don't write the tax code. Congress does. You and I don't set fiscal policy. Congress does. You and I don't control monetary policy. The Federal Reserve Bank does.

One hundred senators, 435 congressmen, one president and nine Supreme Court justices - 545 human beings out of the 235 million [now over 300 million] - are directly, legally, morally and individually responsible for the domestic problems that plague this country.

I excluded the members of the Federal Reserve Board because that problem was created by the Congress. In 1913, Congress delegated its Constitutional duty to provide a sound currency to a federally chartered but private central bank.

I excluded all the special interests and lobbyists for a sound reason. They have no legal authority. They have no ability to coerce a senator, a congressman or a president to do one cotton-picking thing. I don't care if they offer a politician $1 million dollars in cash. The politician has the power to accept or reject it.

No matter what the lobbyist promises, it is the legislator's responsibility to determine how he votes.

A CONFIDENCE CONSPIRACY

Don't you see how the con game is played on the people by the politicians? Those 545 human beings spend much of their energy convincing you that what they did is not their fault. They cooperate in this common con regardless of party.

What separates a politician from a normal human being is an excessive amount of gall. No normal human being would have the gall of Tip O'Neill [retired in 1987], who stood up and criticized Ronald Reagan for creating deficits.

The president can only propose a budget. He cannot force the Congress to accept it. The Constitution, which is the supreme law of the land, gives sole responsibility to the House of Representatives for originating appropriations and taxes.

O'Neill is the speaker of the House. He is the leader of the majority party. He and his fellow Democrats, not the president, can approve any budget they want. If the president vetoes it, they can pass it over his veto.

REPLACE SCOUNDRELS

It seems inconceivable to me that a nation of 235 million [now 300 + million] cannot replace 545 people who stand convicted -- by present facts - of incompetence and irresponsibility.

I can't think of a single domestic problem, from an unfair tax code to defense overruns that is not traceable directly to those 545 people.

When you fully grasp the plain truth that 545 people exercise power of the federal government, then it must follow that what exists is what they want to exist.

If the tax code is unfair, it's because they want it unfair. If the budget is in the red, it's because they want it in the red. If the Marines are in Lebanon, it's because they want them in Lebanon.

There are no insoluble government problems. Do not let these 545 people shift the blame to bureaucrats, whom they hire and whose jobs they can abolish; to lobbyists, whose gifts and advice they can reject; to regulators, to whom they give the power to regulate and from whom they can take it.

Above all, do not let them con you into the belief that there exist disembodied mystical forces like "the economy," "inflation" or "politics" that prevent them from doing what they take an oath to do.

Those 545 people and they alone are responsible. They and they alone have the power. They and they alone should be held accountable by the people who are their bosses - provided they have the gumption to manage their own employees.

We should vote all of them out of office and clean up their mess!

As noted above, this article was first published by the Orlando Sentinel Star newspaper. It was a long time ago but it is still spot on. Tip O'Neill was a man of the 1980's and before, who had honor, and who respected America and Americans.

Thank you Charley

Chapter 26   Familiarity Breeds Contempt

Who do you trust?

People everywhere seem to want to push the bounds of democracy further than their governments will allow. Both former Prime Minister Blair in the UK and former President Bush in the U.S. led incredibly unpopular governments. But, they are of the past and new guys took their places.

Gordon Brown got off to a great start as the #1 in the UK and our own Barack H. Obama was so popular, like Washington, he was almost declared a King and ruler for life. Americans actually loved everything about the Obama's, from the kids to the new dog named Bo. Never had I seen such a high level of satisfaction for any President.

The Brits who had become sick of Tony Blaire and the Iraq War were likewise quite pleased with Gordon Brown, though not at the level of the American love affair with President Obama. Congratulations to both leaders for their fine early showings. Those days too are gone.

After a short while in office, the heads of Presidents and Prime Ministers could be substituted for the moles in the popular carnival game, Whack-A-Mole, and it would probably liven up the game.

In addition to the big new rap of fiscal irresponsibility, the dissatisfaction with the U.S. government at all levels stems from many reasons such as a steady slide in social, economic and environmental conditions in the past 20 years; the increasingly overt nepotism, careerism, cronyism and outright corruption in our political system and in the government itself.

Who do you trust? What once was a Johnny Carson game show title that followed Jack Bailey's afternoon Hit, "Do you trust your wife?" is now a real question that beckons to be answered well but seemingly cannot. In the past six years, more and more blog contributions have been openly asking, "Do you trust your government?"

On top of a major dislike for having unpopular notions rammed down the public's collective throat, much of this is fueled by public revulsion at brain-numbing political campaigns, the blatant disregard for the public in official decision-making, the dominance of big business, big unions, and big government, the flaunting of wealth by the ruling class, and increasingly fat salaries for politicians and government workers at all levels, while regular Americans are looking for just a bit of cake to eat.

Meanwhile the general public (that's us) is chopped liver, theoretically living beyond its means and it has no recourse but to work harder for less money. With the economic collapse of late 2008, from which we have yet to recover, despite orations to the contrary, living beyond ones means has actually taken on new meaning. Many individuals today must live beyond their means just to live.

While making tens of thousands of pages of rules for others to follow each year, the Federal government finds no need to do simple things like balance its own checkbook or follow its own rules. Those of US, trying to balance ours find it a bit disingenuous of our politicians to take pay raises while they are systematically draining the US treasury for their pet reelection projects. When we need a constitutional amendment to balance the budget, how far off the founder's mark have we strayed? Is Nero fiddling again?

We the People have to tighten our belts to compete with those who would take our jobs, while many of the takers are living illegally in the U.S.

Corporations receive no chastisement from our elected officials and no publicity when they move Americans jobs to China, India, or even Russia as well as a host of other developing nations. It's not pretty on the streets. " Let them eat cake" seems to be the government's response. Yet, nobody can afford the coffee needed to down the cake, and the ingredients in a nice "cake" are very expensive.

The public in ever increasing numbers, is also recognizing the structural defects of its political system. The centralization of power within the major parties so that there is no longer a two party system nor room for real independents, is becoming quite obvious.

Bush, Clinton, Bush, Clinton was almost not just a bad joke; it was almost a reality. President Barack Obama benefited from that one. Now, moving to 2016, yet another Bush is ready to take on yet another Clinton. Perhaps Chelsea will take on mom in the primary to give one of them an edge. But, which one?

Add to all of this bad stuff the negativism and personal abuse inherent in adversary partisan politics, the domination of public decision-making by small elites, major party collusion which deprives the public of choice, an institutionalized "broken promise syndrome," the failure of the federal government to be able to handle organized minority groups— legal and illegal—and undemocratic electoral systems and machines where only by chance, and sometimes in spite of devious manipulation, does the resulting government reflect the will of the people.

And did I mention intimidation at the polls by agenda groups carrying riot sticks.

When representatives of the government call citizens at Town
Hall meetings Astroturfers, and disingenuous, while at the
same time they send their bought and paid for thugs and
operatives (yes, the operatives of our legislators against the
people) to combat physically and disrupt the "undue
influence" of John Q Public on the fair and open legislative
process, isn't this really an awful ugly pot calling the kettle
names. Did anybody mention the words "healthcare," and
"government control?" How could it really have gotten this
bad without politicians in control?

Majority Rule

In a democratic republic, it is axiomatic that the majority can
only govern with the consent of the minority. Yet it helps to
have a majority. Our last set of presidential elections shows
that there is a deep divide in this country. Yet the good old
boys in Congress seek bipartisan labels for their "solutions."
They don't want solutions that work for everybody; instead
they want things they can lie about against the people.

It makes no sense since the biggest problem may just well be
the political parties that breed our representatives. They can
never consider electoral matters except in terms of their
partisan advantage. Underlying the alienation and
powerlessness people feel is the lack of a true representative
constitutional democracy, the accelerating rate of change
since the 1980s, the information revolution, the forces of
corporate globalization and the ongoing tyranny of the
minorities. And they, I might add, were the good ole days.

Today, as we now have a president with his first term well
under his belt, and as a country we have been getting change
that is reflective of the rationale about which the founders
engaged in a revolution, risking life and limb, how can
anybody with a brain think things are OK? What would
Jefferson or Franklin say? Would they approve?

And though the above underlying principles and all of the symptoms of no representation that once existed still exist, the debate to many of US has gotten more personal. It has shifted from just plain old poor and often corrupt representation to a new and deep and insidious collusion of the government elite and the otherwise powerful (corporations and unions) against the people. It's time we put it to an end!

These are frightening times as the people wake up to find representatives and unions and corporations and government employees in control, and less and less life, liberty, and the pursuit of happiness in the offing.

Whether it is a fear of full-bore socialism, or a fear of giving up one's whole paycheck or one's own healthcare to get just a piece of it back, the people have been awakened and life for politicians will never be the same. And, that part is good.

But the politicians will not take this sitting down. Will they actually consider taking over the country to keep the will of the people in check?   Will the people be forced to keep the corrupt government they have, if you all work harder to deserve better?

Will we ever be OK again?

When you graduate from dummmy to concerned citizen, life does not get easier, but you feel better. This is a great start to your metamorphosis. Until you overcome the badness and the evil, caused by elected officials, you won't feel completely OK. That can happen and it will. Thanks for joining the cause.

Chapter 27   Elites No Longer Elite—Too Bad!

Why did Edmund Burke know so much?

In 1774 the English Whig Party member and Political philosopher Edmund Burke offered that representatives should be elected to govern rather than the people directly. Burke did not think ordinary people could govern. I think he is right. But, only because as a group; we choose not to "pay attention!

He saw that such "elite" representatives should exercise their superior wisdom and judgment irrespective of the wishes of the electorate. That may be tough to take but consider what we get today. The electorate in Burke's eyes would be easily characterized as "the low information voters," who are a huge part of "We the People." He saw their governance as being aided by an elitist private service -- not a public service. How can people with no concern for government, govern. You tell me!

For Burke, it was not only OK to have elite that actually were virtuous, and who understood the laws; he would deem it very desirable. He believed that the public would always reject the "necessary hard decisions," and thus would be incapable of meaningful governance. Today we would call him naive but back then, there appears to have been a substantially higher level of integrity in the political class, thereby making his ideas more acceptable for the times.

Today, the progressive socialist Marxists pull at the heartstrings of the poor suggesting their days are numbered if an honest government is ever elected. How sick.

Many, including the framers of our Constitution were influenced by Burke but the elitists envisioned by Burke in his writings were not greedy politicians and corporate profiteers who also happened to be wealthy. For Burke, the elitists were in fact the elite of society, the cream of the crop by all standards. They were the best in character, education, and intelligence. They looked for nothing for themselves. They were the ultimate altruists. We can still find such men and women today if we stop listening to the disgusting press.

In their days, they were people you would like if you met them. They were not pretentious. They just happened to be better schooled and in many ways more intelligent and more capable of grappling through the tough decisions. The overall Edmund Burke philosophy is no longer acceptable to a vast number of people, though it is still promulgated by elitist editorialists, bureaucrats and some academicians. It is a great idea!

The problem with this notion is the tacit acceptance of an indefinable inequality and the fact that the good unquoted elite can very easily become members of the bad quoted elite, a group who are well characterized by taking substantially more than they give back. Today's plague of the gullible low information voter is the exact opposite of Burke's Law, yet there are so many in the gullible category, the progressive socialist propagandists suck them in one by one to their ultimate deaths.

As I have used it, you now see the new term that has been popularized by conservatives as "low information voters." This term was created to help define in few words those Americans who have no time to learn the facts, and who are gullible enough to believe everything the corrupt press and the party of progressive socialist Marxists chooses to propagandize to them.

No Secrets!

The more eyes that look at the machinations of government, the safer and more prosperous we all will be. There are many arguments against open government at all levels, but history tells us that secrecy is a formula for corruption and long-term failure. Additionally, secrecy in government all too often provides for the perpetrators to avoid the responsibility and accountability that would be required if their actions were well known.

The fact is that corruption scandals are regular occurrences in governments across the world, and as you examine these failings, secrecy is always a required ingredient. If government is not always open, then what is it? It is closed of course—closed to the people and the press.

If it is truly closed then how is it that in this closed scenario, the secret decision-making is always known by a privileged few who profit from the knowledge?

As open as our government is on paper, secret meetings are commonplace. Thus, we must be wary since these closed sessions occur with "our" representatives at all levels. When they are out of sight in secrecy, we can bet that they are representing somebody other than "We the People."

With a mostly educated populace as exists in the 21st century, it is in fact dangerous to merely trust our representatives with our government. The founders expected the people to not only pay attention, but to give our representatives instructions about how we expected affairs to be conducted. Most Americans today unfortunately are ill equipped to provide those instructions. We must change that.

We can be assured that unwatched representatives will not do the right thing. We must, as Ronald Reagan would say "trust but verify." It is all too easy for elected representatives and

244 America 4 Dummmies!

even their minions, and the bureaucrats, to assume that a shroud of wisdom comes down on them once they have arrived in their chairs.

It is so much easier to serve the private rather than the public interest when dressed in the veil of secrecy, steering clear of accountability. Without a doubt, our most recent history furnishes abundant proof. Open the shades and bring in the light of day. Open the windows, please, and let the stink out of the room--for good. We get the government we deserve.

This Sums it up!

The Representative Democracy that our forefathers brought to this country is clearly not functioning properly in our times. Our elected representatives at all levels of government view the notion of representatives in a much more opportunistic way than intended by the Constitution.

To solve this problem, we must admit that government is out of control and no longer is of the people, for the people, and by thy people. More importantly, we must have the guts to correct it, even if it means not getting something for ourselves from the largesse pile. The time to fix it is now, perhaps before those really in charge become aware of their full power and we never have the opportunity again to regain control. The time is now. We get the government we deserve.

Part VII: Way Too Many Honorables!

Chapter 28   What Happened to Representative Government?

The Issues of Today

Something happened to representative government from the time of the Declaration of Independence and Constitution to the present. Though our representative constitutional democracy (our Republic) has survived for about 230 years, it is not at its healthiest right now. Here are just a few of the major problems that we are facing as a nation presented in alphabetic sequence:

- China preparing for a power grab
- Corporate power and greed
- Crime / Drugs
- Economic hard times not improving
- Education
- Election process corruption
- Energy and oil stagnation
- Excessive legal immigration
- Free trade hurts domestic producers
- Government Health industry power grab
- H-1B and D-1 Foreign National Visas
- Healthcare availability and affordability
- Homeland Security
- Illegal immigration
- Influence of Special Interests

- Institution of marriage
- Iran and North Korean as nuclear powers
- Israel second thinking American promises
- Jobs
- L-1A and L-1B Foreign National Visas
- Labor arbitrage / offshoring
- Lobbying
- Mexico dictating immigration policy
- Over taxation
- Political and corporate corruption
- Private property confiscation
- Respect for life
- Russia out of control; attacking its neighbors
- Social Security / Medicare financial issues
- Syria mocking American red lines
- Threat of Socialism from the Government
- Unfinished wars Iraq, Afghanistan (not really done)
- Unprecedented US weakness on the foreign front
- War on terrorism (whatever they call it now)

No book can attack all of these issues (listed in alphabetic order) and be substantive enough to be informative. This book does not even try. In this book, rather than thump the reader about all of these issues, this book concentrates on the elements of our founding as a country that would be included in any syllabus attempting to teach dummmies about America, and our fundamental principles and beliefs. I hope we do OK

Throughout this book, we present notions that are included in our history and our founding documents that can help you in understanding the lawful solutions to many issues outlined above and even more. But, nobody can handle them all in a single book, no matter what they say. I would answer in the affirmative if queried.

America is a great place with a great set of principles. My objective as I have noted many times between page 1 and this page, is to help all readers appreciate what gifts we have been given at our founding, and why they are important for your liberty and freedom.

And, while we're at it, as a starter, there are few things that we already know about that are intrinsically wrong. I bet nobody out there thinks it is OK that the government is spying on us when we walk, when we talk, and when we use the tools of the day such as the Internet, Facebook, Email, Twitter etc. Who likes the fact that 16,500 new IRS agents have been hired to assure that we are all buying Obamacare? Only an idiot would like any of that. An idiot needs a full education to become a dummmy.

Nobody likes Big Brother; nonetheless Big Brother is growing because trusting Americans give him more and more power over our lives. That is why people like me and many others are writing in blogs, writing articles, and doing what we can to wake up the rest of our little brothers so that together we can save America before America is no more.

Nobody wants to wake up in an America a few years away when we can no longer vote in honest elections. Without honest elections, how will we ever remove the scoundrels who have corrupted our government? Unfortunately, many of the people who do not like what is happening today have yet to experience a voting machine. Folks, it is up to US to make this right again!

You have already been lightly introduced to the notion of a Constitutional Republic / Representative Democracy and you have already heard about the major checks and balances on government authority in the Constitution such as the separation of powers. I hope you have been paying attention.

This book discusses the bottom line reasons for why it is difficult to earn a living today and It presents a unique look at the disdain the founders had for large powerful entities such as unions and corporations and governments. If you think you have a lot of muscle and you need no help, try going against any of the big three in the power list above.

Our congressional representatives, and presidential representatives (Yes, even the president) are supposed to administer the will of the people. With our help, their jobs are to deal with all of the issues in the big list above as well as others that come up daily. The people are in charge!

In the last two elections, while in the midst of the presidential campaigns, through various forms of media, Americans were able to see the opinions and the to-do lists of all presidential aspirants. We saw what they thought about the issues and what they would do to "change" things for the better.

Each election time, the politicos come back home to put on a show with the intention of selling US on putting them back into office. They do not care whether we had gotten anything for our previously spent dime. They hope we do not remember and typically we do not. And, the shame is that most often our dimes are lost.

Hope and change are winners

Going back a ways, change certainly was the theme in 2008's presidential primaries and it continued into the general election. Along the way, we even learned from Mitt Romney that Washington was not only broke; it was broken and needed a quick, yet lasting repair.

Now, with Barack Obama well into term two, the country is even more broke and from looking at his leanings, there is concern that Obama's quick fix may be straight from Carl Marx's playbook, not from the founders. What do you think?

Promises, promises, promises. How can you tell when a politician is lying? The comic answer of course is, "When their lips are moving." That's because there is a big difference in the spoken words of politicians prior to the election and after being elected.

During the election process, promising politicians sell themselves and their ideas to the people using the level of promises necessary to get the vote. Nobody in the campaign team can say anything negative about the candidate or a proposed solution to an issue even if it is the truth.

If you can't get a promise from a politician pre-election, one thing is for sure. You will never get one after the election. Once elected, all bets are off and the truth and facts and real intentions of the politicians take over.

Unfortunately for the American people, when politicians as legislators choose not to fulfill the essence of their promises, we cannot take them back to the store and get a new one. However, if we were to adopt the Recall Amendment to the Constitution, which I discuss numerous times in this book, we would be able to take them back one more time to Washington, and then send them packing. .

In addition to no recalls—at least yet, we cannot assess a penalty for lying to us about their real intentions. Initiative, Referendum, and Recall as we noted are available in 20 states but not at the federal level. So we often wind up being stuck with politicians instead of being supported by our elected representatives. That is why it is important to know who to place on the ballot and who should get out votes long before election day. Pay attention!

Chapter 29

The Honorable Congressman So & So from Such & Such!

When a bad congressman won't go away?

What if we know our Congressman is a bad apple? Then what? Under the current system of platitudes and suckupism, we have to treat them like gold and call them "the honorable so and so." We also must be wary that they do not hurt us too bad if we challenge them, because they have immense power.

Some look the other way, not because of fear, which is acceptable, but because they may want a "favor from them," and would not want them to think poorly of them. That is not acceptable in America.

In the last fifty years—and perhaps longer—the notion of the representative as a noble person (as in "nobility), has been creeping, slowly and subtly back into our etiquette. It is sickening. Yet, not only are most politicians not noble, they are often dishonorable. They are often corrupt and they do not represent the people once elected. We know who they represent—special interests, corporations, unions and the ruling class of elite citizens. In this I mean the current elites, not the virtuous elites of the past.

They tax US and tax US and tax US again; but they do not represent US. They put loopholes in the tax code so their friends and themselves do not have to pay as much as US.

This is clearly taxation without representation but not quite as obvious as it was before the Tea Party.

I have been disturbed about dishonest politicians for quite a long time and it was the reason a number of years ago that I wrote a book about this topic, which I called Taxation Without Representation available at www.bookhawkers.com. The tea is brewing again today in a bigger pot and it is much hotter than when I wrote the first edition of this book six years ago.

Just like before the original Tea Party, which left leaning ideologues today might have you think was a bad thing for America, the regular people on the streets who do not care about the left's ideology are getting more and more riled.

Originally it was the young and the young elected Barack Obama as their answer. He rewarded them by taxing them by health insurance whether they wanted it or not at higher rates so they could pay for somebody else's grandfather. He also stopped their ability to get jobs as he gave them to legal and illegal aliens. Finally, more and more Americans, young and old, see this administration, Democrats and Republicans, as part of the problem; not as part of the solution.

Lack of honest representation is the biggest problem for regular Americans, young and old. It manifests itself in legislation or lack of legislation to protect our most basic rights. In this administration, even with long standing legislation on the side of what is right, the executive branch has chosen in many cases, not to enforce the laws. This may seem nice in a movie but this is not the purview of the executive branch. All branches are equal. This type of action is unconstitutional. .

Among their despicable acts, our representatives have tried to give our healthcare to 50,000,000 more potential voters, while lying through their teeth about their intentions. I call these folks illegal aliens because they are in an illegal status, and they are aliens, meaning foreign nationals. The gifts given to them are paid for by recent college graduates and the rest of Americans.

Our politicos have given our jobs to legal and illegal foreign nationals. Recent college graduates can no longer compete for those jobs. Ironically, with Obamacare, though Americans must pay through the nose for a policy and overcome huge deductibles before they receive any benefits, the illegals who hold their jobs can get their healthcare for free. It simply is not fair to Americans.

Our politicians have also permitted greedy American corporations to swindle stockholders and employees and to take American jobs overseas. Moreover, they have permitted illegal foreign nationals to settle permanently in the U.S. to raise the cost of living quarters, to take the jobs of the young, and to take the jobs of the old.

So Americans collect unemployment for which other Americans pay. While Americans are out of work, those from other countries prosper at our expense; they take our tax money with illegal IDs, and they live just out of reach of the Tax man.

Then, to add insult to injury, our representatives in all areas of the separate powers, have told us that we don't really want our jobs or our own healthcare and that all of these giveaways to non Americans is good for America. It makes no sense and so Americans do not buy in. We all know it is a charade but we stand back hoping George will do it.

Well, if you will pardon me, we have had a number of George's and they cannot make up for an inattentive public that does not call representatives to task. We had George Washington and we had several George Bushes. When we had a George around, at least the arrow was pointing up! Now it is pointing down and we are on a downhill run. Like

Chraley Reese said the only hope for Americans is if we can kick them all out and the sooner the better!

Those Days vs. These Days

Shortly after the Revolutionary War and after the formation of our representative government, there was a problem for the constituency. The problem was simple: somebody had to send representatives to the national forum.

At the federal level, as more states joined the union, it was not too easy for a local farmer to give up his farm in say, Montana, and head off to Washington by wagon or horseback to represent the folks back home. Recognizing this difficulty, and in appreciation for representing the constituency, the neighbors, who were not of the aristocracy but of the commonplace, tended the representative's farm and protected the household while the chosen was doing the duty for all.

They took care of mom and the kids and the animals, until the hero representative would come home and resume his life. During this period of American History, the representatives were clearly honorable, but they did not demand the title. At this time in history, not by exclusion, but by custom, women did their patriotic duty by keeping up the household.

The irony of those days compared to these days is that in those days the representatives performed for their constituency from a sense of duty. In these days, though one cannot strike a broad negative brush on the political class or a good person will never agree to help our cause and run for an official office, it seems that instead of from a sense of duty, today's "politicians" go for the office from a sense of opportunity. That's about it and that is the big problem.

I can probably end this book right here but there are a few more things I must say first.

When one is motivated by the sense of opportunity, one's interests lie mainly in oneself. So, I could rest my case right now but I will continue since we not only need to change the notion that the governors are elite and the governed are subjects, we must convince the best and the brightest of our country to take up the yoke as in days past and do great acts for America from a raging sense of duty, not opportunity... and not for a lifetime.

A Country of Honor

The State of Pennsylvania is not unlike the other 49 states. So, as I speak about PA, I ask you to please think about the similarities with the political business in your own state. Surely some who come to office, come from a sense of duty and they are fine people, while others come from the draw of the opportunity, which the office carries.

Hence, with the dismal track record of politicos from all states and the federal government, it is better for the constituency to not trust any in an elected public office until given proof that such trust is well deserved. Just like your state, the state of Pennsylvania in which I have lived all but two of my years, is a state with a mix of the duty class and the opportunity class.

A number of the names coming up below and perhaps a few more are people who I know from my own area of the state. As I mention names and titles, please do not draw any conclusions at all, on the specific individuals that I mention.

A number of office-holders, such as Martin R. Kane, and William H. Amesbury from my City of Wilkes-Barre, are very good men. However, I admit that I do not know all about even these two. I met Kane as he was serving as a

Justice of the Peace at a wedding of a young man, David Boyle, who was like a son to me. District Justice Martin Kane could have easily dismissed this family's request to travel to the far corners of the county on a sunny holiday morning to marry David and Cindy, but instead, Magistrate Martin Kane welcomed it. We of the hoi polloi appreciate things that are above the norm.

Common Pleas Judge Bill Amesbury and I met in a Little League game when we both were 11 years old. He was a great ball player and later a great coach with his best friend and my one time campaign manager, the late Martin L. Devaney. In all the years that have passed, I still haven't heard a bad word about hizzoner.

I was also friends with a number of recent Wilkes-Barre PA Mayors by happenchance. I became friends with Mayor Tom McLaughlin after he had served well when he was nearing death. I was invited to my great neighborhood friends' Jean and Joe Elinsky's home to a get together in which Tom was present. The event was in the former Mayor's honor. He was a stalwart for righteousness and fun.

I was honored also just to be there because some public servants are honest and worthy of admiration. This Mayor wore a baseball cap to keep his post-treatment look OK, and he clearly projected a positivism that he was going to beat the odds. He did not; but he beat the odds of being a great man and a great Mayor in my City. I had traveled across the street to meet and speak with this fine man and great Mayor. He loved the City and he served it well. In this instance, I was the lucky one.

Another of my favorite Wilkes-Barre Mayor's is Lee Namey, a neighbor, a wonderful man and another great Mayor. As a high school student several years behind Lee, I recognized him as the best athlete I had ever observed in both football and in track. Afterwards and through life whenever we met, always unofficially, he was the finest gentleman. My city prospered while he was the Mayor. Lee always made me know that he and I grew up less than a block away. Just recently, unexpectedly, Lee passed away. He was a great man and a great Mayor.

When I was hardly thirty years old, I built and taught a course in IT personal business computing at King's College, back when PCs were rare, I met WB Councilman Tom McGroarty. He was a student in my class. He was not much more than twenty-one years old. He wanted to learn about computers and business. He was a smart student.

After I had left IBM and was establishing my computer consultancy, Tom McGroarty was awaiting the beginning of his first term as Mayor of Wilkes-Barre. Tom wanted to keep Wilkes-Barre strong and he wanted to have a strong IT department.

Out of nowhere I began to get copied on material, about computers, that was being discussed at City Hall. I was ready to make comment when asked. City Administrator Richard Muessig knew that I had an AS/400 consulting practice and the city used an AS/400 for all of its processing. Mr. Muessig and I, for full disclosure were fellow Meyers High School graduates and both of us were on the Baseball Team. I had been sending him notifications as to how I could help the City, which happened to be my City.

On New Years Eve at the Barney Inn, now called Cris-Nics, in Wilkes-Barre, Tom McGroarty asked me to be the computer consultant for the City of Wilkes-Barre. It was a great honor and a great run. Tom really put his all into making Wilkes-Barre as good as it could be. I respect him immensely for his time as our Mayor.

I met Councilman Leighton during the McGroarty years. When he became Mayor I asked if I could help and he said OK! I did some analysis work for the Mayor, which he appreciated. He will have been Mayor of Wilkes-Barre for 12 years when his term runs out in 2015. Can I be that old?

I never tried to know these Mayors. Yet, I did find myself cheering for them because I felt they were good-fellows and they had stuck their necks out for the citizens of Wilkes-Barre.

As many states in this wonderful nation, the state of Pennsylvania has many politicians bearing the title "The Honorable."

But, are they really "honorable?" That is for their constituencies to examine and decide. It is absolutely amazing how many yeronners and heronners and hizzoners there are in all states, so I have chosen PA, my state, as my example state.

To put some names next to some of those "honorable" representatives, executives, and justices, permit me to use those with whom I am most familiar from a local standpoint from a vantage of several years ago. Then, I will pick others at random the further from my home town they get.

In this work and in the prior section, it is not my desire to unduly adulate or unduly criticize any of the officials who operate close to my home town. I can assure you if they are ignoble people, I will write their names down in subsequent work; but for now, all of the folks I know in PA are off the hook.

For example, the list of PA "Honorables" includes the

- Senator from Pennsylvania, Robert P. Casey,
- Lou Barletta (U.S. House of Representatives),
- Tom Wolfe (Governor, Commonwealth of Pennsylvania),
- Elisabeth J. Baker (PA State Senator),

- Eddie Day Pashinski (PA State House of Representatives),
- Anthony George, Mayor of Wilkes-Barre City,
- Martin R. Kane (District Justice, Luzerne County),
- William T. Amesbury (formerly District Justice, Luzerne County -- who is now a judge of the Common Pleas in Luzerne County). .

With no disrespect intended to any of the above, that is an awful lot of "Honorables" and it doesn't touch the number of hizzoners, heronners, and yeronners in just the state of Pennsylvania.

If you begin a calculation based on current appointees and elected offices, the national total of the "Honorables," would be in the hundreds of thousands.

That's an awful lot of honor that is implicitly taken by this branch of the political class. Think of your own list in your own state and you are probably not surprised that this list is large and in almost all cases, except for Kane and Amesbury, I chose just one of many in the judicial chamber who hold the same office.

For those wondering about America and Dummmies, the big problem as discussed is that the US suffers from taxation and there is no real representation - but somehow all the "representatives" are "honorable."

The situation is quite similar to when King George III and Parliament in the 18th century directly levied taxes on the colonists and the colonists rebelled.

Though outright rebellion is not necessarily right around the corner in the US, the current set of "Honorables," need to pay attention to the mood of the people on this topic because the public mood is not very good. If It were good, you would not be reading this book.

Those representatives, who enjoy the game—need to come to the realization again that the people come first. The dummmies learning of America can take that as one of the big lessons.

Unlike the long past 18th century, however, today there are living representatives. There just isn't real representation. The litmus test is whether that representation is of the people, for the people, and by the people.

Take a look at the Honorable So and So(s) in your home state and in your locale, and ask if you're gifting them with the title of hizzoner has minimized the representation you receive. I say yes it has in most cases, and all of US, myself included must self indict on this issue.

We have overly applauded our representatives.
They would do better for us without our applause.

Chapter 30   Puffery Leads to Improper Allegiances

Creating Better Representatives

The use of platitudes and pufferies to describe elected representatives diminishes their desire to represent the people and increases their desire to represent themselves, the elite and the special interest classes of the elite.

It also decreases the expectation level of the constituency as they, by their own words, place their governors in a higher socio-political class and they submit as subjects to "what comes down the pike."

Can we solve the problem described above? Perhaps this notion of a solution will do:

From henceforth, let the representatives serve as unsung and humble heroes about whom songs of distinction will rarely be raised unless the distinction is truly earned. Let them represent the people and nobody else. Let their inner selves guide their votes and let their inner selves give them praise for jobs well done. Let the pomposity and the arrogance end and end quickly.

Let no special interests be permitted anywhere close to the hallowed chambers of our government and the buildings in which the business of the people is conducted. Keep the lobbyists and those backed by the money of the unknown, including that of the enemies of these United States, from the legislators (our representatives) as they are making laws for the common good of the states.

Lobbyists and those whose income depends on influencing America's lawmakers should be permitted no contact with the representatives of the states, or any local constituency. Such activity in proximity of lawmakers is not for the common good and the lobbyist crowd should not be permitted to intimidate or influence any representative.

The notion of important lobbyists trying to influence legislators can have a negative effect on the clear thinking of the people's elected representatives. Let the lobbyists identify themselves and lobby the governed, not the instruments of their government, their honest representatives.

The notion of lobbyists, however, is just an aside. If our representatives, paid well of course, ($174,000 per year as of 2014 not including expenses --- for each house seat) knew that they could not receive additional compensation from lobbyists, bribers, or whatever you want to call them, ever, even after terms are up, no how, no matter how they voted, they would not be as inclined to favor those private interests against those for public interests. When the lobbyists file their income taxes, they want their contributions to be deductible and so all payments to representatives by law must be noted.

Pay Them Well

Politicians live in elite neighborhoods. This is not good but it would not be right to dictate the neighborhood in which your representative lives as long as it is within your district. Our representatives must be paid well for their service and they should believe that they are being paid well. Otherwise, their honesty may be compromised as they turn to the elite in order to receive additional compensation.

They must be paid well during their terms and their terms must be short so that they do not become untouchable by mere mortals, such as their constituents. The temptation of being for oneself while in office clearly must be minimized. This is a representative democracy and our representatives cannot do well by the people if they represent themselves or those who are not of the people.

It really is that simple. The primary point of this discussion is that we the people must reengage our government within our honorable laws—those that benefit the public. Additionally, we need to get rid of the laws not so honorable.

Minimize the Opportunity for Corruption

Sending our newly elected into a quagmire of corruption and deceit and seeing who survives is not a good recipe for the future of America. Let's figure out how to get rid of the corruption and all the bad that comes with that.

Calling the newly elected "the Honorable" and paying homage to her or him as a new governor of subjects is clearly not the right approach. It is unfortunately today's modus operandi, an operandi that has long failed the people.

Thank-you's are most appropriate for good service. The notion of a required "hizzoner" that starts a period of aristocratic living from the first waltz of the Inaugural Ball breeds just more separation from the people. In a democracy, the rich and the plebeians have the right to a voice in their government. So, what do we do?

Well, first of all we must realize that nothing is going to change for the better unless the people are very insistent. Corruption begins as the corrupt begin to believe in themselves and not the mission of helping their whole constituency. Rule # 1 for the people is to pay attention.

Unfortunately as innocuous as it may seem this notion of "The Honorable" and all that it means is ingrained deeply into the fabric of American political culture and etiquette. Until recently, however, one could also rely on the ethics and morals of the representatives as an additional inhibitor to corruption, and thus assuring proper action. It seems that in the latter part of the 20th century the culture of "anything goes" has permeated American society and its morals and its ethics.

Not all politicians are corrupt but it is easy for our representatives to get sucked in to something that is much bigger then even themselves. Therefore, one can no longer count on one's own ethics and one's own morals if elected to serve as a countervailing force against bad representation.

Consequently, it is up to the people to create an environment, which is more personally rewarding for our representatives to do their jobs, than it would be to accept praise for merely being elected.

Political corruption can be prevented but only by a vigilant people. We caution the people to pay attention because without such attention, politicians are given a green light to chicanery and debauchery. Who is there to stop them when we the people say it is OK?

When it was once safe to speak of religious values in this country without fear of reprisal or a lawsuit, there was an apparent social conscience with which to gauge all other actions. Today it is not so easy.

In fact today on the news it was reported that a group of Muslim parents were outraged that the local church distributed fliers to public school students for an Eggstravaganza (Easter Egg Hunt) to be held at the church. They claimed that it was against the Constitution. Tolerance goes both ways.

Ironically, the same Muslims from Dearborn Michigan have no problem using the public schools as a battle-ground for Islamic supremacists and Muslim law and they have made many inroads and have been given many accommodations. But an Easter Egg Hunt is too much to ask?

For example, there are Islamic prayer rooms, prayer times, special Friday prayer accommodation, halal food in school cafeterias, Islamic proselytizing curriculums, and Muslim hajj accommodation. All of these have been imposed on public schools in Michigan and across the country. Muslim parents demand that students be excused from music and co-ed phys-ed classes.

I would hope that one day we can all get along but ladies and gentlemen, this is America and in all fairness, it was not founded by Muslims. There are Muslim countries and US citizens do not try to influence their culture in their countries.

There is nothing of which I am aware that is as peaceful as the Christianity. I have read and have observed that Hinduism and Buddhism are also very peaceful religions. Maybe while we are reexamining how to bring back the country we should bring back the Christian principles of our founders. I am not talking about making the government practice Christianity but if we take the Christian label off the values and principles of the Ten Commandments, which are simply ten rules about how to treat deities and our fellow man, we would be making a great start. Remove the Christian label if we must be. Call them the values of honesty but bring them forth.

Much of the writing of the Founding Fathers reflects a Christian bias for example. This country was founded by Christians. The underlying Christian faith, which is not the US Faith, since there is no national church, has had a role in assuring that all political actors must act well. It assumes that they would act in the nature of themselves, which is for

268 America 4 Dummmies!

themselves and friends, but it also suggests that they be good and honest and forthright in their lives.

The Christian faith, as Buddhism and Hinduism, would be acknowledged by all well-thinking persons, to have its very basis in love and honesty and goodness. As such, whether this is a religious notion or a notion of a good-fellow, it is not bad? It is a good model, upon which to form a government. Would it not be nice if all of US were honest?

Ethics and Morals

As our representatives get further removed from their original neighborhoods and become rich in one way or another because of their public service, removal of Christian religious precepts and norms may have helped the representatives in their selfish quest, but it has not helped the people. In many ways, it gives the representatives a license that the public does not want them to have.

One teaching of the Christian church for example, is the "eye of the needle" analogy. Christianity holds that this is bad news for the rich, because it is easier for a camel to pass through the eye of a needle than for a rich man to enter the kingdom of Heaven. I am the last to suggest that the rich earn unjustly or they should not keep theirs. When they take on power that belongs to the people for their own enrichment, however, the rich and I part company.

So, according to Christian teaching (the faith of the founding fathers), the tendency of a politician to work with the well-to-do and live in their neighborhoods while becoming rich themselves makes them less likely to be worthy of Heaven.

Less likely for Heaven means more likely for corruption and so, if honor is given in any form, perhaps it should be from the people to our representatives -- those representatives who stay in the regular neighborhoods and live humble lives.

Being in the neighborhood would be honoring the people and would give representatives more of an opportunity to pass the needle test. Besides, they may actually meet some constituents in person, rather than having to send out form letters.

Representatives of the people at all levels of government are of the people and must therefore be for the people so that our laws can be recognized clearly as being by the people. When situations occur that exalt the representative, regardless of their service or lack of service to the people--merely by their elected office, this is reprehensible. Laws put forth under these circumstances should be viewed with jaded eyes accordingly and scorned.

How can a pack of nothing but "Honorables," who have distanced and disconnected themselves from the ordinary folk who elected them, represent US fairly as our government?

The fact is that as a whole, today's representatives are not doing the people's business. They are doing their own business and the business of their elite sponsors. This problem could be the very essence and the rationale of many a book. In our case, we have more to cover about the goodness of America as our main purpose. The more we know about America, the more prepared we will be to assure the goodness of those who we elect to serve US.

Thomas Jefferson had great disdain and mistrust for the propensity of man, once given the power to rule, to use that power for the good of the people rather than oneself. He warned of what could happen when such people create issues for society that require more and more debt and ultimately more taxation, with the implication of poor representation. With historically high deficits and mounting national debt, we seemingly have not learned Jefferson's lesson well, though we have had over two hundred years of training to do it right:

"We must not let our rulers load us with perpetual debt. We must make our election between economy and liberty or profusion and servitude. If we run into such debt, as that we must be taxed in our meat and in our drink, in our necessaries and our comforts, in our labors and our amusements, for our calling and our creeds...we [will] have no time to think, no means of calling our miss-managers to account but be glad to obtain subsistence by hiring ourselves to rivet their chains on the necks of our fellow-sufferers. And this is the tendency of all human governments. A departure from principle in one instance becomes a precedent till the bulk of society is reduced to be mere automatons of misery. And the foreshores of this frightful team is public debt. Taxation follows that, and in its train wretchedness and oppression."
Thomas Jefferson

Does it not seem in these words that Thomas Jefferson is looking at us from the grave, knowing his words have been unheeded and working for God now to make sure we get his message and we act accordingly?

Chapter 31   Too Many Honorables

Solving the problem of "Honorables"

The solution to the "Honorables" is quite simple. Our elected representatives, while in Washington or in the state assemblies and even in the courtrooms and the lower legislatures, executive branch chambers, and councils should be treated with respect and should have amenities to compensate them well for their time away from home.

However, they are not entitled to the title, "honorable" merely by taking the oath of office one time or even many times. The title "honorable" no longer can be an expected gift from the public to the representatives without them having earned the title. It is the legislators, executives, and justices themselves who should strip themselves of the title immediately and be done with it. It is nonsense and should be ceased immediately. If the people in unison choose to honor somebody, let it be a one-time gift as the honors which we all temporarily receive.

Additional Thoughts

Those once in office but no longer in office, who still get a kick out of being called the "honorable," can receive a replacement title if it is that important to them, from the body from which they retired. Ex-presidents and ex-Governors and Ex-Mayors can request the title from an ad-hoc committee respectively made up of ex-Presidents, ex-Governors, and ex-Mayors. A suitable respectable title that does not imply honor can be created, such as "public servant" or the "friend of the people," and this can be used in etiquette from henceforth rather than force a vote about honor for each public official above a certain level of office.

A different term for judges than "Your Honor," should be instituted and while in session. Judges would be greeted as "Your Judgeship," while presiding officially in a courtroom. This is proper since "judgeship" accurately reflects the high respect needed for the position of judge, not the person behind the robes.

In all social events other than those purely political in nature and sponsored by politicians or friends of politicians, all of our duly elected servants should not be greeted as "the Honorable" or by their official title. In a democracy, if these people are of the people, and they are—or should be, they should be addressed as all of the people in their constituency are addressed.

If we think about it, we are all pretending about the elected being honorable anyway and that is just silly. It's actually pretty stupid besides. It is pure puffery at its best and in this day and age, in which the constituency is questioning the loyalty of its representatives, considering ones-self as "the honorable," is not the side of the puff on which a representative should want to find himself.

Others have checked out the notion of the "honorable so and so from such and such," and they have found it most often does not fit and it is too much to give to a public servant.

For example, Mary K. Mewborn, writing in the November 19, 1999 edition of Washington Life Magazine, in an article aptly titled "Too Many Honorables?" has done most of my work for me in forming valid conclusions and recommendations.

The solution remains the stoppage of haphazardly bestowing the title of "Honorable" - period. Ms. Mewborn notes the asininity involved in granting such a title in her first examples. Here are three priceless misuses of the title from Ms. Mewborn:

- "A socialite in Wesley Heights thinks it adds personal distinction to her many listings on fundraising invitations."
- "A former ambassador living at the Watergate uses it to remind others of his long-ago diplomatic posting to a small Caribbean nation."
- "Appointees to even the most minor Presidential commissions are apt to believe it bestows instant social cachet- with invitations to A-list parties sure to follow."

It all has to do with self aggrandizement and those who love it most are narcissists. Mewborn points out in this article that it is illegal to take the title "honorable," although she acknowledges that which cannot be gained legally can be gained by political process. In other words, the politicians can do what they want once they run the country—and they do—and they have—and quite frankly that's why she and I and you are upset!

Let us now test the reasonableness of no longer conferring the title honorable on our representatives by reading the following several paragraphs, again taken from Mary K. Mewborn's timeless article about "Too Many Honorables." Before the paragraphs, there is the URL of the article, Mewborn wrote, available online for your surfing. It's a fun read.

http://www.washingtonlife.com/backissues/archives/99nov/honorab les.htm

Whether it is the roster of the Board of Governors of the Smithsonian Institution or the benefit committee of a typical Washington charity gala, there are always a number of names preceded by "Honorable," instead of the usual Mr., Mrs., Miss or Ms. How this came about in a country whose Constitution expressly forbids the granting of titles amuses some and irritates others. At the very least its widespread usage raises some eyebrows.

Traditionally the British use the "Hon." (originally abbreviated from "The Right Honorable Magnificence of Nobles"), to identify certain family members of hereditary barons and earls, i.e., their daughters, younger sons and the younger sons' wives. In America, however, such inherited titles were rare among the early colonists, and after independence there was no king to grant new ones.
...

Political primacy is now well-established in matters of protocol and etiquette and is, according to the U.S. Government, a matter of procedure and form. Consequently, it would be very improper indeed to refer to the "Hon. Bill Gates," even though he may have billions in the bank and pay his taxes, or to the "Hon. Cindy Crawford," although what man wouldn't hope to flatter her? Nobel Prizes and great humanitarian deeds won't make you Honorable either, though getting elected Mayor of Bladensburg, Md. definitely will.

By the rules of etiquette,... Once you are made an Honorable, you stay that way for life, regardless of what an independent counsel or district attorney may subsequently uncover about any untoward activities. "In Washington, as Betty Beale, longtime social columnist and observer of the Washington social scene, bluntly puts it, "The title `Honorable' has nothing to do either with honor or character."

Copious research work permitted Ms. Mewborn to uncover the fact that the title "honorable" is not and cannot be a conferred title and therefore it is a title that is improperly used to refer to the people's representatives merely because of their representation. The raw data from her research is not here for US to examine but there is enough in her article to suffice as data well collected.

Moreover, you and I have observed the notion of the "Honorables" in our daily lives and we have also seen the impact of such pomposity in the behavior of our elected officials. If you have looked at the same news accounts as I over many years, it is clear that our representatives have become so honorable that there is now so much honor, there is no longer any room for shame.

In the Federal Government, it is clear that Senators are further away from the people than members of the House of Representatives. They behave as Lords from old England and have a major disconnect with the people. Even when they commit a crime, they believe they are better than the represented.

Among just about every highlight reel from several years ago, is the story of a US senator who said he would resign in the midst of scandal surrounding his arrest in a police sting targeting lewd behavior in a men's public restroom. But, then he flip-flopped believing his own admission of guilt was not enough to prove he was guilty.

Remember Republican Senator Larry Craig, 62 at the time, who had been arrested in June, 2007 and then pleaded guilty in August to a lesser charge - disorderly conduct. He apparently paid the $500 fine, and was given a 10-day suspended sentence and a year's probation. But, he was only kidding...Really?

Another class act is Democratic Congressman William "the Freezer" Jefferson of Louisiana from the Katrina days. Jefferson has been dubbed the "Freezer" though he has no major football skills. The "Freezer" stashed his sack with $90,000 in a freezer in his home to cool them off a bit since they represented hot illegal tender. Yes folks, cash can freeze.

He's in jail now. He got 13 years for his role in the taking of roughly $500,000 in bribes. But, he was seeking millions more in exchange for using his influence to broker business deals in Africa. Perhaps his defense was that his constituents had given him the cash from a number of lemonade sales they undertook to help him with his future defense.

OK, he simply was a thief. The cash he had hidden came from marked FBI bills. He received them from an FBI informant. Turns out the bills were still marked in the freezer and they were not frozen enough to keep Representative Jefferson out of the slammer.

There are others such as Republican Duke Cunningham, Republican Bob Ney, and Democrat Jim Traficant and probably hundreds more like them. It has become easy to presume guilt because the blamed politicians are usually guilty. As noted previously, "How can you tell if a politician is lying? He's moving his lips." That says it all and it helps to repeat it often to remember it.

Dr. Gerhard Falk, writing an article in blog form on http://jbuff.com/c012705.htm performed his research and collected data in order to shed some light on the subject of respect for politicians. Whether you agree with all of what he says or not, Falk certainly catches the spirit of the great disdain with which our leaders are held. Not much has changed since his diatribe.

Mewborn and Falk and many others with whom we would probably agree, note that the "Honorables" have created an ironically dishonorable circumstance. Some is because of their conduct outside of office and some is simply because of their poor representation. The moniker of "Honorable" being used to describe those looked upon as of questionable repute does not help matters. Dr. Falk adds his own few words about the "Honorables" to the mix as he discusses the vile of politicians in his blog:

Politicians of all parties are evidently convinced that the whole world revolves only around them. They do not want to meet the voters, i.e. the ordinary taxpayers, for fear that they may be asked what they do all day and what happened to our money. They call themselves "the honorable" this and that...

...

Politicians love to aggrandize themselves. Bill Clinton spent $42 million on his second inauguration and George W. Bush spent $40 million more. [Of course Obama's 1st inauguration cost double that and his second double again]. These expensive theatrics are obscene and have no place in our democracy. Read the life of George Washington. He was sworn in for a second time as President of the United States on March 4, 1793. His speech was only 134 words and he then walked home alone. No parade. No speeches. No dances. No gross exhibition of ego.

Before he wrote this piece, Falk had not met Barack Obama, the first combination Sultan, King, Dictator, and President of the US. Because of the triple duty, Obama was forced to spend upwards of $170 million for his inauguration. Was it inflation or excessive love? I think we know!

The problem of self aggrandizement and the notion of self-importance are well documented and well observed even without deploying a scientific method. Will the inability to use the title "honorable" actually solve the problem of (1) inappropriate claiming of title and (2) the resultant lack of true representation of the people for the people and by the representatives of the people?

Unfortunately, we cannot pre-observe the results of blocking of the use of the title, since there is no real data and no true table upon which to experiment. For conclusions based on the future, we might be able to conjure the spirit of Rod Serling of Alfred Hitchcock, but otherwise, we have only logic to use.

However, since this problem limits itself to part 1 of 2 above, the answer is logically clear that if the title "honorable" can no longer be used in a whimsical manner by any politician at any time, then the problem is solved by a proper conclusion based on the hypothesis. We can thus stage the data analysis to draw the conclusions outlined below.

Looking at what we have been discussing objectively, we can deduce some information directly and we can draw some fairly accurate conclusions. If politicians are no longer bestowed the title of honorable merely by gaining an office or an appointment, the problem of "too many Honorables" and not enough honor will be solved.

Once politicians can no longer use the title, "honorable," their egos will no longer be instantly stroked and the people will have eliminated one major source of puffery for our duly elected representatives. Let honor be reserved for honorable deeds and not because politicians may be offended if there is not an aura of puff surrounding their entrance on the scene. So we can say this conclusion that the use of honorable as a title for these charlatans should cease immediately if not sooner. I would suggest that we should say it loudly.

But is puffery really the problem?

Heavens no! But, puffery is a big problem since it is the arrogant, puffed-up politician who is more likely to choose to disrespect the will of the people and go on his way to legislate for the good of special interests. Politicians go out of their way to bring wonderful legislative gifts to the privileged class and the special interests. The current "honorables" have a hard time saying "no" to friends in high places. Most Americans feel the puffery is unwarranted.

I received a number of emails this year from cohorts who, like you are interested in this U.S. government succeeding. Most, like you and I find major fault with such a representation process that puts so many buffoons in office.

We all know intuitively that the notion of humor is the quality that appeals to a sense of the ludicrous or absurdly incongruous. For those schooled in high school geometry, it's like when CPCT (corresponding parts of congruent triangles) is not equal. When things do not add up and nobody is hurt, at least at the time of the adding, it sure can be funny and it can induce a big belly laugh.

The puffery that comes with political office and the buffoonery of many of the "Honorables," is what I will attribute to this email that I received from one of my friends. I have no idea of the original source of this email but it sure captures what I have been trying to say about the perception of character of our elected officials.

Subject: Haircut

One day a florist goes to a barber for a haircut. After the cut he asked about his bill and the barber replies, "I cannot accept money from you. I'm doing community service this week." The florist was pleased and left the shop. When the barber goes to open his shop the next morning there is a 'thank you' card and a dozen roses waiting for him at his door.

Later, a cop comes in for a haircut, and when he tries to pay his bill, the barber again replies, "I cannot accept money from you. I'm doing community service this week." The cop is happy and leaves the shop. The next morning when the barber goes to open up there is a 'thank you' card and a dozen donuts waiting for him at his door.

Later that day, a college professor comes in for a haircut, and when he tries to pay his bill, the barber again replies, "I cannot accept money from you. I'm doing community service this week." The professor is very happy and leaves the shop. The next morning when the barber opens his shop, there is a 'thank you' card and a dozen different books, such as "How to Improve Your Business" and Becoming More Successful."

"Then, a Congressman comes in for a haircut, and when he goes to pay his bill the barber again replies, "I cannot

accept money from you. I'm doing community service this week." The Congressman is very happy and leaves the shop. The next morning when the barber goes to open up, there are a dozen Congressmen lined up waiting for a free haircut.

And that, my friends, illustrates the fundamental difference between the citizens of our country and the members of our Congress

This little email joke may not say it all but it sure says a lot about the breakdown in respect that the people have for the representatives of the people. The intent of this book is not to hammer our legislators, though clearly it is mostly their fault, and the people are at fault for putting them in office. Our intent of course is to help make Americans aware so that we do not get snookered again and again by politicians.

Therefore, the message for any dummmy trying to learn more about America is that a set of rules, whether they be in a document known as the Articles of Confederation, or a better and more perfect document known as the Constitution are needed to protect Americans from being hoodwinked by politicians always looking out for themselves. It is a real concern and not just a matter of puff.

"Honorables" Summary

In this chapter we talked a lot about whether there was a real problem with all of the fluff and puff that is associated with our political class. The use of the word "honorable" was the point that was debated in this chapter. Should our elected representatives be entitled to the title "honorable" merely by being elected?

Using logic and lots of anecdotes and real facts, we concluded that the answer is no. We also concluded that the abuse of the system by politicians hurts our democratic system of representative egalitarian government to suggest that all men are not equal. Let me borrow and convolute for impact a phrase from Orwell's Animal Farm:

"Some people are less equal than others—to the people they are known as politicians." Would it not be nice on their own; if politicians would choose to improve? Then again, it would be nice if there really was a Tooth Ferry.

Now that we have reached the end of all our lessons in this book, I have one more thing for you to do. Go ahead and open all your windows and shout out at the top of your lungs: "I'm as mad as hell, and I'm not going to take this anymore!" Amen!

Part VIII: Appendices – Founding Documents

Appendix A: The Declaration of Rights and Grievances

At the First Continental Congress, the delegates drafted several documents, and several drafts of documents, one of which was the Declaration of Rights and Grievances. This was a statement of American complaints. It was sent to King George III, to whom, at the time, many of the delegates remained loyal. It was not sent to Parliament since the delegates did not have the same level of loyalty to this body. Quite frankly, The document implored King George III to step in and rescue the colonies from the English Parliament.

The radical delegates were critical of this particular *Declaration* because it continued to concede the right of Parliament to regulate colonial trade, a view that was losing favor in the mid-1770s. Many suggest that the actual cause of the American Revolution is found in this major historical document.

Thus, In the First Continental Congress, which met in September and October 1774, the delegates of the Congress made several major decisions. Among those was to send King George III this Declaration of Rights and Grievances, which is shown below: .

In Congress, at Philadelphia, October 14, 1774
Whereas, since the close of the last war, the British Parliament, claiming a power of right to bind the people of America, by statute, all cases whatsoever, hath in some acts expressly imposed taxes on them and in others, under various pretenses, but in fact for the purpose raising a revenue, hath imposed rates and duties payable in these colonies established a board of commissioners, with unconstitutional powers, and extended the jurisdiction of courts of admiralty, not only for collecting the said duties, but for the trial of causes merely arising within the body of a county.

And whereas, in consequence of other statutes, judges, who before held only estates at will in their offices, have been made dependent on the Crown alone for their salaries, and standing armies kept in time of peace:

And whereas, it has lately been resolved in Parliament, that by force of a statute, made in the thirty-fifth year of the reign of Henry the Eighth, colonists may be transported to England, and tried there upon accusations for treasons, and misprisions, or concealments of treasons committed in the colonies, and by a late statute, such trials have been directed in cases therein mentioned.

And whereas, in the last session of Parliament, three statutes were made; one, entitled "An act to discontinue, in such manner and for such time as are therein mentioned, the landing and discharging, lading, or shipping of goods, wares and merchandise, at the town, and within the harbor of Boston, in the province of Massachusetts Bay, in North America"; and another, entitled "An act for the better regulating the government of the province of the Massachusetts Bay in New England"; and another, entitled "An act for the impartial administration of justice, in the cases of persons questioned for any act done by them in the execution of the law, or for the suppression of riots and tumults in the province of the Massachusetts Bay, in New England." And another statute was then made, "for making more effectual provision for the government of the province of Quebec, etc." All which statutes are impolitic, unjust and cruel, as well as unconstitutional, and most dangerous and destructive of American rights.

And whereas, assemblies have been frequently dissolved, contrary to the rights of the people, when they attempted to deliberate on grievances; and their dutiful, humble, loyal, and reasonable petitions to the Crown for redress, have been repeatedly treated with contempt by His Majesty's ministers of state:

The good people of the several colonies of New Hampshire, Massachusetts Bay, Rhode Island and Providence Plantations, Connecticut, New York, New Jersey, Pennsylvania, New Castle, Kent and Sussex on Delaware, Maryland, Virginia, North Carolina, and South Carolina, justly alarmed at these arbitrary proceedings of Parliament and administration, have severally elected, constituted, and appointed deputies to meet and sit in general congress, in the city of Philadelphia, in order to obtain such establishment, as that their religion, laws, and liberties may not be subverted.

Whereupon the deputies so appointed being now assembled, in a full and free representation of these colonies, taking into their most serious consideration, the best means of attaining the ends aforesaid, do, in the first place, as Englishmen, their ancestors in like cases have usually done, for asserting and vindicating their rights and liberties, declare,

That the inhabitants of the English colonies in North America, by the immutable laws of nature, the principles of the English Constitution, and the several charters or compacts, have the following rights:

1. That they are entitled to life, liberty, and property, and they have never ceded to any sovereign power whatever, a right to dispose of either without their consent.

2. That our ancestors, who first settled these colonies, were at the time of their emigration from the mother country, entitled to all the rights, liberties, and immunities of free and natural-born subjects, within the realm of England.

3. That by such emigration they by no means forfeited, surrendered, or lost any of those rights, but that they were, and their descendants now are, entitled to the exercise and enjoyment of all such of them, as their local and other circumstances enable them, to exercise and enjoy.

4. That the foundation of English liberty, and of all free government, is a right in the people to participate in their legislative council: and as the English colonists are not represented, and from their local and other circumstances, can not properly be represented in the British Parliament, they are entitled to a free and exclusive power of legislation in their several provincial legislatures, where their right of representation can alone be preserved, in all cases of taxation and internal polity, subject only to the negative of their sovereign, in such manner as has been heretofore used and accustomed. But, from the necessity of the case, and a regard to the mutual interest of both countries, we cheerfully consent to the operation of such acts of the British Parliament, as are bona fide, restrained to the regulation of our external commerce, for the purpose of securing the commercial advantages of the whole empire to the mother country, and the commercial benefits of its respective members; excluding every idea of taxation, internal or eternal, for raising a revenue on the subjects in America, without their consent.

5. That the respective colonies are entitled to the common law of England, and more especially to the great and inestimable privilege of being tried by their peers of the vicinage, according to the course of that law.

6. That they are entitled to the benefit of such of the English statutes as existed at the time of their colonization; and which they have, by experience, respectively found to be applicable to their several local and other circumstances.

7. That these, His Majesty's colonies, are likewise entitled to all the immunities and privileges granted and confirmed to them by royal charters, or secured by their several codes of provincial laws.

8. That they have a right peaceably to assemble, consider of their grievances, and petition the King; and that all prosecutions, prohibitory proclamations, and commitment for the same, are illegal.

9. That the keeping a standing army in these colonies, in times of peace, without the consent of the legislature of that colony, in which such army is kept, is against law.

10. It is indispensably necessary to good government, and rendered essential by the English constitution, that the constituent branches of the legislature be independent of each other; that, therefore, the exercise of legislative power in several colonies, by a council appointed, during pleasure by the Crown, is unconstitutional, dangerous, and destructive to the freedom of American legislation.

All and each of which the aforesaid deputies, in behalf of themselves and their constituents, do claim, demand, and insist on, as their indubitable rights and liberties; which can not be legally taken from them, altered or abridged by any power whatever, without their own consent, by their representatives in their several provincial legislatures.

In the course of our inquiry, we find many infringements and violations of the foregoing rights, which, from an ardent desire, that harmony and mutual intercourse of affection and interest may be restored, we pass over for the present, and proceed to state such acts and measures as have been adopted since the last war, which demonstrate a system formed to enslave America. Resolved, N. C. D. That the following acts of Parliament are infringements and violations of the rights of the colonists; and that the repeal of them is essentially necessary in order to restore harmony between Great Britain and the American colonies, viz;

The several acts of 4 Geo. 3. ch. 15, and ch. 34.--5 Geo. 3. ch. 25.--6 Geo. 3. ch. 52.--7 Geo. 3. ch. 41, and ch. 46.--8 Geo. 3. ch. 22, which impose duties for the purpose of raising a revenue in America, extend the powers of the admiralty court beyond their ancient limits, deprive the American subject of trial by jury, authorize the judges' certificate to indemnify the prosecutor from damages, that he might otherwise be liable to, requiring oppressive security from a claimant of ships and goods seized, before he shall be allowed to defend his property, and are subversive of American rights.

Also the 12 Geo. 3. ch. 24, entitled "An act for the better securing His Majesty's dock yards, magazines, ships, ammunition, and stores," which declares a new offense in America, and deprives the American subject of a constitutional trial by jury of the vicinage, by authorizing the trial of any person, charged with the committing any offense described in the said act, out of the realm, to be indicted and tried for the same in any shire or county within the realm.

Also the three acts passed in the last session of Parliament, for stopping the port and blocking up the harbor of Boston, for altering the charter and government of the Massachusetts Bay, and that which is entitled "An act for the better administration of justice," etc.

Also the act passed in the same session for establishing the Roman Catholic religion in the province of Quebec, abolishing the equitable system of English laws, and erecting a tyranny there, to the great danger, from so total a dissimilarity of religion, law, and government of the neighboring British colonies, by the assistance of whose blood and treasure the said country was conquered from France.

Also the act passed in the same session for the better providing suitable quarters for officers and soldiers in His Majesty's service in North America.

Also, that the keeping a standing army in several of these colonies, in time of peace, without the consent of the legislature of that colony in which such army is kept, is against law.

To these grievous acts and measures, Americans can not submit, but in hopes that their fellow subjects in Great Britain will, on a revision of them, restore us to that state in which both countries found happiness and prosperity, we have for the present only resolved to pursue the following peaceable measures:

1st. To enter into a non-importation, non-consumption, and non exportation agreement or association.

2. To prepare an address to the people of Great Britain, and a memorial to the inhabitants of British America, and

3. To prepare a loyal address to His Majesty; agreeable to resolutions already entered into.

Appendix B   The Articles of Association

The Articles of Association

October 20, 1774

We, his majesty's most loyal subjects, the delegates of the several colonies of New-Hampshire, Massachusetts-Bay, Rhode-Island, Connecticut, New-York, New-Jersey, Pennsylvania, the three lower counties of Newcastle, Kent and Sussex on Delaware, Maryland, Virginia, North-Carolina, and South-Carolina, deputed to represent them in a continental Congress, held in the city of Philadelphia, on the 5th day of September, 1774, avowing our allegiance to his majesty, our affection and regard for our fellow-subjects in Great-Britain and elsewhere, affected with the deepest anxiety, and most alarming apprehensions, at those grievances and distresses, with which his Majesty's American subjects are oppressed; and having taken under our most serious deliberation, the state of the whole continent, find, that the present unhappy situation of our affairs is occasioned by a ruinous system of colony administration, adopted by the British ministry about the year 1763, evidently calculated for enslaving these colonies, and, with them, the British Empire. In prosecution of which system, various acts of parliament have been passed, for raising a revenue in America, for depriving the American subjects, in many instances, of the constitutional trial by jury, exposing their lives to danger, by directing a new and illegal trial beyond the seas, for crimes alleged to have been committed in America: And in prosecution of the same system, several late, cruel, and oppressive acts have been passed, respecting the town of Boston and the Massachusetts-Bay, and also an act for extending the province of Quebec, so as to border on the western frontiers of these colonies, establishing an arbitrary government therein, and discouraging the settlement of British subjects in that wide extended country; thus, by the influence of civil principles and ancient prejudices, to dispose the inhabitants to act with hostility against the free Protestant colonies, whenever a wicked ministry shall choose so to direct them.

To obtain redress of these grievances, which threaten destruction to the lives liberty, and property of his majesty's subjects, in North-America, we are of opinion, that a non-importation, non-consumption, and non-exportation agreement, faithfully adhered to, will prove the most speedy, effectual, and peaceable measure: And, therefore, we do, for ourselves, and the inhabitants of the several colonies, whom we represent, firmly agree and associate, under the sacred ties of virtue, honour and love of our country, as follows:

1. That from and after the first day of December next, we will not import, into British America, from Great-Britain or Ireland, any goods, wares, or merchandise whatsoever, or from any other place, any such goods, wares, or merchandise, as shall have been exported from Great-Britain or Ireland; nor will we, after that day, import any East-India tea from any part of the world; nor any molasses, syrups, paneles, coffee, or pimento, from the British plantations or from Dominica; nor wines from Madeira, or the Western Islands; nor foreign indigo.

2. We will neither import nor purchase, any slave imported after the first day of December next; after which time, we will wholly discontinue the slave trade, and will neither be concerned in it ourselves, nor will we hire our vessels, nor sell our commodities or manufactures to those who are concerned in it.

3. As a non-consumption agreement, strictly adhered to, will be an effectual security for the observation of the non-importation, we, as above, solemnly agree and associate, that from this day, we will not purchase or use any tea, imported on account of the East-India company, or any on which a duty bath been or shall be paid; and from and after the first day of March next, we will not purchase or use any East-India tea whatever; nor will we, nor shall any person for or under us, purchase or use any of those goods, wares, or merchandise, we have agreed not to import, which we shall know, or have cause to suspect, were imported after the first day of December, except such as come under the rules and directions of the tenth article hereafter mentioned.

4. The earnest desire we have not to injure our fellow-subjects in Great-Britain, Ireland, or the West-Indies, induces us to suspend a non-exportation, until the tenth day of September, 1775; at which time, if the said acts and parts of acts of the British parliament herein after mentioned, are not repealed, we will not directly or indirectly, export any merchandise or commodity whatsoever to Great-Britain, Ireland, or the West-Indies, except rice to Europe.

5. Such as are merchants, and use the British and Irish trade, will give orders, as soon as possible, to their factors, agents and correspondents, in Great-Britain and Ireland, not to ship any goods to them, on any pretence whatsoever, as they cannot be received in America; and if any merchant, residing in Great-Britain or Ireland, shall directly or indirectly ship any goods, wares or merchandize, for America, in order to break the said non-importation agreement, or in any manner contravene the same, on such unworthy conduct being well attested, it ought to be made public; and, on the same being so done, we will not, from thenceforth, have any commercial connexion with such merchant.

6. That such as are owners of vessels will give positive orders to their captains, or masters, not to receive on board their vessels any goods prohibited by the said non-importation agreement, on pain of immediate dismission from their service.

7. We will use our utmost endeavours to improve the breed of sheep, and increase their number to the greatest extent; and to that end, we will kill them as seldom as may be, especially those of the most profitable kind; nor will we export any to the West-Indies or elsewhere; and those of us, who are or may become overstocked with, or can conveniently spare any sheep, will dispose of them to our neighbours, especially to the poorer sort, on moderate terms.

8. We will, in our several stations, encourage frugality, economy, and industry, and promote agriculture, arts and the manufactures of this country, especially that of wool; and will discountenance and discourage every species of extravagance and dissipation, especially all horse-racing, and all kinds of games, cock fighting, exhibitions of shews, plays, and other expensive diversions and entertainments; and on the death of any relation or friend, none of us, or any of our families will go into any further mourning-dress, than a black crepe or ribbon on the arm or hat, for gentlemen, and a black ribbon and necklace for ladies, and we will discontinue the giving of gloves and scarves at funerals.

9. Such as are venders of goods or merchandize will not take advantage of the scarcity of goods, that may be occasioned by this association, but will sell the same at the rates we have been respectively accustomed to do, for twelve months last past. -And if any vender of goods or merchandise shall sell such goods on higher terms, or shall, in any manner, or by any device whatsoever, violate or depart from this agreement, no person ought, nor will any of us deal with any such person, or his or her factor or agent, at any time thereafter, for any commodity whatever.

10. In case any merchant, trader, or other person, shall import any goods or merchandize, after the first day of December, and before the first day of February next, the same ought forthwith, at the election of the owner, to be either re-shipped or delivered up to the committee of the country or town, wherein they shall be imported, to be stored at the risque of the importer, until the non-importation agreement shall cease, or be sold under the direction of the committee aforesaid; and in the last-mentioned case, the owner or owners of such goods shall be reimbursed out of the sales, the first cost and charges, the profit, if any, to be applied towards relieving and employing such poor inhabitants of the town of Boston, as are immediate sufferers by the Boston port-bill; and a particular account of all goods so returned, stored, or sold, to be inserted in the public papers; and if any goods or merchandizes shall be imported after the said first day of February, the same ought forthwith to be sent back again, without breaking any of the packages thereof.

11. That a committee be chosen in every county, city, and town, by those who are qualified to vote for representatives in the legislature, whose business it shall be attentively to observe the conduct of all persons touching this association; and when it shall be made to appear, to the satisfaction of a majority of any such committee, that any person within the limits of their appointment has violated this association, that such majority do forthwith cause the truth of the case to be published in the gazette; to the end, that all such foes to the rights of British-America may be publicly known, and universally contemned as the enemies of American liberty; and thenceforth we respectively will break off all dealings with him or her.

12. That the committee of correspondence, in the respective colonies, do frequently inspect the entries of their customhouses, and inform each other, from time to time, of the true state thereof, and of every other material circumstance that may occur relative to this association.

13. That all manufactures of this country be sold at reasonable prices, so- that no undue advantage be taken of a future scarcity of goods.

14. And we do further agree and resolve that we will have no trade, commerce, dealings or intercourse whatsoever, with any colony or province, in North-America, which shall not accede to, or which shall hereafter violate this association, but will hold them as unworthy of the rights of freemen, and as inimical to the liberties of their country.

And we do solemnly bind ourselves and our constituents, under the ties aforesaid, to adhere to this association, until such parts of the several acts of parliament passed since the close of the last war, as impose or continue duties on tea, wine, molasses, syrups paneles, coffee, sugar, pimento, indigo, foreign paper, glass, and painters' colours, imported into America, and extend the powers of the admiralty courts beyond their ancient limits, deprive the American subject of trial by jury, authorize the judge's certificate to indemnify the prosecutor from damages, that he might otherwise be liable to from a trial by his peers, require oppressive security from a claimant of ships or goods seized, before he shall be allowed to defend his property, are repealed.-And until that part of the act of the 12 G. 3. ch. 24, entitled "An act for the better securing his majesty's dock-yards magazines, ships, ammunition, and stores," by which any persons charged with committing any of the offenses therein described, in America, may be tried in any shire or county within the realm, is repealed-and until the four acts, passed the last session of parliament, viz. that for stopping the port and blocking up the harbour of Boston-that for altering the charter and government of the Massachusetts-Bay-and that which is entitled "An act for the better administration of justice, &c."-and that "for extending the limits of Quebec, &c." are repealed. And we recommend it to the provincial conventions, and to the committees in the respective colonies, to establish such farther regulations as they may think proper, for carrying into execution this association.

The foregoing association being determined upon by the Congress, was ordered to be subscribed by the several members thereof; and thereupon, we have hereunto set our respective names accordingly.

IN CONGRESS, PHILADELPHIA, October 20, 1774.
PEYTON RANDOLPH, President.

New Hampshire
John Sullivan, Nathaniel Folsom

Massachusetts Bay
Thomas Cushing, Samuel Adams, John Adams, Robert Treat Paine

Rhode Island
Stephen Hopkins, Samuel Ward

Connecticut
Eliphalet Dyer, Roger Sherman, Silas Deane

New York
Isaac Low, John Alsop, John Jay, James Duane, Philip Livingston, William Floyd, Henry Wisner, Simon. Boerum

New Jersey

James. Kinsey, William. Livingston, Stephen Crane, Richard. Smith,
John De Hart

Pennsylvania
Joseph Galloway, John Dickinson , Charles Humphreys, Thomas Mifflin,
Edward Biddle, John Morton, George Ross

The Lower Counties New Castle
Cæsar Rodney, Thomas. M: Kean, George Read

Maryland
Matthew Tilghman, Thomas Johnson Junior, William Paca, Samuel Chase

Virginia
Richard Henry Lee, George Washington, Patrick Henry, Junior, Richard Bland,
Benjamin Harrison, Edmund Pendleton

North-Carolina
William Hooper, Joseph Hewes, Richard Caswell

South-Carolina
Henry Middleton, Thomas Lynch, Christopher Gadsden,
John Rutledge, Edward Rutledge

Appendix C   The Declaration of Independence

IN CONGRESS, JULY 4, 1776

The Unanimous Declaration of the thirteen United States of America

When in the Course of human events it becomes necessary for one people to dissolve the political bands which have connected them with another and to assume among the powers of the earth, the separate and equal station to which the Laws of Nature and of Nature's God entitle them, a decent respect to the opinions of mankind requires that they should declare the causes which impel them to the separation.

We hold these truths to be self-evident, that all men are created equal, that they are endowed by their Creator with certain unalienable Rights, that among these are Life, Liberty and the pursuit of Happiness. — That to secure these rights, Governments are instituted among Men, deriving their just powers from the consent of the governed, — That whenever any Form of Government becomes destructive of these ends, it is the Right of the People to alter or to abolish it, and to institute new Government, laying its foundation on such principles and organizing its powers in such form, as to them shall seem most likely to effect their Safety and Happiness. Prudence, indeed, will dictate that Governments long established should not be changed for light and transient causes; and accordingly all experience hath shewn that mankind are more disposed to suffer, while evils are sufferable than to right themselves by abolishing the forms to which they are accustomed. But when a long train of abuses and usurpations, pursuing invariably the same Object evinces a design to reduce them under absolute Despotism, it is their right, it is their duty, to throw off such Government, and to provide new Guards for their future security. — Such has been the patient sufferance of these Colonies; and such is now the necessity which constrains them to alter their former Systems of Government. The history of the present King of Great Britain is a history of repeated injuries and usurpations, all having in direct object the establishment of an absolute Tyranny over these States. To prove this, let Facts be submitted to a candid world.

He has refused his Assent to Laws, the most wholesome and necessary for the public good.

He has forbidden his Governors to pass Laws of immediate and pressing importance, unless suspended in their operation till his Assent should be obtained; and when so suspended, he has utterly neglected to attend to them.

He has refused to pass other Laws for the accommodation of large districts of people, unless those people would relinquish the right of Representation in the Legislature, a right inestimable to them and formidable to tyrants only.

He has called together legislative bodies at places unusual, uncomfortable, and distant from the depository of their Public Records, for the sole purpose of fatiguing them into compliance with his measures.

He has dissolved Representative Houses repeatedly, for opposing with manly firmness his invasions on the rights of the people.

He has refused for a long time, after such dissolutions, to cause others to be elected, whereby the Legislative Powers, incapable of Annihilation, have returned to the People at large for their exercise; the State remaining in the mean time exposed to all the dangers of invasion from without, and convulsions within.

He has endeavoured to prevent the population of these States; for that purpose obstructing the Laws for Naturalization of Foreigners; refusing to pass others to encourage their migrations hither, and raising the conditions of new Appropriations of Lands.

He has obstructed the Administration of Justice by refusing his Assent to Laws for establishing Judiciary Powers.

He has made Judges dependent on his Will alone for the tenure of their offices, and the amount and payment of their salaries.

He has erected a multitude of New Offices, and sent hither swarms of Officers to harass our people and eat out their substance.

He has kept among us, in times of peace, Standing Armies without the Consent of our legislatures.

He has affected to render the Military independent of and superior to the Civil Power.

He has combined with others to subject us to a jurisdiction foreign to our constitution, and unacknowledged by our laws; giving his Assent to their Acts of pretended Legislation:

For quartering large bodies of armed troops among us:

For protecting them, by a mock Trial from punishment for any Murders which they should commit on the Inhabitants of these States:

For cutting off our Trade with all parts of the world:

For imposing Taxes on us without our Consent:

For depriving us in many cases, of the benefit of Trial by Jury:

For transporting us beyond Seas to be tried for pretended offences:

For abolishing the free System of English Laws in a neighbouring Province, establishing therein an Arbitrary government, and enlarging its Boundaries so as to render it at once an example and fit instrument for introducing the same absolute rule into these Colonies

For taking away our Charters, abolishing our most valuable Laws and altering fundamentally the Forms of our Governments:

For suspending our own Legislatures, and declaring themselves invested with power to legislate for us in all cases whatsoever.

He has abdicated Government here, by declaring us out of his Protection and waging War against us.

He has plundered our seas, ravaged our coasts, burnt our towns, and destroyed the lives of our people.

He is at this time transporting large Armies of foreign Mercenaries to compleat the works of death, desolation, and tyranny, already begun with circumstances of Cruelty & Perfidy scarcely paralleled in the most barbarous ages, and totally unworthy the Head of a civilized nation.

He has constrained our fellow Citizens taken Captive on the high Seas to bear Arms against their Country, to become the executioners of their friends and Brethren, or to fall themselves by their Hands.

He has excited domestic insurrections amongst us, and has endeavoured to bring on the inhabitants of our frontiers, the merciless Indian Savages whose known rule of warfare, is an undistinguished destruction of all ages, sexes and conditions.

In every stage of these Oppressions We have Petitioned for Redress in the most humble terms: Our repeated Petitions have been answered only by repeated injury. A Prince, whose character is thus marked by every act which may define a Tyrant, is unfit to be the ruler of a free people.

Nor have We been wanting in attentions to our British brethren. We have warned them from time to time of attempts by their legislature to extend an unwarrantable jurisdiction over us. We have reminded them of the circumstances of our emigration and settlement here. We have appealed to their native justice and magnanimity, and we have conjured them by the ties of our common kindred to disavow these usurpations, which would inevitably interrupt our connections and correspondence. They too have been deaf to the voice of justice and of consanguinity. We must, therefore, acquiesce in the necessity, which denounces our Separation, and hold them, as we hold the rest of mankind, Enemies in War, in Peace Friends.

We, therefore, the Representatives of the united States of America, in General Congress, Assembled, appealing to the Supreme Judge of the world for the rectitude of our intentions, do, in the Name, and by Authority of the good People of these Colonies, solemnly publish and declare, That these united Colonies are, and of Right ought to be Free and Independent States, that they are Absolved from all Allegiance to the British Crown, and that all political connection between them and the State of Great Britain, is and ought to be totally dissolved; and that as Free and Independent States, they have full Power to levy War, conclude Peace, contract Alliances, establish Commerce, and to do all other Acts and Things which Independent States may of right do. — And for the support of this Declaration, with a firm reliance on the protection of Divine Providence, we mutually pledge to each other our Lives, our Fortunes, and our sacred Honor.

— John Hancock

New Hampshire:
Josiah Bartlett, William Whipple, Matthew Thornton

Massachusetts:
John Hancock, Samuel Adams, John Adams, Robert Treat Paine, Elbridge Gerry

Rhode Island:
Stephen Hopkins, William Ellery

Connecticut:
Roger Sherman, Samuel Huntington, William Williams, Oliver Wolcott

New York:
William Floyd, Philip Livingston, Francis Lewis, Lewis Morris

New Jersey:
Richard Stockton, John Witherspoon, Francis Hopkinson, John Hart, Abraham Clark

Pennsylvania:
Robert Morris, Benjamin Rush, Benjamin Franklin, John Morton, George Clymer, James Smith, George Taylor, James Wilson, George Ross

Delaware:
Caesar Rodney, George Read, Thomas McKean

Maryland:
Samuel Chase, William Paca, Thomas Stone, Charles Carroll of Carrollton

Virginia:
George Wythe, Richard Henry Lee, Thomas Jefferson, Benjamin Harrison, Thomas Nelson, Jr., Francis Lightfoot Lee, Carter Braxton

North Carolina:
William Hooper, Joseph Hewes, John Penn

South Carolina:
Edward Rutledge, Thomas Heyward, Jr., Thomas Lynch, Jr., Arthur Middleton

Georgia:
Button Gwinnett, Lyman Hall, George Walton

Appendix D   The Articles of Confederation

The Articles of Confederation

Agreed to by Congress November 15, 1777; ratified and in force, March 1, 1781.

Preamble:
To all to whom these Presents shall come, we the undersigned Delegates of the States affixed to our Names send greeting.

Articles of Confederation and perpetual Union between the States of New Hampshire, Massachusetts bay, Rhode Island and Providence Plantations, Connecticut, New York, New Jersey, Pennsylvania, Delaware, Maryland, Virginia, North Carolina, South Carolina and Georgia.

Article I. The Stile of this Confederacy shall be "The United States of America."

Article II. Each state retains its sovereignty, freedom, and independence, and every power, jurisdiction, and right, which is not by this Confederation expressly delegated to the United States, in Congress assembled.

Article III. The said States hereby severally enter into a firm league of friendship with each other, for their common defense, the security of their liberties, and their mutual and general welfare, binding themselves to assist each other, against all force offered to, or attacks made upon them, or any of them, on account of religion, sovereignty, trade, or any other pretense whatever.

Article IV. The better to secure and perpetuate mutual friendship and intercourse among the people of the different States in this Union, the free inhabitants of each of these States, paupers, vagabonds, and fugitives from justice excepted, shall be entitled to all privileges and immunities of free citizens in the several States; and the people of each State shall free ingress and regress to and from any other State, and shall enjoy therein all the privileges of trade and commerce, subject to the same duties, impositions, and restrictions as the inhabitants thereof respectively, provided that such restrictions shall not extend so far as to prevent the removal of property imported into any State, to any other State, of which the owner is an inhabitant; provided also that no imposition, duties or restriction shall be laid by any State, on the property of the United States, or either of them.

If any person guilty of, or charged with, treason, felony, or other high misdemeanor in any State, shall flee from justice, and be found in any of the United States, he shall, upon demand of the Governor or executive power of the State from which he fled, be delivered up and removed to the State having jurisdiction of his offense.

Full faith and credit shall be given in each of these States to the records, acts, and judicial proceedings of the courts and magistrates of every other State.

Article V. For the most convenient management of the general interests of the United States, delegates shall be annually appointed in such manner as the legislatures of each State shall direct, to meet in Congress on the first Monday in November, in every year, with a power reserved to each State to recall its delegates, or any of them, at any time within the year, and to send others in their stead for the remainder of the year.

No State shall be represented in Congress by less than two, nor more than seven members; and no person shall be capable of being a delegate for more than three years in any term of six years; nor shall any person, being a delegate, be capable of holding any office under the United States, for which he, or another for his benefit, receives any salary, fees or emolument of any kind.

Each State shall maintain its own delegates in a meeting of the States, and while they act as members of the committee of the States.

In determining questions in the United States in Congress assembled, each State shall have one vote.

Freedom of speech and debate in Congress shall not be impeached or questioned in any court or place out of Congress, and the members of Congress shall be protected in their persons from arrests or imprisonments, during the time of their going to and from, and attendance on Congress, except for treason, felony, or breach of the peace.

Article VI. No State, without the consent of the United States in Congress assembled, shall send any embassy to, or receive any embassy from, or enter into any conference, agreement, alliance or treaty with any King, Prince or State; nor shall any person holding any office of profit or trust under the United States, or any of them, accept any present, emolument, office or title of any kind whatever from any King, Prince or foreign State; nor shall the United States in Congress assembled, or any of them, grant any title of nobility.

No two or more States shall enter into any treaty, confederation or alliance whatever between them, without the consent of the United States in Congress assembled, specifying accurately the purposes for which the same is to be entered into, and how long it shall continue.

No State shall lay any imposts or duties, which may interfere with any stipulations in treaties, entered into by the United States in Congress assembled, with any King, Prince or State, in pursuance of any treaties already proposed by Congress, to the courts of France and Spain.

No vessel of war shall be kept up in time of peace by any State, except such number only, as shall be deemed necessary by the United States in Congress assembled, for the defense of such State, or its trade; nor shall any body of forces be kept up by any State in time of peace, except such number only, as in the judgement of the United States in Congress assembled, shall be deemed requisite to garrison the forts necessary for the defense of such State;

but every State shall always keep up a well-regulated and disciplined militia, sufficiently armed and accoutered, and shall provide and constantly have ready for use, in public stores, a due number of filed pieces and tents, and a proper quantity of arms, ammunition and camp equipage.

No State shall engage in any war without the consent of the United States in Congress assembled, unless such State be actually invaded by enemies, or shall have received certain advice of a resolution being formed by some nation of Indians to invade such State, and the danger is so imminent as not to admit of a delay till the United States in Congress assembled can be consulted; nor shall any State grant commissions to any ships or vessels of war, nor letters of marque or reprisal, except it be after a declaration of war by the United States in Congress assembled, and then only against the Kingdom or State and the subjects thereof, against which war has been so declared, and under such regulations as shall be established by the United States in Congress assembled, unless such State be infested by pirates, in which case vessels of war may be fitted out for that occasion, and kept so long as the danger shall continue, or until the United States in Congress assembled shall determine otherwise.

Article VII. When land forces are raised by any State for the common defense, all officers of or under the rank of colonel, shall be appointed by the legislature of each State respectively, by whom such forces shall be raised, or in such manner as such State shall direct, and all vacancies shall be filled up by the State which first made the appointment.

Article VIII. All charges of war, and all other expenses that shall be incurred for the common defense or general welfare, and allowed by the United States in Congress assembled, shall be defrayed out of a common treasury, which shall be supplied by the several States in proportion to the value of all land within each State, granted or surveyed for any person, as such land and the buildings and improvements thereon shall be estimated according to such mode as the United States in Congress assembled, shall from time to time direct and appoint.
The taxes for paying that proportion shall be laid and levied by the authority and direction of the legislatures of the several States within the time agreed upon by the United States in Congress assembled.

Article IX. The United States in Congress assembled, shall have the sole and exclusive right and power of determining on peace and war, except in the cases mentioned in the sixth article — of sending and receiving ambassadors — entering into treaties and alliances, provided that no treaty of commerce shall be made whereby the legislative power of the respective States shall be restrained from imposing such imposts and duties on foreigners, as their own people are subjected to, or from prohibiting the exportation or importation of any species of goods or commodities whatsoever — of establishing rules for deciding in all cases, what captures on land or water shall be legal, and in what manner prizes taken by land or naval forces in the service of the United States shall be divided or appropriated — of granting letters of marque and reprisal in times of peace — appointing courts for the trial of piracies and felonies committed on the high seas and establishing courts for receiving and determining finally appeals in all cases of captures, provided that no member of Congress shall be appointed a judge of any of the said courts.

The United States in Congress assembled shall also be the last resort on appeal in all disputes and differences now subsisting or that hereafter may arise between two or more States concerning boundary, jurisdiction or any other causes whatever; which authority shall always be exercised in the manner following. Whenever the legislative or executive authority or lawful agent of any State in controversy with another shall present a petition to Congress stating the matter in question and praying for a hearing, notice thereof shall be given by order of Congress to the legislative or executive authority of the other State in controversy, and a day assigned for the appearance of the parties by their lawful agents, who shall then be directed to appoint by joint consent, commissioners or judges to constitute a court for hearing and determining the matter in question: but if they cannot agree, Congress shall name three persons out of each of the United States, and from the list of such persons each party shall alternately strike out one, the petitioners beginning, until the number shall be reduced to thirteen; and from that number not less than seven, nor more than nine names as Congress shall direct, shall in the presence of Congress be drawn out by lot, and the persons whose names shall be so drawn or any five of them, shall be commissioners or judges, to hear and finally determine the controversy, so always as a major part of the judges who shall hear the cause shall agree in the determination: and if either party shall neglect to attend at the day appointed, without showing reasons, which Congress shall judge sufficient, or being present shall refuse to strike, the Congress shall proceed to nominate three persons out of each State, and the secretary of Congress shall strike in behalf of such party absent or refusing; and the judgment and sentence of the court to be appointed, in the manner before prescribed, shall be final and conclusive; and if any of the parties shall refuse to submit to the authority of such court, or to appear or defend their claim or cause, the court shall nevertheless proceed to pronounce sentence, or judgment, which shall in like manner be final and decisive, the judgment or sentence and other proceedings being in either case transmitted to Congress, and lodged among the acts of Congress for the security of the parties concerned: provided that every commissioner, before he sits in judgment, shall take an oath to be administered by one of the judges of the supreme or superior court of the State, where the cause shall be tried, 'well and truly to hear and determine the matter in question, according to the best of his judgment, without favor, affection or hope of reward': provided also, that no State shall be deprived of territory for the benefit of the United States.

All controversies concerning the private right of soil claimed under different grants of two or more States, whose jurisdictions as they may respect such lands, and the States which passed such grants are adjusted, the said grants or either of them being at the same time claimed to have originated antecedent to such settlement of jurisdiction, shall on the petition of either party to the Congress of the United States, be finally determined as near as may be in the same manner as is before prescribed for deciding disputes respecting territorial jurisdiction between different States.

The United States in Congress assembled shall also have the sole and exclusive right and power of regulating the alloy and value of coin struck by their own authority, or by that of the respective States — fixing the standards of weights and measures throughout the United States — regulating the trade and managing all affairs with the Indians, not members of any of the States, provided that the legislative right of any State within its own limits be not infringed or violated — establishing or regulating post offices from one State to another, throughout all the United States, and exacting such postage on the papers passing through the same as may be requisite to defray the expenses of the said office — appointing all officers of the land forces, in the service of the United States, excepting regimental officers — appointing all the officers of the naval forces, and commissioning all officers whatever in the service of the United States — making rules for the government and regulation of the said land and naval forces, and directing their operations.

The United States in Congress assembled shall have authority to appoint a committee, to sit in the recess of Congress, to be denominated 'A Committee of the States', and to consist of one delegate from each State; and to appoint such other committees and civil officers as may be necessary for managing the general affairs of the United States under their direction — to appoint one of their members to preside, provided that no person be allowed to serve in the office of president more than one year in any term of three years; to ascertain the necessary sums of money to be raised for the service of the United States, and to appropriate and apply the same for defraying the public expenses — to borrow money, or emit bills on the credit of the United States, transmitting every half-year to the respective States an account of the sums of money so borrowed or emitted — to build and equip a navy — to agree upon the number of land forces, and to make requisitions from each State for its quota, in proportion to the number of white inhabitants in such State; which requisition shall be binding, and thereupon the legislature of each State shall appoint the regimental officers, raise the men and cloath, arm and equip them in a solid- like manner, at the expense of the United States; and the officers and men so cloathed, armed and equipped shall march to the place appointed, and within the time agreed on by the United States in Congress assembled. But if the United States in Congress assembled shall, on consideration of circumstances judge proper that any State should not raise men, or should raise a smaller number of men than the quota thereof, such extra number shall be raised, officered, cloathed, armed and equipped in the same manner as the quota of each State, unless the legislature of such State shall judge that such extra number cannot be safely spread out in the same, in which case they shall raise, officer, cloath, arm and equip as many of such extra number as they judge can be safely spared. And the officers and men so cloathed, armed, and equipped, shall march to the place appointed, and within the time agreed on by the United States in Congress assembled.

The United States in Congress assembled shall never engage in a war, nor grant letters of marque or reprisal in time of peace, nor enter into any treaties or alliances, nor coin money, nor regulate the value thereof, nor ascertain the sums and expenses necessary for the defense and welfare of the United States, or any of them, nor emit bills, nor borrow money on the credit of the United States, nor appropriate money, nor agree upon the number of vessels of war, to be built or purchased, or the number of land or sea forces to be raised, nor appoint a commander in chief of the army or navy, unless nine States assent to the same: nor shall a question on any other point, except for adjourning from day to day be determined, unless by the votes of the majority of the United States in Congress assembled.

The Congress of the United States shall have power to adjourn to any time within the year, and to any place within the United States, so that no period of adjournment be for a longer duration than the space of six months, and shall publish the journal of their proceedings monthly, except such parts thereof relating to treaties, alliances or military operations, as in their judgement require secrecy; and the yeas and nays of the delegates of each State on any question shall be entered on the journal, when it is desired by any delegates of a State, or any of them, at his or their request shall be furnished with a transcript of the said journal, except such parts as are above excepted, to lay before the legislatures of the several States.

Article X. The Committee of the States, or any nine of them, shall be authorized to execute, in the recess of Congress, such of the powers of Congress as the United States in Congress assembled, by the consent of the nine States, shall from time to time think expedient to vest them with; provided that no power be delegated to the said Committee, for the exercise of which, by the Articles of Confederation, the voice of nine States in the Congress of the United States assembled be requisite.

Article XI. Canada acceding to this confederation, and adjoining in the measures of the United States, shall be admitted into, and entitled to all the advantages of this Union; but no other colony shall be admitted into the same, unless such admission be agreed to by nine States.

Article XII. All bills of credit emitted, monies borrowed, and debts contracted by, or under the authority of Congress, before the assembling of the United States, in pursuance of the present confederation, shall be deemed and considered as a charge against the United States, for payment and satisfaction whereof the said United States, and the public faith are hereby solemnly pledged.

Article XIII. Every State shall abide by the determination of the United States in Congress assembled, on all questions which by this confederation are submitted to them. And the Articles of this Confederation shall be inviolably observed by every State, and the Union shall be perpetual; nor shall any alteration at any time hereafter be made in any of them; unless such alteration be agreed to in a Congress of the United States, and be afterwards confirmed by the legislatures of every State.

And Whereas it hath pleased the Great Governor of the World to incline the hearts of the legislatures we respectively represent in Congress, to approve of, and to authorize us to ratify the said Articles of Confederation and perpetual Union. Know Ye that we the undersigned delegates, by virtue of the power and authority to us given for that purpose, do by these presents, in the name and in behalf of our respective constituents, fully and entirely ratify and confirm each and every of the said Articles of Confederation and perpetual Union, and all and singular the matters and things therein contained: And we do further solemnly plight and engage the faith of our respective constituents, that they shall abide by the determinations of the United States in Congress assembled, on all questions, which by the said Confederation are submitted to them. And that the Articles thereof shall be inviolably observed by the States we respectively represent, and that the Union shall be perpetual.

In Witness whereof we have hereunto set our hands in Congress. Done at Philadelphia in the State of Pennsylvania the ninth day of July in the Year of our Lord One Thousand Seven Hundred and Seventy-Eight, and in the Third Year of the independence of America.

On the part and behalf of the State of New Hampshire:
Josiah Bartlett, John Wentworth Junior. August 8th 1778

On the part and behalf of The State of Massachusetts Bay:
John Hancock, Samuel Adams, Elbridge Gerry, Francis Dana, James Lovell, Samuel Holten

On the part and behalf of the State of Rhode Island and Providence Plantations:
William Ellery, Henry Marchant, John Collins

On the part and behalf of the State of Connecticut:
Roger Sherman, Samuel Huntington, Oliver Wolcott, Titus Hosmer, Andrew Adams

On the part and behalf of the State of New York:
James Duane, Francis Lewis, William Duer, Gouv Morris

On the part and behalf of the State of New Jersey: November 26, 1778.
John Witherspoon, Nathan Scudder

On the part and behalf of the State of Pennsylvania:
Robert Morris, Daniel Roberdeau, John Bayard Smith, William Clingan, Joseph Reed 22nd July 1778

On the part and behalf of the State of Delaware:
Thomas Mckean February 12, 1779, John Dickinson May 5th 1779, Nicholas Van Dyke

On the part and behalf of the State of Maryland:
John Hanson March 1 1781, Daniel Carroll

On the part and behalf of the State of Virginia:
Richard Henry Lee, John Banister, Thomas Adams, John Harvie, Francis Lightfoot Lee

On the part and behalf of the State of No Carolina:
John Penn July 21st 1778, Cornelius Harnett, John Williams

On the part and behalf of the State of South Carolina:
Henry Laurens, William Henry Drayton, John Mathews, Richard Hutson, Thomas Heyward Junior

On the part and behalf of the State of Georgia:
John Walton 24th July 1778, Edward Telfair, Edward Langworthy

Appendix E The Constitution of the United States of America

The Constitution of the United States: A Transcription

Note: The following text is a transcription of the Constitution in its original form. Items that are hyperlinked have since been amended or superseded.

We the People of the United States, in Order to form a more perfect Union, establish Justice, insure domestic Tranquility, provide for the common defence, promote the general Welfare, and secure the Blessings of Liberty to ourselves and our Posterity, do ordain and establish this Constitution for the United States of America.

Article. I.
Section. 1.
All legislative Powers herein granted shall be vested in a Congress of the United States, which shall consist of a Senate and House of Representatives.

Section. 2.
The House of Representatives shall be composed of Members chosen every second Year by the People of the several States, and the Electors in each State shall have the Qualifications requisite for Electors of the most numerous Branch of the State Legislature.

No Person shall be a Representative who shall not have attained to the Age of twenty five Years, and been seven Years a Citizen of the United States, and who shall not, when elected, be an Inhabitant of that State in which he shall be chosen.

Representatives and direct Taxes shall be apportioned among the several States which may be included within this Union, according to their respective Numbers, which shall be determined by adding to the whole Number of free Persons, including those bound to Service for a Term of Years, and excluding Indians not taxed, three fifths of all other Persons. The actual Enumeration shall be made within three Years after the first Meeting of the Congress of the United States, and within every subsequent Term of ten Years, in such Manner as they shall by Law direct. The Number of Representatives shall not exceed one for every thirty Thousand, but each State shall have at Least one Representative; and until such enumeration shall be made, the State of New Hampshire shall be entitled to chuse three, Massachusetts eight, Rhode-Island and Providence Plantations one, Connecticut five, New-York six, New

Jersey four, Pennsylvania eight, Delaware one, Maryland six, Virginia ten, North Carolina five, South Carolina five, and Georgia three.

When vacancies happen in the Representation from any State, the Executive Authority thereof shall issue Writs of Election to fill such Vacancies.

The House of Representatives shall chuse their Speaker and other Officers; and shall have the sole Power of Impeachment.

Section. 3.
The Senate of the United States shall be composed of two Senators from each State, chosen by the Legislature thereof for six Years; and each Senator shall have one Vote.

Immediately after they shall be assembled in Consequence of the first Election, they shall be divided as equally as may be into three Classes. The Seats of the Senators of the first Class shall be vacated at the Expiration of the second Year, of the second Class at the Expiration of the fourth Year, and of the third Class at the Expiration of the sixth Year, so that one third may be chosen every second Year; and if Vacancies happen by Resignation, or otherwise, during the Recess of the Legislature of any State, the Executive thereof may make temporary Appointments until the next Meeting of the Legislature, which shall then fill such Vacancies.

No Person shall be a Senator who shall not have attained to the Age of thirty Years, and been nine Years a Citizen of the United States, and who shall not, when elected, be an Inhabitant of that State for which he shall be chosen.

The Vice President of the United States shall be President of the Senate, but shall have no Vote, unless they be equally divided.

The Senate shall chuse their other Officers, and also a President pro tempore, in the Absence of the Vice President, or when he shall exercise the Office of President of the United States.

The Senate shall have the sole Power to try all Impeachments. When sitting for that Purpose, they shall be on Oath or Affirmation. When the President of the United States is tried, the Chief Justice shall preside: And no Person shall be convicted without the Concurrence of two thirds of the Members present.

Judgment in Cases of Impeachment shall not extend further than to removal from Office, and disqualification to hold and enjoy any Office of honor, Trust or Profit under the United States: but the Party convicted shall nevertheless be liable and subject to Indictment, Trial, Judgment and Punishment, according to Law.

Section. 4.
The Times, Places and Manner of holding Elections for Senators and Representatives, shall be prescribed in each State by the Legislature thereof; but the Congress may at any time by Law make or alter such Regulations, except as to the Places of chusing Senators.

The Congress shall assemble at least once in every Year, and such Meeting shall be on the first Monday in December, unless they shall by Law appoint a different Day.

Section. 5.
Each House shall be the Judge of the Elections, Returns and Qualifications of its own Members, and a Majority of each shall constitute a Quorum to do Business; but a smaller Number may adjourn from day to day, and may be authorized to compel the Attendance of absent Members, in such Manner, and under such Penalties as each House may provide.

Each House may determine the Rules of its Proceedings, punish its Members for disorderly Behaviour, and, with the Concurrence of two thirds, expel a Member.

Each House shall keep a Journal of its Proceedings, and from time to time publish the same, excepting such Parts as may in their Judgment require Secrecy; and the Yeas and Nays of the Members of either House on any question shall, at the Desire of one fifth of those Present, be entered on the Journal.

Neither House, during the Session of Congress, shall, without the Consent of the other, adjourn for more than three days, nor to any other Place than that in which the two Houses shall be sitting.

Section. 6.
The Senators and Representatives shall receive a Compensation for their Services, to be ascertained by Law, and paid out of the Treasury of the United States. They shall in all Cases, except Treason, Felony and Breach of the Peace, be privileged from Arrest during their Attendance at the Session of their respective Houses, and in going to and returning from the same; and for any Speech or Debate in either House, they shall not be questioned in any other Place.

No Senator or Representative shall, during the Time for which he was elected, be appointed to any civil Office under the Authority of the United States, which shall have been created, or the Emoluments whereof shall have been encreased during such time; and no Person holding any Office under the United States, shall be a Member of either House during his Continuance in Office.

Section. 7.
All Bills for raising Revenue shall originate in the House of Representatives; but the Senate may propose or concur with Amendments as on other Bills.

Every Bill which shall have passed the House of Representatives and the Senate, shall, before it become a Law, be presented to the President of the United States: If he approve he shall sign it, but if not he shall return it, with his Objections to that House in which it shall have originated, who shall enter the Objections at large on their Journal, and proceed to reconsider it. If after such Reconsideration two thirds of that House shall agree to pass the Bill, it shall be sent, together with the Objections, to the other House, by which it shall likewise be reconsidered, and if approved by two thirds of that House, it shall become a Law. But in all such Cases the Votes of both Houses shall be determined by yeas and Nays, and the Names of the Persons voting for and against the Bill shall be entered on the Journal of each House respectively. If any Bill shall not be returned by the President within ten Days (Sundays excepted) after it shall have been presented to him, the Same shall be a Law, in like Manner as if he had signed it, unless the Congress by their Adjournment prevent its Return, in which Case it shall not be a Law.

Every Order, Resolution, or Vote to which the Concurrence of the Senate and House of Representatives may be necessary (except on a question of Adjournment) shall be presented to the President of the United States; and before the Same shall take Effect, shall be approved by him, or being disapproved by him, shall be repassed by two thirds of the Senate and House of Representatives, according to the Rules and Limitations prescribed in the Case of a Bill.

Section. 8.
The Congress shall have Power To lay and collect Taxes, Duties, Imposts and Excises, to pay the Debts and provide for the common Defence and general Welfare of the United States; but all Duties, Imposts and Excises shall be uniform throughout the United States;

*To borrow Money on the credit of the United States;
*To regulate Commerce with foreign Nations, and among the several States, and with the Indian Tribes;
*To establish an uniform Rule of Naturalization, and uniform Laws on the subject of Bankruptcies throughout the United States;
*To coin Money, regulate the Value thereof, and of foreign Coin, and fix the Standard of Weights and Measures;
*To provide for the Punishment of counterfeiting the Securities and current Coin of the United States;
*To establish Post Offices and post Roads;
*To promote the Progress of Science and useful Arts, by securing for limited Times to Authors and Inventors the exclusive Right to their respective Writings and Discoveries;
*To constitute Tribunals inferior to the supreme Court;
*To define and punish Piracies and Felonies committed on the high Seas, and Offences against the Law of Nations;
*To declare War, grant Letters of Marque and Reprisal, and make Rules concerning Captures on Land and Water;
*To raise and support Armies, but no Appropriation of Money to that Use shall be for a longer Term than two Years;
*To provide and maintain a Navy;
*To make Rules for the Government and Regulation of the land and naval Forces;
*To provide for calling forth the Militia to execute the Laws of the Union, suppress Insurrections and repel Invasions;
*To provide for organizing, arming, and disciplining, the Militia, and for governing such Part of them as may be employed in the Service of the United States, reserving to the States respectively, the Appointment of the Officers, and the Authority of training the Militia according to the discipline prescribed by Congress;
*To exercise exclusive Legislation in all Cases whatsoever, over such District (not exceeding ten Miles square) as may, by Cession of particular States, and

the Acceptance of Congress, become the Seat of the Government of the United States, and to exercise like Authority over all Places purchased by the Consent of the Legislature of the State in which the Same shall be, for the Erection of Forts, Magazines, Arsenals, dock-Yards, and other needful Buildings;--And

*To make all Laws which shall be necessary and proper for carrying into Execution the foregoing Powers, and all other Powers vested by this Constitution in the Government of the United States, or in any Department or Officer thereof.

Section. 9.

The Migration or Importation of such Persons as any of the States now existing shall think proper to admit, shall not be prohibited by the Congress prior to the Year one thousand eight hundred and eight, but a Tax or duty may be imposed on such Importation, not exceeding ten dollars for each Person.

The Privilege of the Writ of Habeas Corpus shall not be suspended, unless when in Cases of Rebellion or Invasion the public Safety may require it.

No Bill of Attainder or ex post facto Law shall be passed.

No Capitation, or other direct, Tax shall be laid, unless in Proportion to the Census or enumeration herein before directed to be taken.

No Tax or Duty shall be laid on Articles exported from any State.

No Preference shall be given by any Regulation of Commerce or Revenue to the Ports of one State over those of another; nor shall Vessels bound to, or from, one State, be obliged to enter, clear, or pay Duties in another.

No Money shall be drawn from the Treasury, but in Consequence of Appropriations made by Law; and a regular Statement and Account of the Receipts and Expenditures of all public Money shall be published from time to time.

No Title of Nobility shall be granted by the United States: And no Person holding any Office of Profit or Trust under them, shall, without the Consent of the Congress, accept of any present, Emolument, Office, or Title, of any kind whatever, from any King, Prince, or foreign State.

Section. 10.

No State shall enter into any Treaty, Alliance, or Confederation; grant Letters of Marque and Reprisal; coin Money; emit Bills of Credit; make any Thing but gold and silver Coin a Tender in Payment of Debts; pass any Bill of Attainder, ex post facto Law, or Law impairing the Obligation of Contracts, or grant any Title of Nobility.

No State shall, without the Consent of the Congress, lay any Imposts or Duties on Imports or Exports, except what may be absolutely necessary for executing it's inspection Laws: and the net Produce of all Duties and Imposts, laid by any State on Imports or Exports, shall be for the Use of the Treasury of the United States; and all such Laws shall be subject to the Revision and Controul of the Congress.

No State shall, without the Consent of Congress, lay any Duty of Tonnage, keep Troops, or Ships of War in time of Peace, enter into any Agreement or Compact with another State, or with a foreign Power, or engage in War, unless actually invaded, or in such imminent Danger as will not admit of delay.

Article. II.
Section. 1.
The executive Power shall be vested in a President of the United States of America. He shall hold his Office during the Term of four Years, and, together with the Vice President, chosen for the same Term, be elected, as follows:

Each State shall appoint, in such Manner as the Legislature thereof may direct, a Number of Electors, equal to the whole Number of Senators and Representatives to which the State may be entitled in the Congress: but no Senator or Representative, or Person holding an Office of Trust or Profit under the United States, shall be appointed an Elector.

The Electors shall meet in their respective States, and vote by Ballot for two Persons, of whom one at least shall not be an Inhabitant of the same State with themselves. And they shall make a List of all the Persons voted for, and of the Number of Votes for each; which List they shall sign and certify, and transmit sealed to the Seat of the Government of the United States, directed to the President of the Senate. The President of the Senate shall, in the Presence of the Senate and House of Representatives, open all the Certificates, and the Votes shall then be counted. The Person having the greatest Number of Votes shall be the President, if such Number be a Majority of the whole Number of Electors appointed; and if there be more than one who have such Majority, and have an equal Number of Votes, then the House of Representatives shall immediately chuse by Ballot one of them for President; and if no Person have a Majority, then from the five highest on the List the said House shall in like Manner chuse the President. But in chusing the President, the Votes shall be taken by States, the Representation from each State having one Vote; A quorum for this purpose shall consist of a Member or Members from two thirds of the States, and a Majority of all the States shall be necessary to a Choice. In every Case, after the Choice of the President, the Person having the greatest Number of Votes of the Electors shall be the Vice President. But if there should remain two or more who have equal Votes, the Senate shall chuse from them by Ballot the Vice President.

The Congress may determine the Time of chusing the Electors, and the Day on which they shall give their Votes; which Day shall be the same throughout the United States.

No Person except a natural born Citizen, or a Citizen of the United States, at the time of the Adoption of this Constitution, shall be eligible to the Office of President; neither shall any Person be eligible to that Office who shall not have attained to the Age of thirty five Years, and been fourteen Years a Resident within the United States.

In Case of the Removal of the President from Office, or of his Death, Resignation, or Inability to discharge the Powers and Duties of the said Office, the Same shall devolve on the Vice President, and the Congress may by Law provide for the Case of Removal, Death, Resignation or Inability, both of the President and Vice President, declaring what Officer shall then act as President, and such Officer shall act accordingly, until the Disability be removed, or a President shall be elected.

The President shall, at stated Times, receive for his Services, a Compensation, which shall neither be increased nor diminished during the Period for which he shall have been elected, and he shall not receive within that Period any other Emolument from the United States, or any of them.

Before he enter on the Execution of his Office, he shall take the following Oath or Affirmation:--"I do solemnly swear (or affirm) that I will faithfully execute the Office of President of the United States, and will to the best of my Ability, preserve, protect and defend the Constitution of the United States."

Section. 2.
The President shall be Commander in Chief of the Army and Navy of the United States, and of the Militia of the several States, when called into the actual Service of the United States; he may require the Opinion, in writing, of the principal Officer in each of the executive Departments, upon any Subject relating to the Duties of their respective Offices, and he shall have Power to grant Reprieves and Pardons for Offences against the United States, except in Cases of Impeachment.

He shall have Power, by and with the Advice and Consent of the Senate, to make Treaties, provided two thirds of the Senators present concur; and he shall nominate, and by and with the Advice and Consent of the Senate, shall appoint Ambassadors, other public Ministers and Consuls, Judges of the supreme Court, and all other Officers of the United States, whose Appointments are not herein otherwise provided for, and which shall be established by Law: but the Congress may by Law vest the Appointment of such inferior Officers, as they think proper, in the President alone, in the Courts of Law, or in the Heads of Departments.

The President shall have Power to fill up all Vacancies that may happen during the Recess of the Senate, by granting Commissions which shall expire at the End of their next Session.

Section. 3.
He shall from time to time give to the Congress Information of the State of the Union, and recommend to their Consideration such Measures as he shall judge necessary and expedient; he may, on extraordinary Occasions, convene both Houses, or either of them, and in Case of Disagreement between them, with Respect to the Time of Adjournment, he may adjourn them to such Time as he shall think proper; he shall receive Ambassadors and other public Ministers; he shall take Care that the Laws be faithfully executed, and shall Commission all the Officers of the United States.

Section. 4.
The President, Vice President and all civil Officers of the United States, shall be removed from Office on Impeachment for, and Conviction of, Treason, Bribery, or other high Crimes and Misdemeanors.

Article III.

Section. 1.
The judicial Power of the United States shall be vested in one supreme Court, and in such inferior Courts as the Congress may from time to time ordain and establish. The Judges, both of the supreme and inferior Courts, shall hold their Offices during good Behaviour, and shall, at stated Times, receive for their Services a Compensation, which shall not be diminished during their Continuance in Office.

Section. 2.
The judicial Power shall extend to all Cases, in Law and Equity, arising under this Constitution, the Laws of the United States, and Treaties made, or which shall be made, under their Authority;--to all Cases affecting Ambassadors, other public Ministers and Consuls;--to all Cases of admiralty and maritime Jurisdiction;--to Controversies to which the United States shall be a Party;--to Controversies between two or more States;-- between a State and Citizens of another State;--between Citizens of different States;--between Citizens of the same State claiming Lands under Grants of different States, and between a State, or the Citizens thereof, and foreign States, Citizens or Subjects.

In all Cases affecting Ambassadors, other public Ministers and Consuls, and those in which a State shall be Party, the supreme Court shall have original Jurisdiction. In all the other Cases before mentioned, the supreme Court shall have appellate Jurisdiction, both as to Law and Fact, with such Exceptions, and under such Regulations as the Congress shall make.

The Trial of all Crimes, except in Cases of Impeachment, shall be by Jury; and such Trial shall be held in the State where the said Crimes shall have been committed; but when not committed within any State, the Trial shall be at such Place or Places as the Congress may by Law have directed.

Section. 3.
Treason against the United States, shall consist only in levying War against them, or in adhering to their Enemies, giving them Aid and Comfort. No Person shall be convicted of Treason unless on the Testimony of two Witnesses to the same overt Act, or on Confession in open Court.

The Congress shall have Power to declare the Punishment of Treason, but no Attainder of Treason shall work Corruption of Blood, or Forfeiture except during the Life of the Person attainted.

Article. IV.

Section. 1.
Full Faith and Credit shall be given in each State to the public Acts, Records, and judicial Proceedings of every other State. And the Congress may by general Laws prescribe the Manner in which such Acts, Records and Proceedings shall be proved, and the Effect thereof.

Section. 2.

The Citizens of each State shall be entitled to all Privileges and Immunities of Citizens in the several States.

A Person charged in any State with Treason, Felony, or other Crime, who shall flee from Justice, and be found in another State, shall on Demand of the executive Authority of the State from which he fled, be delivered up, to be removed to the State having Jurisdiction of the Crime.

No Person held to Service or Labour in one State, under the Laws thereof, escaping into another, shall, in Consequence of any Law or Regulation therein, be discharged from such Service or Labour, but shall be delivered up on Claim of the Party to whom such Service or Labour may be due.

Section. 3.
New States may be admitted by the Congress into this Union; but no new State shall be formed or erected within the Jurisdiction of any other State; nor any State be formed by the Junction of two or more States, or Parts of States, without the Consent of the Legislatures of the States concerned as well as of the Congress.

The Congress shall have Power to dispose of and make all needful Rules and Regulations respecting the Territory or other Property belonging to the United States; and nothing in this Constitution shall be so construed as to Prejudice any Claims of the United States, or of any particular State.

Section. 4.
The United States shall guarantee to every State in this Union a Republican Form of Government, and shall protect each of them against Invasion; and on Application of the Legislature, or of the Executive (when the Legislature cannot be convened), against domestic Violence.

Article. V.

The Congress, whenever two thirds of both Houses shall deem it necessary, shall propose Amendments to this Constitution, or, on the Application of the Legislatures of two thirds of the several States, shall call a Convention for proposing Amendments, which, in either Case, shall be valid to all Intents and Purposes, as Part of this Constitution, when ratified by the Legislatures of three fourths of the several States, or by Conventions in three fourths thereof, as the one or the other Mode of Ratification may be proposed by the Congress; Provided that no Amendment which may be made prior to the Year One thousand eight hundred and eight shall in any Manner affect the first and fourth Clauses in the Ninth Section of the first Article; and that no State, without its Consent, shall be deprived of its equal Suffrage in the Senate.

Article. VI.

All Debts contracted and Engagements entered into, before the Adoption of this Constitution, shall be as valid against the United States under this Constitution, as under the Confederation.

This Constitution, and the Laws of the United States which shall be made in Pursuance thereof; and all Treaties made, or which shall be made, under the Authority of the United States, shall be the supreme Law of the Land; and the

Judges in every State shall be bound thereby, any Thing in the Constitution or Laws of any State to the Contrary notwithstanding.

The Senators and Representatives before mentioned, and the Members of the several State Legislatures, and all executive and judicial Officers, both of the United States and of the several States, shall be bound by Oath or Affirmation, to support this Constitution; but no religious Test shall ever be required as a Qualification to any Office or public Trust under the United States.

Article. VII.

The Ratification of the Conventions of nine States, shall be sufficient for the Establishment of this Constitution between the States so ratifying the Same.

The Word, "the," being interlined between the seventh and eighth Lines of the first Page, the Word "Thirty" being partly written on an Erazure in the fifteenth Line of the first Page, The Words "is tried" being interlined between the thirty second and thirty third Lines of the first Page and the Word "the" being interlined between the forty third and forty fourth Lines of the second Page. Attest William Jackson Secretary

Done in Convention by the Unanimous Consent of the States present the Seventeenth Day of September in the Year of our Lord one thousand seven hundred and Eighty seven and of the Independence of the United States of America the Twelfth In witness whereof We have hereunto subscribed our Names,

George Washington
President and Deputy from Virginia

Delaware
Geo Read, Gunning Bedford, John Dickinson, Richard Bassett, Jaco Broom

Maryland
James McHenry, Dan of St Thos. Jenifer Daniel Carroll

Virginia
John Blair, James Madison Jr.

North Carolina
William Blount, Richard Dobbs Spaight, Hume Williamson

South Carolina
J. Rutledge, Charles Cotesworth Pinckney, Charles Pinckney, Pierce Butler

Georgia
William Few, Abraham Baldwin

New Hampshire
John Langdon, Nicholas Gilman,

Massachusetts

Nathaniel Gorham, Rufus King

Connecticut
William. Samuel Johnson, Roger Sherman

New York
Alexander Hamilton,

New Jersey
William Livingston, David Brearley, William Paterson, Jonathan Dayton

Pennsylvania
Ben Franklin, Thomas Mifflin, Robert. Morris, George. Clymer, Thomas. FitzSimons, Jared Ingersoll, James Wilson, Gouv Morris

http://www.archives.gov/national-archives-experience/charters/constitution_transcript.html

Appendix F The Bill of Rights & Constitutional Amendments

The Preamble to the Bill of Rights

Congress of the United States -- begun and held at the City of New-York, on Wednesday the fourth of March, one thousand seven hundred and eighty nine.

THE Conventions of a number of the States, having at the time of their adopting the Constitution, expressed a desire, in order to prevent misconstruction or abuse of its powers, that further declaratory and restrictive clauses should be added: And as extending the ground of public confidence in the Government, will best ensure the beneficent ends of its institution.

RESOLVED by the Senate and House of Representatives of the United States of America, in Congress assembled, two thirds of both Houses concurring, that the following Articles be proposed to the Legislatures of the several States, as amendments to the Constitution of the United States, all, or any of which Articles, when ratified by three fourths of the said Legislatures, to be valid to all intents and purposes, as part of the said Constitution; viz.

ARTICLES in addition to, and Amendment of the Constitution of the United States of America, proposed by Congress, and ratified by the Legislatures of the several States, pursuant to the fifth Article of the original Constitution.

The Bill of Rights: A Transcription

The Preamble to The Bill of Rights-- Congress of the United States, begun and held at the City of New-York, on Wednesday the fourth of March, one thousand seven hundred and eighty nine.

THE Conventions of a number of the States, having at the time of their adopting the Constitution, expressed a desire, in order to prevent misconstruction or abuse of its powers, that further declaratory and restrictive clauses should be added: And as extending the ground of public confidence in the Government, will best ensure the beneficent ends of its institution.

RESOLVED by the Senate and House of Representatives of the United States of America, in Congress assembled, two thirds of both Houses concurring, that the following Articles be proposed to the Legislatures of the several States, as amendments to the Constitution of the United States, all, or any of which Articles, when ratified by three fourths of the said Legislatures, to be valid to all intents and purposes, as part of the said Constitution; viz.

ARTICLES in addition to, and Amendment of the Constitution of the United States of America, proposed by Congress, and ratified by the Legislatures of the several States, pursuant to the fifth Article of the original Constitution.

Note: The following text is a transcription of the first ten amendments to the Constitution in their original form. These amendments were ratified December 15, 1791, and form what is known as the "Bill of Rights."

Amendment I

Congress shall make no law respecting an establishment of religion, or prohibiting the free exercise thereof; or abridging the freedom of speech, or of the press; or the right of the people peaceably to assemble, and to petition the Government for a redress of grievances.

Amendment II

A well regulated Militia, being necessary to the security of a free State, the right of the people to keep and bear Arms, shall not be infringed.

Amendment III

No Soldier shall, in time of peace be quartered in any house, without the consent of the Owner, nor in time of war, but in a manner to be prescribed by law.

Amendment IV

The right of the people to be secure in their persons, houses, papers, and effects, against unreasonable searches and seizures, shall not be violated, and no Warrants shall issue, but upon probable cause, supported by Oath or affirmation, and particularly describing the place to be searched, and the persons or things to be seized. [No fishing expeditions]

Amendment V

No person shall be held to answer for a capital, or otherwise infamous crime, unless on a presentment or indictment of a Grand Jury, except in cases arising in the land or naval forces, or in the Militia, when in actual service in time of War or public danger; nor shall any person be subject for the same offence to be twice put in jeopardy of life or limb; nor shall be compelled in any criminal case to be a witness against himself, nor be deprived of life, liberty, or property, without due process of law; nor shall private property be taken for public use, without just compensation.

Amendment VI

In all criminal prosecutions, the accused shall enjoy the right to a speedy and public trial, by an impartial jury of the State and district wherein the crime shall have been committed, which district shall have been previously ascertained by law, and to be informed of the nature and cause of the accusation; to be confronted with the witnesses against him; to have compulsory process for obtaining witnesses in his favor, and to have the Assistance of Counsel for his defence.

Amendment VII

In Suits at common law, where the value in controversy shall exceed twenty dollars, the right of trial by jury shall be preserved, and no fact tried by a jury, shall be otherwise re-examined in any Court of the United States, than according to the rules of the common law.

Amendment VIII

Excessive bail shall not be required, nor excessive fines imposed, nor cruel and unusual punishments inflicted.

Amendment IX

The enumeration in the Constitution, of certain rights, shall not be construed to deny or disparage others retained by the people.

Amendment X

The powers not delegated to the United States by the Constitution, nor prohibited by it to the States, are reserved to the States respectively, or to the people.

The Constitution: Amendments 11-27

Constitutional Amendments 1-10 above—make up what is known as The Bill of Rights. Amendments 11-27 are listed below.

AMENDMENT XI
Passed by Congress March 4, 1794. Ratified February 7, 1795.
Note: Article III, section 2, of the Constitution was modified by amendment 11.
The Judicial power of the United States shall not be construed to extend to any suit in law or equity, commenced or prosecuted against one of the United States by Citizens of another State, or by Citizens or Subjects of any Foreign State.

AMENDMENT XII
Passed by Congress December 9, 1803. Ratified June 15, 1804.

Note: A portion of Article II, section 1 of the Constitution was superseded by the 12th amendment.

The Electors shall meet in their respective states and vote by ballot for President and Vice-President, one of whom, at least, shall not be an inhabitant of the same state with themselves; they shall name in their ballots the person voted for as President, and in distinct ballots the person voted for as Vice-President, and they shall make distinct lists of all persons voted for as President, and of all persons voted for as Vice-President, and of the number of votes for each, which lists they shall sign and certify, and transmit sealed to the seat of the government of the United States, directed to the President of the Senate; -- the President of the Senate shall, in the presence of the Senate and House of Representatives, open all the certificates and the votes shall then be counted; -- The person having the greatest number of votes for President, shall be the President, if such number be a majority of the whole number of Electors appointed; and if no person have such majority, then from the persons having the highest numbers not exceeding three on the list of those voted for as President, the House of Representatives shall choose immediately, by ballot, the President. But in choosing the President, the votes shall be taken by states, the representation from each state having one vote; a quorum for this purpose shall consist of a member or members from two-thirds of the states, and a majority of all the states shall be necessary to a choice. [And if the House of Representatives shall not choose a President whenever the right of choice shall devolve upon them, before the fourth day of March next following, then the Vice-President shall act as President, as in case of the death or other constitutional disability of the President. --]* The person having the greatest number of votes as Vice-President, shall be the Vice-President, if such number be a majority of the whole number of Electors appointed, and if no person have a majority, then from the two highest numbers on the list, the Senate shall choose the Vice-President; a quorum for the purpose shall consist of two-thirds of the whole number of Senators, and a majority of the whole number shall be necessary to a choice. But no person constitutionally ineligible to the office of President shall be eligible to that of Vice-President of the United States.

*Later Superseded by section 3 of the 20th amendment.

AMENDMENT XIII
Passed by Congress January 31, 1865. Ratified December 6, 1865.

Note: A portion of Article IV, section 2, of the Constitution was superseded by the 13th amendment.

Section 1.
Neither slavery nor involuntary servitude, except as a punishment for crime whereof the party shall have been duly convicted, shall exist within the United States, or any place subject to their jurisdiction.

Section 2.
Congress shall have power to enforce this article by appropriate legislation.

AMENDMENT XIV
Passed by Congress June 13, 1866. Ratified July 9, 1868.
Note: Article I, section 2, of the Constitution was modified by section 2 of the 14th amendment.

Section 1.
All persons born or naturalized in the United States, and subject to the jurisdiction thereof, are citizens of the United States and of the State wherein they reside. No State shall make or enforce any law which shall abridge the privileges or immunities of citizens of the United States; nor shall any State

deprive any person of life, liberty, or property, without due process of law; nor deny to any person within its jurisdiction the equal protection of the laws.

Section 2.

Representatives shall be apportioned among the several States according to their respective numbers, counting the whole number of persons in each State, excluding Indians not taxed. But when the right to vote at any election for the choice of electors for President and Vice-President of the United States, Representatives in Congress, the Executive and Judicial officers of a State, or the members of the Legislature thereof, is denied to any of the male inhabitants of such State, being twenty-one years of age,* and citizens of the United States, or in any way abridged, except for participation in rebellion, or other crime, the basis of representation therein shall be reduced in the proportion which the number of such male citizens shall bear to the whole number of male citizens twenty-one years of age in such State.

Section 3.

No person shall be a Senator or Representative in Congress, or elector of President and Vice-President, or hold any office, civil or military, under the United States, or under any State, who, having previously taken an oath, as a member of Congress, or as an officer of the United States, or as a member of any State legislature, or as an executive or judicial officer of any State, to support the Constitution of the United States, shall have engaged in insurrection or rebellion against the same, or given aid or comfort to the enemies thereof. But Congress may by a vote of two-thirds of each House, remove such disability.

Section 4.

The validity of the public debt of the United States, authorized by law, including debts incurred for payment of pensions and bounties for services in suppressing insurrection or rebellion, shall not be questioned. But neither the United States nor any State shall assume or pay any debt or obligation incurred in aid of insurrection or rebellion against the United States, or any claim for the loss or emancipation of any slave; but all such debts, obligations and claims shall be held illegal and void.

Section 5.

The Congress shall have the power to enforce, by appropriate legislation, the provisions of this article.

*Later Changed by section 1 of the 26th amendment.

AMENDMENT XV

Passed by Congress February 26, 1869. Ratified February 3, 1870.

Section 1.

The right of citizens of the United States to vote shall not be denied or abridged by the United States or by any State on account of race, color, or previous condition of servitude--

Section 2.

The Congress shall have the power to enforce this article by appropriate legislation.

AMENDMENT XVI

Passed by Congress July 2, 1909. Ratified February 3, 1913.
Note: Article I, section 9, of the Constitution was modified by amendment 16.
The Congress shall have power to lay and collect taxes on incomes, from whatever source derived, without apportionment among the several States, and without regard to any census or enumeration.

AMENDMENT XVII

Passed by Congress May 13, 1912. Ratified April 8, 1913.
Note: Article I, section 3, of the Constitution was modified by the 17th amendment.
---The Senate of the United States shall be composed of two Senators from each State, elected by the people thereof, for six years; and each Senator shall have one vote. The electors in each State shall have the qualifications requisite for electors of the most numerous branch of the State legislatures.
---When vacancies happen in the representation of any State in the Senate, the executive authority of such State shall issue writs of election to fill such vacancies: Provided, That the legislature of any State may empower the executive thereof to make temporary appointments until the people fill the vacancies by election as the legislature may direct.
---This amendment shall not be so construed as to affect the election or term of any Senator chosen before it becomes valid as part of the Constitution.

AMENDMENT XVIII

Passed by Congress December 18, 1917. Ratified January 16, 1919.
Repealed by amendment 21.

Section 1.
After one year from the ratification of this article the manufacture, sale, or transportation of intoxicating liquors within, the importation thereof into, or the exportation thereof from the United States and all territory subject to the jurisdiction thereof for beverage purposes is hereby prohibited.

Section 2.
The Congress and the several States shall have concurrent power to enforce this article by appropriate legislation.

Section 3.
This article shall be inoperative unless it shall have been ratified as an amendment to the Constitution by the legislatures of the several States, as provided in the Constitution, within seven years from the date of the submission hereof to the States by the Congress.

AMENDMENT XIX

Passed by Congress June 4, 1919. Ratified August 18, 1920.
The right of citizens of the United States to vote shall not be denied or abridged by the United States or by any State on account of sex.
Congress shall have power to enforce this article by appropriate legislation.

AMENDMENT XX

Passed by Congress March 2, 1932. Ratified January 23, 1933.

Note: Article I, section 4, of the Constitution was modified by section 2 of this amendment. In addition, a portion of the 12th amendment was superseded by section 3.

Section 1.

The terms of the President and the Vice President shall end at noon on the 20th day of January, and the terms of Senators and Representatives at noon on the 3d day of January, of the years in which such terms would have ended if this article had not been ratified; and the terms of their successors shall then begin.

Section 2.

The Congress shall assemble at least once in every year, and such meeting shall begin at noon on the 3d day of January, unless they shall by law appoint a different day.

Section 3.

If, at the time fixed for the beginning of the term of the President, the President elect shall have died, the Vice President elect shall become President. If a President shall not have been chosen before the time fixed for the beginning of his term, or if the President elect shall have failed to qualify, then the Vice President elect shall act as President until a President shall have qualified; and the Congress may by law provide for the case wherein neither a President elect nor a Vice President shall have qualified, declaring who shall then act as President, or the manner in which one who is to act shall be selected, and such person shall act accordingly until a President or Vice President shall have qualified.

Section 4.

The Congress may by law provide for the case of the death of any of the persons from whom the House of Representatives may choose a President whenever the right of choice shall have devolved upon them, and for the case of the death of any of the persons from whom the Senate may choose a Vice President whenever the right of choice shall have devolved upon them.

Section 5.

Sections 1 and 2 shall take effect on the 15th day of October following the ratification of this article.

Section 6.

This article shall be inoperative unless it shall have been ratified as an amendment to the Constitution by the legislatures of three-fourths of the several States within seven years from the date of its submission.

AMENDMENT XXI

Passed by Congress February 20, 1933. Ratified December 5, 1933.
Section 1.
The eighteenth article of amendment to the Constitution of the United States is hereby repealed.

Section 2.

The transportation or importation into any State, Territory, or Possession of the United States for delivery or use therein of intoxicating liquors, in violation of the laws thereof, is hereby prohibited.

Section 3.
This article shall be inoperative unless it shall have been ratified as an amendment to the Constitution by conventions in the several States, as provided in the Constitution, within seven years from the date of the submission hereof to the States by the Congress.

AMENDMENT XXII
Passed by Congress March 21, 1947. Ratified February 27, 1951.
Section 1.
No person shall be elected to the office of the President more than twice, and no person who has held the office of President, or acted as President, for more than two years of a term to which some other person was elected President shall be elected to the office of President more than once. But this Article shall not apply to any person holding the office of President when this Article was proposed by Congress, and shall not prevent any person who may be holding the office of President, or acting as President, during the term within which this Article becomes operative from holding the office of President or acting as President during the remainder of such term.

Section 2.
This article shall be inoperative unless it shall have been ratified as an amendment to the Constitution by the legislatures of three-fourths of the several States within seven years from the date of its submission to the States by the Congress.

AMENDMENT XXIII
Passed by Congress June 16, 1960. Ratified March 29, 1961.

Section 1.
The District constituting the seat of Government of the United States shall appoint in such manner as Congress may direct:
---A number of electors of President and Vice President equal to the whole number of Senators and Representatives in Congress to which the District would be entitled if it were a State, but in no event more than the least populous State; they shall be in addition to those appointed by the States, but they shall be considered, for the purposes of the election of President and Vice President, to be electors appointed by a State; and they shall meet in the District and perform such duties as provided by the twelfth article of amendment.

Section 2.
The Congress shall have power to enforce this article by appropriate legislation.

AMENDMENT XXIV
Passed by Congress August 27, 1962. Ratified January 23, 1964.
Section 1.
The right of citizens of the United States to vote in any primary or other election for President or Vice President, for electors for President or Vice

President, or for Senator or Representative in Congress, shall not be denied or abridged by the United States or any State by reason of failure to pay poll tax or other tax.

Section 2.
The Congress shall have power to enforce this article by appropriate legislation.

AMENDMENT XXV
Passed by Congress July 6, 1965. Ratified February 10, 1967.
Note: Article II, section 1, of the Constitution was affected by the 25th amendment.
Section 1.
In case of the removal of the President from office or of his death or resignation, the Vice President shall become President.

Section 2.
Whenever there is a vacancy in the office of the Vice President, the President shall nominate a Vice President who shall take office upon confirmation by a majority vote of both Houses of Congress.

Section 3.
Whenever the President transmits to the President pro tempore of the Senate and the Speaker of the House of Representatives his written declaration that he is unable to discharge the powers and duties of his office, and until he transmits to them a written declaration to the contrary, such powers and duties shall be discharged by the Vice President as Acting President.

Section 4.
Whenever the Vice President and a majority of either the principal officers of the executive departments or of such other body as Congress may by law provide, transmit to the President pro tempore of the Senate and the Speaker of the House of Representatives their written declaration that the President is unable to discharge the powers and duties of his office, the Vice President shall immediately assume the powers and duties of the office as Acting President.
---Thereafter, when the President transmits to the President pro tempore of the Senate and the Speaker of the House of Representatives his written declaration that no inability exists, he shall resume the powers and duties of his office unless the Vice President and a majority of either the principal officers of the executive department or of such other body as Congress may by law provide, transmit within four days to the President pro tempore of the Senate and the Speaker of the House of Representatives their written declaration that the President is unable to discharge the powers and duties of his office. Thereupon Congress shall decide the issue, assembling within forty-eight hours for that purpose if not in session. If the Congress, within twenty-one days after receipt of the latter written declaration, or, if Congress is not in session, within twenty-one days after Congress is required to assemble, determines by two-thirds vote of both Houses that the President is unable to discharge the powers and duties of his office, the Vice President shall continue to discharge the same as Acting President; otherwise, the President shall resume the powers and duties of his office.

AMENDMENT XXVI
Passed by Congress March 23, 1971. Ratified July 1, 1971.
Note: Amendment 14, section 2, of the Constitution was modified by section 1
of the 26th amendment.
Section 1.
The right of citizens of the United States, who are eighteen years of age or
older, to vote shall not be denied or abridged by the United States or by any
State on account of age.

Section 2.
The Congress shall have power to enforce this article by appropriate
legislation.

AMENDMENT XXVII
Originally proposed Sept. 25, 1789. Ratified May 7, 1992.
No law, varying the compensation for the services of the Senators and
Representatives, shall take effect, until an election of representatives shall
have intervened.
http://www.archives.gov/national-archives-
experience/charters/constitution_amendments_11-27.html

Appendix G Constitutional Amendments Not Ratified

These are the proposed amendments to the Constitution—not ratified by the States.

During the course of our history, in addition to the 27 amendments that have been ratified by the required three-fourths of the States, six other amendments have been submitted to the States but have not been ratified by them.

Beginning with the proposed Eighteenth Amendment, Congress has customarily included a provision requiring ratification within seven years from the time of the submission to the States. The Supreme Court in Coleman v. Miller, 307 U.S. 433 (1939), declared that the question of the reasonableness of the time within which a sufficient number of States must act is a political question to be determined by the Congress.

In 1789, twelve proposed articles of amendment were submitted to the States. Of these, Articles III through XII were ratified and became the first ten amendments to the Constitution, popularly known as the Bill of Rights. In 1992, proposed Article II was ratified and became the 27th amendment to the Constitution. Proposed Article I which was not ratified is as follows:

"Article the first"

"After the first enumeration required by the first article of the Constitution, there shall be one Representative for every thirty thousand, until the number shall amount to one hundred, after which the proportion shall be so regulated by Congress, that there shall be not less than one hundred Representatives, nor less than one Representative for every forty thousand persons, until the number of Representatives shall amount to two hundred; after which the proportion shall be so regulated by Congress, that there shall not be less than two hundred Representatives, nor more than one Representative for every fifty thousand persons."

Thereafter, in the 2d session of the Eleventh Congress, the Congress proposed the following article of amendment to the Constitution relating to acceptance by citizens of the United States of titles of nobility from any foreign government.

The proposed amendment, which was not ratified by three-fourths of the States, is as follows:

Resolved by the Senate and House of Representatives of the United States of America in Congress assembled, two thirds of both houses concurring, That the following section be submitted to the legislatures of the several states, which, when ratified by the legislatures of three fourths of the states, shall be valid and binding, as a part of the constitution of the United States.

> If any citizen of the United States shall accept, claim, receive or retain any title of nobility or honour, or shall, without the consent of Congress, accept and retain any present, pension, office or emolument of any kind whatever, from any emperor, king, prince or foreign power, such person shall cease to be a citizen of the United States, and shall be incapable of holding any office of trust or profit under them, or either of them.

The following amendment to the Constitution relating to slavery was proposed by the 2d session of the Thirty-sixth Congress on March 2, 1861, when it passed the Senate, having previously passed the House on February 28, 1861. It is interesting to note in this connection that this is the only proposed (and not ratified) amendment to the Constitution to have been signed by the President. The President's signature is considered unnecessary because of the constitutional provision that on the concurrence of two-thirds of both Houses of Congress the proposal shall be submitted to the States for ratification.

> Resolved by the Senate and House of Representatives of the United States of America in Congress assembled, That the following article be proposed to the Legislatures of the several States as an amendment to the Constitution of the United States, which, when ratified by three-fourths of said Legislatures, shall be valid, to all intents and purposes, as part of the said Constitution, viz:
>
> **"Article Thirteen**
>
> "No amendment shall be made to the Constitution which will authorize or give to Congress the power to abolish or interfere, within any State, with the domestic institutions thereof, including that of persons held to labor or service by the laws of said State."

A child labor amendment was proposed by the 1st session of the Sixty-eighth Congress on June 2, 1926, when it passed the Senate, having previously passed the House on April 26, 1926. The proposed amendment, which has been ratified by 28 States, to date, is as follows:

Joint Resolution Proposing an Amendment to the Constitution of the United States

> Resolved by the Senate and House of Representatives of the United States of America in Congress assembled (two-thirds of each House concurring therein), That the following article is proposed as an amendment to the Constitution of the United States, which, when ratified by the legislatures of three-fourths of the several States, shall be valid to all intents and purposes as a part of the Constitution:
>
> **"Article—[no number given].**
>
> "Section 1. The Congress shall have power to limit, regulate, and prohibit the labor of persons under eighteen years of age.

"Section 2. The power of the several States is unimpaired by this article except that the operation of State laws shall be suspended to the extent necessary to give effect to legislation enacted by the Congress."

HOUSE JOINT RESOLUTION 208

An amendment relative to equal rights for men and women was proposed by the 2d session of the Ninety-second Congress on March 22, 1972, when it passed the Senate, having previously passed the House on October 12, 1971. The seven-year deadline for ratification of the proposed amendment was extended to June 30, 1982, by the 2d session of the Ninety-fifth Congress. The proposed amendment, which was not ratified by three-fourths of the States by June 30, 1982, is as follows:

Joint Resolution Proposing an Amendment to the Constitution of the United States Relative to Equal Rights for Men and Women

Resolved by the Senate and House of Representatives of the United States of America in Congress assembled (two-thirds of each House concurring therein), That the following article is proposed as an amendment to the Constitution of the United States, which shall be valid to all intents and purposes as part of the Constitution when ratified by the legislatures of three-fourths of the several States within seven years from the date of its submission by the Congress:

"Article—[No number given]

"Section 1. Equality of rights under the law shall not be denied or abridged by the United States or by any State on account of sex.

"Section. 2. The Congress shall have the power to enforce, by appropriate legislation, the provisions of this article.

"Section. 3. This amendment shall take effect two years after the date of ratification."

HOUSE JOINT RESOLUTION 554

An amendment relative to voting rights for the District of Columbia was proposed by the 2d session of the Ninety-fifth Congress on August 22, 1978, when it passed the Senate, having previously passed the House on March 2, 1978. The proposed amendment, which was not ratified by three-fourths of the States within the specified seven-year period, is as follows:

Joint Resolution Proposing an Amendment to the Constitution To Provide for Representation of the District of Columbia in the Congress

Resolved by the Senate and House of Representatives of the United States of America in Congress assembled (two-thirds of each House concurring therein), That the following article is proposed as an amendment to the Constitution of the United States, which shall be valid to all intents and purposes as part of the Constitution when ratified by the legislatures of three-fourths of the several States within seven years from the date of its submission by the Congress:

"Article—[No number given]

"Section 1. For purposes of representation in the Congress, election of the President and Vice President, and article V of this Constitution, the District constituting the seat of government of the United States shall be treated as though it were a State.

"Section. 2. The exercise of the rights and powers conferred under this article shall be by the people of the District constituting the seat of government, and as shall be provided by the Congress.

"Section. 3. The twenty-third article of amendment to the Constitution of the United States is hereby repealed.

"Section. 4. This article shall be inoperative, unless it shall have been ratified as an amendment to the Constitution by the legislatures of three-fourths of the several States within seven years from the date of its submission."

Books by Brian W. Kelly
www.letsgopublish.com; Sold at

www.bookhawkers.com
Email info@ letsgopublish.com for specific ordering info. Our titles include the following:

Great Moments in Notre Dame Football The story about the beginning of US football and ND football in the US as well as the great moemnts and great coaches and players ove the years.

Thank You IBM The story of how IBM helped today's technology millionaires and billionaires gain their vast fortunes

WineDiets.Com Presents The Wine Diet Learn how to lose weight while having fun. Four specific diets and some great anecdotes fill this book with fun.

Wilkes-Barre, PA; Return to Glory Wilkes-Barre City's return to glory begins with dreams and ideas. Along with plans and actions, this equals leadership.

The Lifetime Guest Plan. This is a plan which if deployed today would immediately solve the problem of 60 million illegal aliens in the United States.

Geoffrey Parsons' Epoch... The Land of Fair Play Better than the original. The greatest re-mastering of the greatest book ever written on American Civics. It was built for all Americans as the best govt. design in the history of the world.

The Bill of Rights 4 Dummmies This is the best book to learn about your rights. Be the first, to have a "Rights Fest" on your block. You will win for sure!

Sol Bloom's Epoch ...Story of the Constitution This work by Sol Bloom was written to commemorate the Sesquicentennial celebration of the Constitution. It has been remastered by Lets Go Publish! – an excellent read!

The Constitution 4 Dummmies This is the best book to learn about the Constitution. Learn all about the fundamental laws of America.

America for Dummmies!
All Americans should read to learn about this great country.

Just Say No to Chris Christie for President!
Discusses the reasons why Chris Christie is a poor choice for US President

The Federalist Papers by Hamilton, Jay, Madison w/ intro by Brian Kelly
Complete unabridged, easier to read version of the original Federalist Papers

Bring On the American Party!
Demonstrates how Americans can be free from Parties of wimps by starting our own national party called the American Party.

Saving America
This how-to book is about saving our country using strong mercantilist principles. These are the same principles that helped the country from its founding.

RRR:
A unique plan for economic recovery and job creation

Kill the EPA
The EPA seems to hate mankind and love nature. They are also making it tough for asthmatics to breathe and for those with malaria to live. It's time they go.

Taxation Without Representation Second Edition
At the time of the Boston Tea Party, there was no representation. Now, there is no representation again but there are "representatives."

Healthcare Accountability
Who should pay for your healthcare? Whose healthcare should you pay for? Is it a lifetime free ride on others or should those once in need of help have to pay it back when their lives improve?

Jobs! Jobs! Jobs!
Where have all the American Jobs gone and how can we get them back?

IBM I Technical Books

The All Everything Operating System:
The story about IBM's finest operating system, its facilities, and how it came to be.

The All-Everything Machine
The story about IBM's finest computer server.

Chip Wars
The story of the ongoing war between Intel and AMD and the upcoming was between Intel and IBM. This book may cause you to buy or sell somebody's stock.

Can the AS/400 Survive IBM?
Exciting book about the AS/400 in an System i5 World.

The IBM i Pocket SQL Guide.
Complete Pocket Guide to SQL as implemented on System i5. A must have for SQL developers new to System i5. It is very compact yet very comprehensive and it is example driven. Written in a part tutorial and part reference style, this book has tons of SQL coding samples, from the simple to the sublime.

The IBM i Pocket Query Guide.
If you have been spending money for years educating your Query users, and you find you are still spending, or you've given up, this book is right for you. This one QuikCourse covers all Query options.

The IBM I Pocket RPG & RPG IV Guide.
Comprehensive RPG & RPGIV Textbook -- Over 900 pages. This is the one RPG book to have if you are not having more than one. All areas of the language covered smartly in a convenient sized book Annotated PowerPoint's available for self-study (extra fee for self-study package)

www.ingramcontent.com/pod-product-compliance
Lightning Source LLC
Chambersburg PA
CBHW072109270326
41931CB00010B/1497